World City Growth

J H Lowry M.A. B.Sc.(Econ.)

Senior Geography Master, Cranleigh School

Edward Arnold

© J H Lowry 1975

First published 1975
by Edward Arnold (Publishers) Ltd
25 Hill Street, London W1X 8LL

ISBN 0 7131 1968 3

Maps and diagrams by :
  Art Innovations
  Nicholas Rous
  Cartographic Enterprises

Set in 10 on 11 point Imprint by
Photoprint Plates Ltd, Rayleigh, Essex
and printed in Great Britain by
Unwin Brothers Ltd, Old Woking, Surrey

Preface

It is the experience of the author that there is a dearth of geography text-books written specifically for the upper school. This is especially the case in the field of Human Geography, where students have perforce to use texts intended primarily for undergraduates. In Urban Geography this is particularly unsatisfactory because many advanced texts, excellent though they are for the specialist reader, deal only with limited aspects of the subject. The aim of this book is therefore to give a clear and concise account, at Sixth Form level, of the principal factors involved in the study of Urban Geography.

The approach is basically non-mathematical, but where appropriate reference is made to analytical methods, considerable attention being given, for example, to techniques of delimiting a Central Business District. Theories of urban structure and of central place are also covered. It is hoped that the extended Sections dealing with urban problems and planning will encourage students to think constructively about the many critical choices now facing urban man.

J.H.L.

Contents

Preface   iii

Section 1   **The urban phenomenon**
    1   The urban 'explosion'   1

Section 2   **Early urban growth**
    2   Cities in history   12
    3   The pre-industrial city   24

Section 3   **The impact of technology**
    4   The factory system   29
    5   The metropolitan expansion   31
    6   The transport revolution   33

Section 4   **Modern urbanism**
    7   The city centre   37
    8   The location of industry   47
    9   Residential areas   52

Section 5   **Urban patterns**
    10   Theories of urban structure   63
    11   The size and spacing of
       settlements   82

Section 6   **Some urban problems**   114
    12   Water supply   118
    13   The disposal of wastes   124
    14   Health hazards and crime   130
    15   Traffic in cities

Section 7   **Urban planning**   141
    16   The garden idea   142
    17   New towns and 'overspill'
       152

Bibliography

Acknowledgments   153

Index   154

Section 1 The urban phenomenon

1 The urban 'explosion'

Figures 1–3 focus attention on one of the most extraordinary developments currently affecting human society, i.e. the extent to which it is becoming increasingly urbanized. By urbanized is meant the proportion of a population living in towns or cities. How far it is possible to differentiate precisely between urban and rural settlements is discussed overleaf: diagrams include only settlements

with a minimum of 5000 people. Towns of this size are by no means new: the photograph below shows the remains of the great city of Karnak which in 1400 B.C. contained no less than 100 000 inhabitants. The first cities in fact appeared over 5000 years ago, but throughout history until the nineteenth century only a very small proportion of persons were town dwellers, and before 1850 no society was predominantly urbanized.

The first country to be affected by large-scale urbanization was Great Britain, where the progressive concentration of people into rapidly growing towns was a concomitant of the Industrial Revolution. Prior to the mid-eighteenth century the great majority of people in Britain depended upon agriculture for their livelihood and lived in isolated farms, hamlets and villages in rural surroundings. The first census took place in 1801 after several decades of industrial growth and revealed that already 9·9% of the population of England and Wales lived in really large

Figure 1
Rapid urbanization of the world's population is evident in this comparison of total population (unbroken line) with the population in cities of more than 100,000 inhabitants (broken curve) over more than a century and a half.

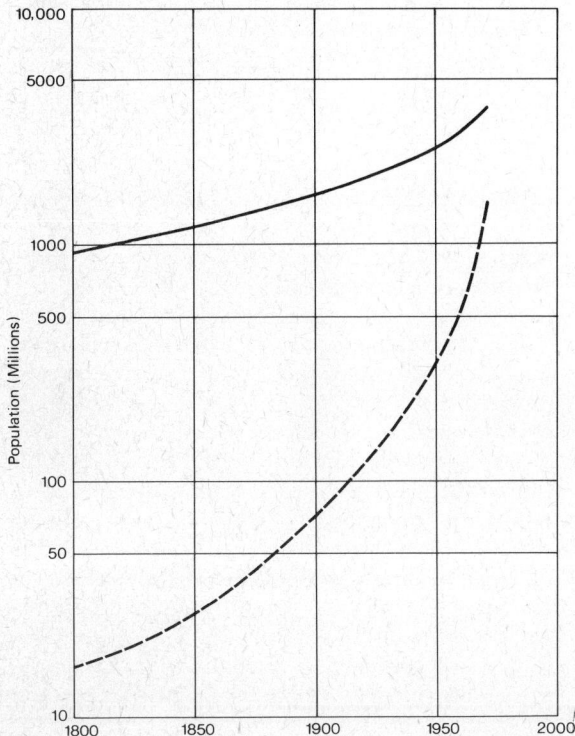

Photo 1
Karnak, Upper Egypt. Karnak contains the northern half of the ruins of Thebes, the capital of the ancient Egyptian Empire. During its heyday in the fourteenth century B.C. Thebes was a city of great wealth, with a population of well over 100 000, including 87 000 slaves.

Area	Populations (millions)		Number of cities over 100 000		Percentage population classified as urban ☐ Early '60s ■ Early '70s	
	1963	1972	Early 1960s	Early 1970s		
Africa	289	364	59	122		
Anglo America	208	233	169	264		
Middle America	75	99	37	53		
South America	157	201	88	150		
Asia	1754	2154	481	627		
Europe	437	469	308	401		
U.S.S.R	225	248	220	233		
Oceania	17	20	12	15		
World total	3162	3782	1374	1865		

0   10   20   30   40   50   60   70   80

Per cent

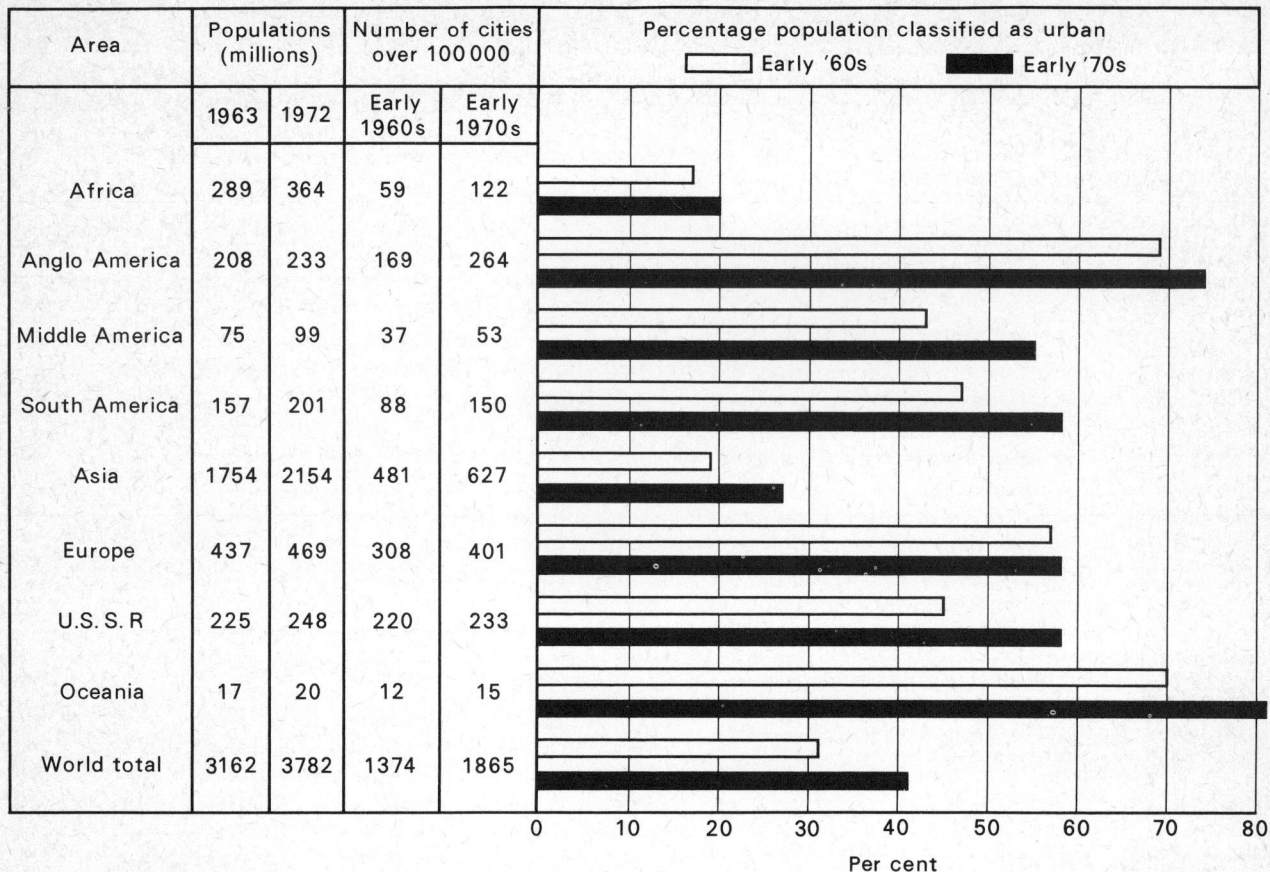

Figure 2
Urbanization trends in various regions of the world. (*Source:* UN Statistics)

towns of over 100 000. The startling increase in this percentage during the past 170 years is shown in figure 4. By 1861 the rural portion of the population was in a minority, and the urban majority has continued to grow until today it includes 78% of the total population.

There is evidence to suggest that urbanization is a finite process and that in certain advanced societies such as Great Britain, Germany and the United States, the end of the cycle may well be in sight. This curve shows, for example, that there has recently been a slight decline in the rate of urbanization in England and Wales. The main reason is that for two centuries so many people have moved out of farming and into city jobs that the supply of rural migrants has virtually dried up. On the other hand the slowing down of urbanization may be more apparent than real, for it

is becoming increasingly difficult to differentiate between urban and rural settlements. This is mainly because the number of non-farming residents in the countryside is rapidly increasing, but also because some farm workers now choose to live in urban surroundings. In both cases the key to the situation is modern transport, above all the ownership of private cars, which allows people to live many miles from their place of work. The growth of the suburban fringe and of commuter living entail an 'invasion' of hamlets, villages and small country towns by hundreds of thousands of former city dwellers, inevitably bringing urban sophistication to settings which once were unmistakably rural. In the space of a few years farming communities can change into 'dormitory villages', acquiring new shopping facilities and an accretion of

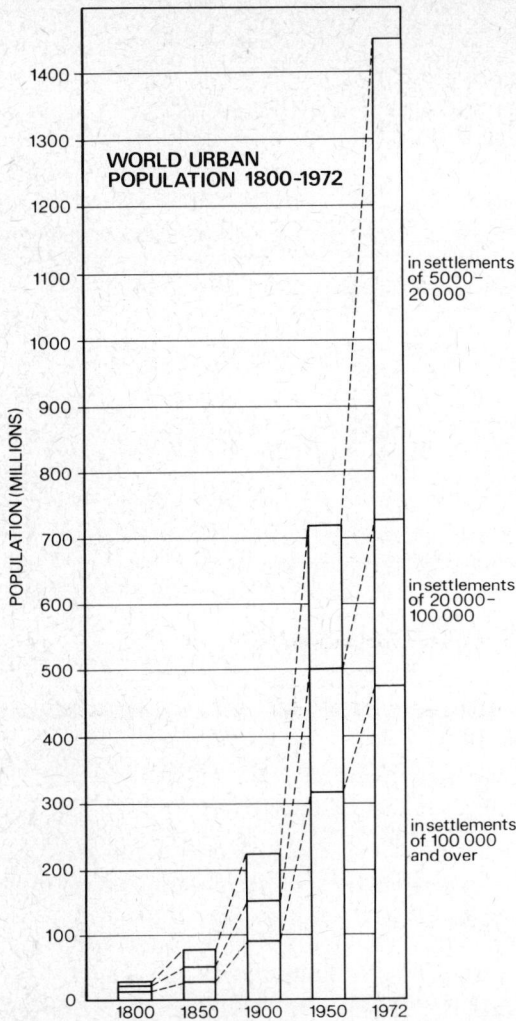

WORLD URBAN POPULATION 1800-1972

POPULATION (MILLIONS)

in settlements of 5000–20 000

in settlements of 20 000–100 000

in settlements of 100 000 and over

Figure 3
World urban population 1800–1972. (*Sources:* Beaujeu-Garnier and Chabot, and UN Statistics)

modern housing estates which give them the appearance of city suburbs. At the same time many well laid out low-density housing estates at the edge of cities are deliberately built in a 'rural' style. Where city leaves off and the countryside begins therefore becomes increasingly difficult to establish and the very terms *rural* and *urban* tend to become meaningless. Many predict that in time the whole of Great Britain will become one vast semi-rural suburban sprawl, with very few tracts of truly open countryside. This entirely novel situation would have the most profound effects on our quality of living and illustrates the vital importance of town and country planning.

In developed countries the net reproduction rates of rural inhabitants have exceeded those of people living in towns through most of the period of urbanization. Such urbanization was therefore only made possible by a continuous substantial flow of persons into the towns. Towards the end of the cycle, however, this imbalance tends to disappear, for net reproduction rates in cities go up while those in the country go down. Reasons include (i) a decline in death rates in modern cites brought about by improved hygiene, housing, health services and reduced atmospheric pollution; (ii) the greater fertility of city populations which, because migrants to cities are

Figure 4
Trends towards urbanization in certain countries. (*Source:* UN Statistics)

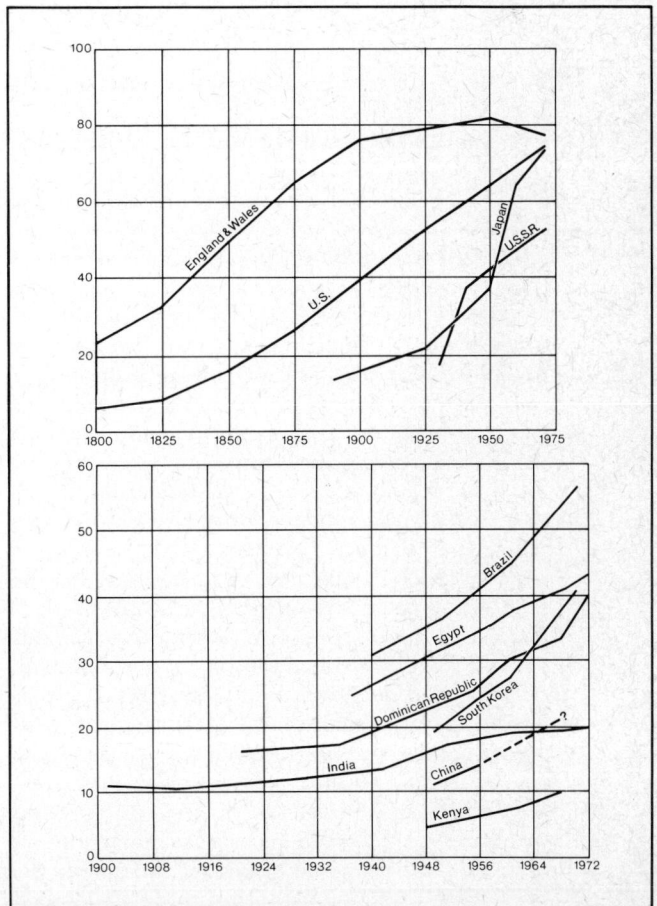

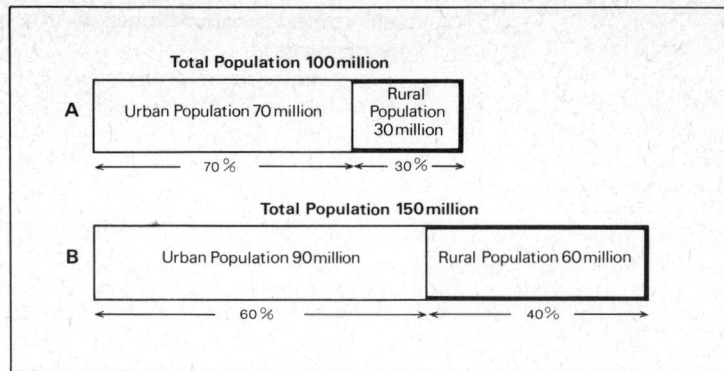

Figure 5
Total population increase and urbanization. This diagram illustrates the point that it is possible for the total urban population of a region to increase substantially, even though the region is becoming less urbanized.

mainly young, often include a larger proportion of people of child-bearing age; and (iii) the adoption of urban ideas, including the use of contraception, by farmers and other rural residents. In time, therefore, urbanization may continue by virtue of a very small net flow of migrants into the towns from the surrounding countryside.

It should be noted that although urbanization involves an *increase* in the proportion of a population living in towns it is possible for the process to cease, or even go into reverse, whilst the *absolute* numbers and size of towns may continue to increase, sometimes very rapidly. This is due to the natural increase of urban dwellers themselves, and in the current situation whereby the world population of over 4000 million is multiplying annually by some 75 million, the total increase of both urban and rural populations is staggering.

Until recent decades urbanization on a significant scale affected only those countries like Great Britain, Germany and the United States which began to industrialize in the eighteenth or nineteenth centuries and which acquired the technology distinctive of advanced societies over a long period of time. In currently underdeveloped countries such as Brazil, Zambia, India and Pakistan, the proportion of the population living in cities is also rising, in some cases very quickly, but there are some significant ways in which their urbanization differs from that formerly undergone by countries now reaching the end of the cycle. In other words the underdeveloped

regions are not in a stage of urban development exactly analagous to that of, say, Great Britain in the early nineteenth century. For one thing urbanization in such regions is somewhat more rapid, with a gain of about 20% per decade, compared with a fastest rate of 15% per decade which the industrialized countries once experienced. Another difference is that rural as well as town populations are growing in an unprecedented fashion, and this, by keeping down the *rate* of urbanization tends to obscure the fact that many towns in underdeveloped lands are growing at alarming speeds. Furthermore, except for the very large cities which have a powerful magnetic effect, the main factor today tends to be not rural–urban migration but a sheer net increase affecting both towns and country. *(See, e.g. figure 6(b).)* During the period of rapid growth of the advanced countries there were very substantial drops in the numbers of rural inhabitants *(see figure 6(a).)* During the difficult period of farm mechanization and rationalization it was possible for displaced peasants, tenant farmers and labourers to move with their families into the growing towns where there was plenty of employment. Today the story is disturbingly different, for the great bulk of displaced farmers in underdeveloped regions have nowhere to go and nothing to do—new jobs in towns being snapped up as soon as they occur by unemployed persons who were themselves born in the towns.

Despite the fact that the big cities of underdeveloped regions offer very limited opportunities of employment, their 'bright lights' constitute an almost fatal fascination for poverty stricken farmers. Rapid rural population increases put a very great strain on agricultural resources, and conditions in the countryside are often very bad. Overcrowding, land-fragmentation, over-grazing, soil-erosion, drought, pests, all these ills lead to chronic underemployment and distress, forcing peasants to abandon their plots and move into the towns. Caracas, Rio de Janeiro, Brazzaville, Calcutta, Rangoon, Manila . . . cities such as these become the goals of hundreds of thousands of rural migrants, people without land, jobs, money or possessions, for whom the remote chance of finding an urban occupation is a last remaining hope. Very large numbers of peasants therefore drift towards the metropolitan centres, pausing en route at various smaller towns where they fail to take root, and arriving destitute and homeless at their final destination. Such unfortunate people become squatters wherever there are unoccupied and unprotected sites, and the ramshackle hovels which they build for themselves out of discarded tins, packing cases, plastic bags and fragments of wood and galvanized iron form a commonplace feature of many 'emerging' cities—the *shanty towns* of Johannesburg, the *bidonvilles*

Photo 2
A West African rural family with seven children. Mounting population pressure on limited resources causes migration to urban centres.

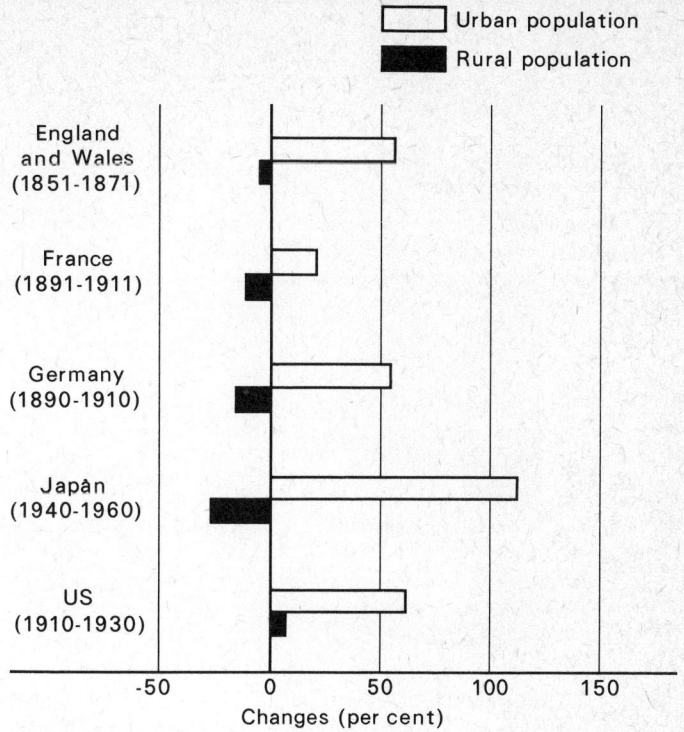

Figure 6(a)
Urban and rural population changes (per cent) in certain developed countries.

Figure 6(b)
Urban and rural population changes (per cent) in certain underdeveloped countries between 1968 and 1972.

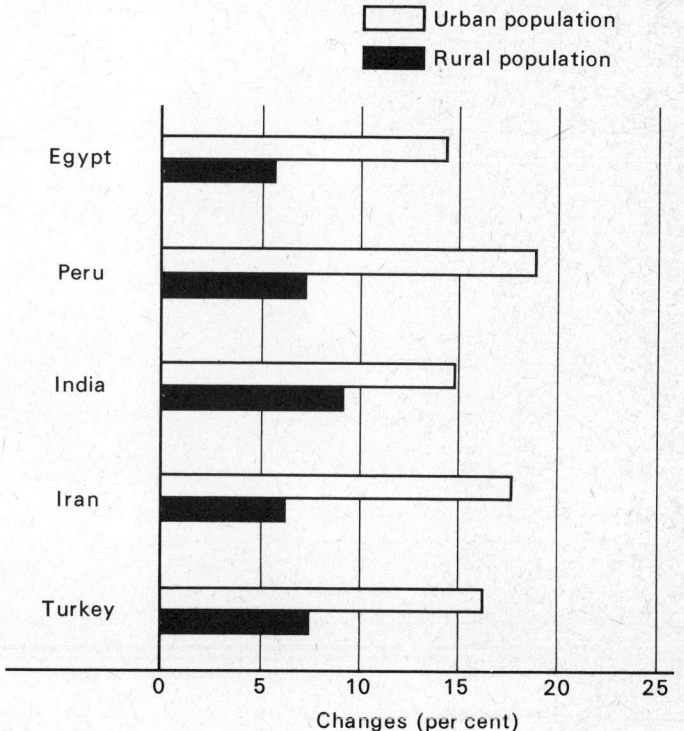

Photo 3
Tembiza Township, an African shanty town near Edenvale, Transvaal.

Photo 4
Shanty town, Bombay.

of Algiers, the *cardboard towns* of Khartoum, the *jacoles* of Mexico City and so on. Yet the advantages of towns in underdeveloped regions is for the most part quite illusory, for '. . . appalling and virtually unchanging poverty, still largely of a rural type, and itself . . . a considerable anti-developmental factor, is a major characteristic of the urban areas.'*

In Southeast Asia . . . a fragile and insufficient superstructure of modern industry is being erected. . . . upon a foundation of a largely stagnant agricultural sector. In these circumstances, even a small increase in industrial development may cause disproportionate urban growth. From smaller towns in which the effect of establishing one factory or other modern enterprise is observable, it has been reported that the increment in employment resulting specifically from such a project may well be accompanied by an increase in unemployment and in casual or irregular employment within the town. This is because the new source of wealth attracts large numbers from the countryside seeking to obtain some benefit from it, usually indirectly in rendering some form of service to those employed in the new enterprise. It is for reasons such as these that the proportion of the economically active population recorded in 'service' occupations is characteristically so large in the Asian city. This tends to give a false picture of the prosperity of the cities because in the West a full tertiary sector is usually associated with a high level of economic development. In Asia the reverse tends to be the case. Many more persons are supported in the cities than the economic base warrants through what is essentially a shared poverty system. . . . (Thus) if a great proportion of the urban population is not to starve, a much larger number of jobs has to be created than is reconcilable with efficient management. For the masses of immigrants from the countryside who now crowd into the cities, the urban standard of living must remain only marginally above

*Dr D. J. Dwyer, 'The city in the developing world and the example of Southeast Asia', *Geography*, No. 241.

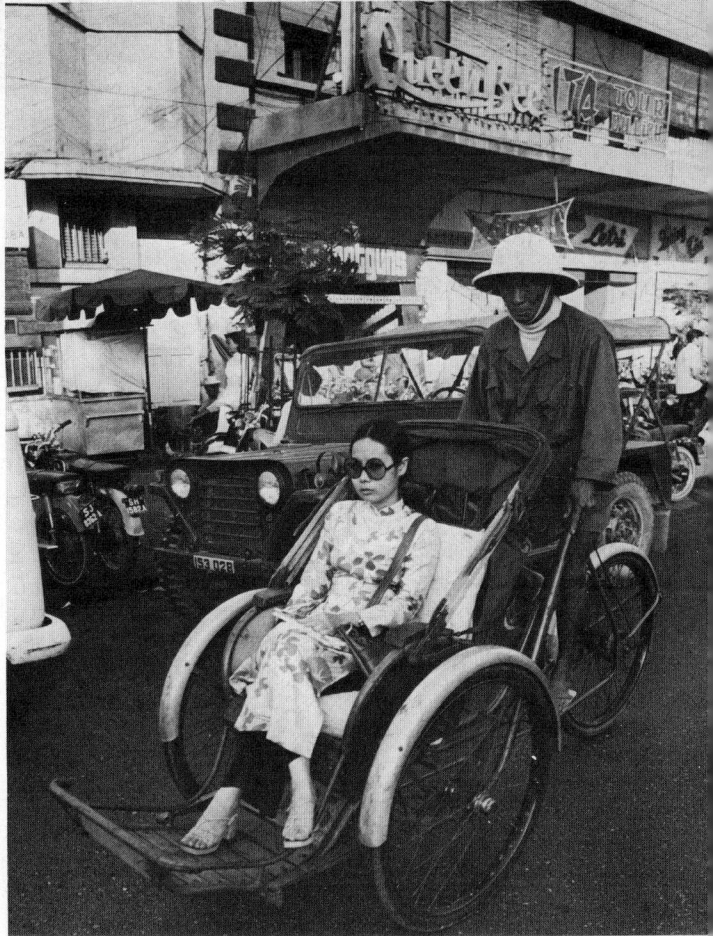

Photo 5
A pedicab in Saigon. Pedicab driving is a typical 'do-it-yourself' service occupation in South-east Asian cities with underemployment problems.

that which they can obtain in their home villages, an abysmally low level, in order to be acceptable. Hence street-sellers abound; there are many more pedicab drivers than are really needed; large numbers of domestic servants are kept; and there are far too many office employees. The process extends even into official administration. There are many middlemen in commerce also, each taking a small share of the profit on the movement of goods.*

As well as massive unemployment problems most of these cities also suffer from chronic maladministration, typified by the following account of conditions in the

Great numbers of those who fetch up in cities like Manila remain essentially *rural* in outlook: illiterate and apathetic, they build rural-type shacks and follow a hand-to-mouth subsistence life more akin to that of a peasant farmer than a wage-earning industrial worker. City populations and institutions thus tend to become permeated by a lethargy born of rural apathy and the cities fail to act as effective catalysts for economic expansion. The persistence of rural ideals and aspirations is accentuated wherever new migrants to a city congregate in squatter communities. The only obvious solution is to transfer mixed groups of the newcomers to specially built low cost houses scattered throughout the city, in the hope that they will gradually become assimilated and urbanized. An example of what can be

Photo 6
This rural migrant to Chandigarh, Punjab, has set up a flimsy pavement home from which he sells drinking water to passers-by.

Photo 7
Recently constructed housing blocks, Hong Kong. These apartments form part of the Colony's re-settlement project for its teeming homeless. *(See also text and cover photo.)*

Philippines: 'In the past twelve months Manila has had a water shortage in which some 70% of the metropolitan area was without regular service . . . it has had a garbage crisis . . . there has been a school crisis, though a minor one this year . . . electric services went through a bad period some months ago . . . mail is in a continual state of crisis and in general it seems better to give up trying to use the telephone . . . police and fire protection are unreliable . . . the constantly increasing burden of traffic and the conditions of the roads discourage one from venturing beyond walking distance. In other words, social organization in the Manila area has not been able to maintain these services in the face of population increase and normal wear and tear on facilities; and at times it appears we are returning to *barrio* (village) -type existence.'*
This last remark is especially significant, for in such near-chaotic situation there can be no development of a truly urban ethos, no sense of progress or hope for future material rewards such as fired the imagination of migrants into European cities in the nineteenth century.

*J. J. Carroll, 'Philippine social organization and national development', *Philippine Studies*, Vol. 14, pp. 573–90.

Photo 8
Slum house and re-settlement blocks, Zanzibar.

Table A

Table A
**Annual rate of population increase (%)
in certain undeveloped countries**

Algeria	3·5	Mexico	3·5
Egypt	2·5	Peru	3·1
Ghana	2·9	India	2·2
Zambia	2·6	Pakistan	2·4
Brazil	2·9	South Korea	2·1
Venezuela	3·4	Iran	3·0

each multiplied threefold during the past decade. There are substantial, and locally massive, rural–urban movements of population in all such countries, which combined with an overall population growth rate exceeding 2% p.a. *(see Table A)* makes the potential expansion of their cities a most serious economic, social and political problem.

Accra is typical of many rapidly growing cities in underdeveloped regions. It was the main centre of administration during British colonial rule, becoming the capital of the Gold Coast in 1870 and subsequently of Ghana in 1948. As the country's natural outlet for trade it soon became the main focus of road and rail routes and these made the city a

done in this respect is provided by Hong Kong, where since 1952 the Resettlement Department alone has re-housed more than 1 in 4 of the total population of 3·8 millions.

Yet despite these sometimes frightening problems the urbanization of underdeveloped regions continues with undiminished vigour, and an unprecedented number of their people now live in giant cities, many of which show astonishing rates of growth. During the past 30 years, for example, Caracas, Teheran, Seoul and Karachi have all increased their populations by 7–8 times and Dehli, Lima and Kowloon by 5–6 times. A further nine cities—Bombay, Bogata, Calcutta, Peking, São Paulo, Mexico City, Buenos Aires, Santiago and Cairo—have grown by 3–4 times, whilst Accra, Algiers and Nairobi have

Table B
Population of Accra

1901	15 000
1948	133 000
1960	338 000
1966	600 000
1971	740 000

Table C

Ghana. Unemployment rates (% of total population)

	Male	Female
Accra	11·0	9·1
Elsewhere in Ghana (except Niger and Upper Volta)	6·5	3·5

natural target for rural migrants. Since the country gained independence in 1948 Accra's population has multiplied more than fivefold, from 133 000 to 740 000. In 1970 there were 116 000 people in Accra from other parts of Ghana and 60 000 from other African countries. Its population includes a large proportion (64%) of males, attracted into the city by a wide range of employment opportunities in manufacturing and construction. Even so the city has considerable unemployment as the Table *(left)* shows. Accra also has acute housing problems, the numbers of persons per house having risen from 12·6 to 18·5 over the period from 1948 to 1970. The map shows the growth of Accra since 1900.

Some of the more serious problems faced by

Figure 7
The growth of Accra. (*After* Amoah and Hilton)

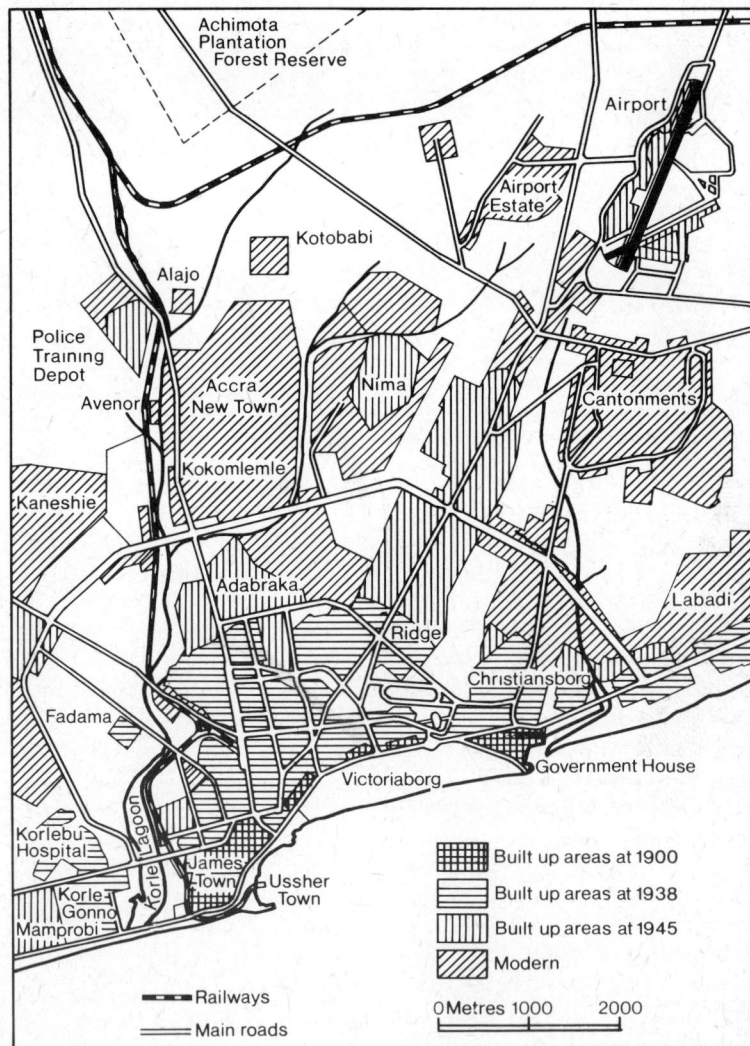

Table D

Some problems associated with urbanization

Atmospheric pollution and associated diseases, e.g. lung cancer, chronic bronchitis.

Industrial waste disposal and pollution of waterways.

Sewage disposal.

Traffic congestion.

Overcrowding and associated epidemics, e.g. cholera and influenza.

Social rootlessness and associated violence.

Stress illnesses, e.g. hypertension, some heart diseases and mental disorders.

employment in an urban environment. Gigantic city agglomerations are predicted with New York, for example, possibly reaching 30 million by the year 2000, and world cities of 50–100 million becoming commonplace in the twenty-first century. Such estimates postulate the virtual disappearance of pure countryside and raise questions about how such a completely urbanized humanity could obtain its food and fibres. Perhaps agriculture as it is now practised will be completely replaced by highly intensive 'factory farming' and the production of synthetic foods. Large-scale urbanization is bound to affect the *quality* of living and unless urgent efforts are made both to foresee and to tackle its problems it seems inevitable that future changes in mankind's environment will be for the worse.

urbanized societies are indicated above. These problems are discussed at length in Section 6. Here it should be noted that many of these dislocations are novel in human experience. Furthermore, little is known of the long-term deleterious physical and mental effects on Man of living in a desperately overcrowded and stressful environment, but recent medical reports and predictions are far from reassuring.* Solutions to the problems of urban living are still largely at the experimental stage, e.g. urban heavy goods traffic might eventually be reduced by sending goods in containers along pressurized underground tunnels. Such projects take a long while to test and even longer to put into effect and time is running out. Meanwhile the emergence of giant cities of 5–15 million is adding a new dimension to urbanization and virtually every human society is becoming more urbanized. Such trends seem certain to continue, for a large majority of mankind inhabits the underdeveloped lands where urbanization is in its early stages. India, for example, with some 12% of its population of 605 million in cities of over 20 000 is at a stage equivalent to that reached by European countries such as Austria and Switzerland in 1890. Some experts predict a situation where 85–90% of the entire world population will live in settlements of over 5000 and find

*See, for example, René Dubos, 'The human environment', *Science Journal*, Vol. 5A, No. 4, October 1969

Section 2 **Early urban growth**

2 Cities in history

These photographs and that on page 1 show the remains of some of the world's earliest known cities. All of them were built about 5000 years ago in the river basins of the Nile and Mesopotamia. *(See figure 8.)* This location resulted from the fact that city construction followed the technological changes of Neolithic times, during which men acquired the art of cultivation. The development of farming made it possible to accumulate food surpluses, a factor of crucial importance for the evolution of cities.*

In a pre-urban society everyone is directly involved almost continuously in collecting or hunting for food. Such a society must necessarily be nomadic and there is neither time nor

*This assumption and the argument in the next three paragraphs follows the conventional explanations of city growth. See, however, page 15, for an alternative viewpoint.

Photo 9
All that remains of a city which flourished three millenia ago on the banks of the Gurgan River, Iran. Air photos may reveal details of buildings and streets which are barely recognisable on the ground. The total population of such a city can be inferred from the number of dwellings which show up in the ruins.

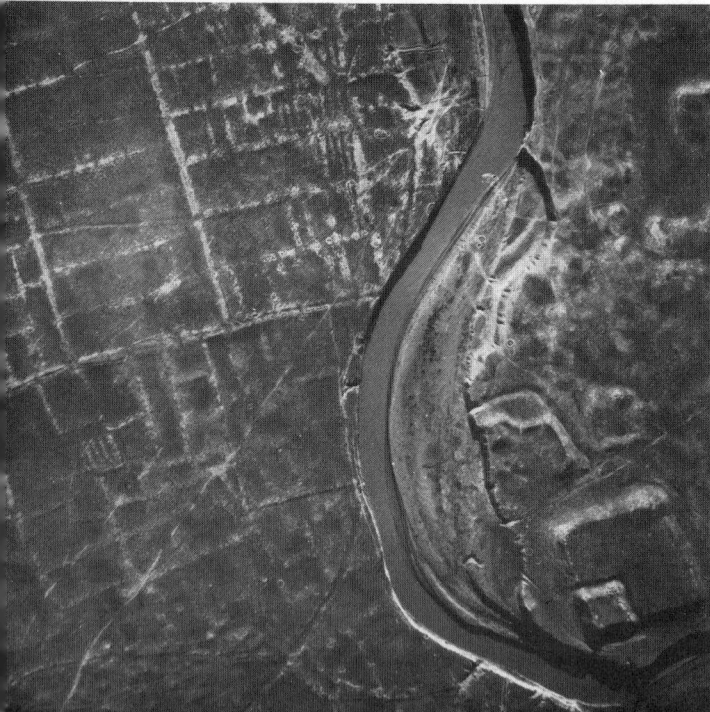

Photo 10
The ruins of Babylon. The city stood on a bank of the River Euphrates at a point where a relatively narrow strip of land separates it from the River Tigris. The nodal position of Babylon enabled it to intercept traffic between Syria and the Persian Gulf and to dominate trade routes between the Euphrates and Tigris. Already by the eighteenth century B.C. Babylon controlled the greater part of Mesopotamia. The present ruins date back to the early sixteenth century B.C. when the city was rebuilt and when it attained its greatest fame.

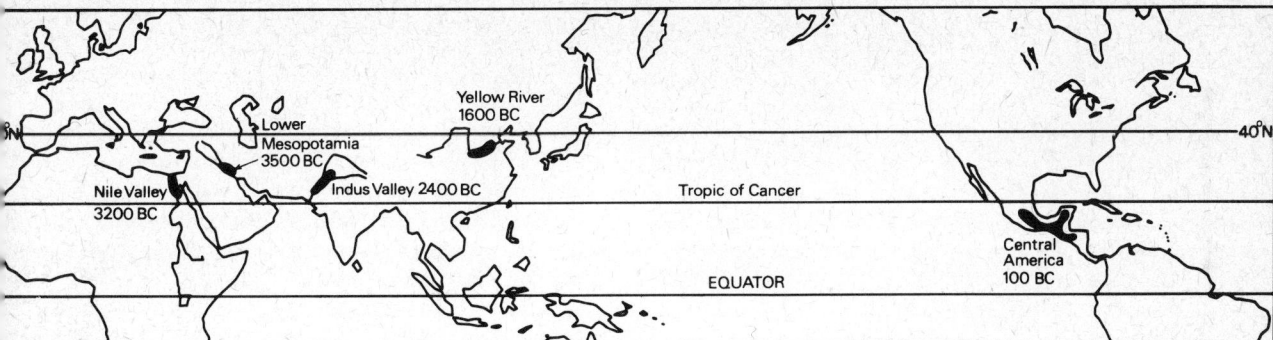

Figure 8
Locations of earliest city growth.

incentive for the construction of anything more than temporary shelters. Peoples such as the Boro of Amazonia and the Bushmen of the Kalahari still live in this way. The discovery of agriculture probably took place simultaneously on the fertile flood plains of the Nile, Tigris and Euphrates and later spread to the Indus and Yellow River valleys. The first grain crops were wild grasses, from which new plants, e.g. the Emmer wheats, were gradually evolved. In these ancient civilizations a variety of technological innovations (*see right*) made it possible for a people to become sedentary, build up food surpluses and allow a minority to specialize in tasks

other than those concerned with food production. These specialist artisans—potters,

Table E
Some technical innovations which favoured urban growth

Use of tools, e.g. stone hoes and later metal axes, sickles and digging sticks.

Invention of writing and numeracy and the keeping of accounts.

Harnessing of animal and human muscle power, e.g. ox-drawn plough.

Irrigation.

Wheeled vehicles.

Photo 11
Persepolis, the ancient capital of the Archaemenian kings of Persia. These ruins date back to the fourth century B.C. and lie 50 kilometres north-east of Shiraz in south-western Iran. Persepolis was captured and partly destroyed by the Greeks under Alexander the Great in 330 B.C.

13

Photo 12
Afghan nomad tents.

Photo 13
Nomad huts, Somalia.

weavers, metallurgists, builders and so on—
were directed by a wealthy élite composed of
religious leaders and traders. The latter
obtained their wealth and power by appro-
priating part of the produce of the agrarian
majority. Thus evolved static, partly urban-

ized, feudal societies, with a rigid class
structure and division of labour.

The inhabitants of these first cities formed a
tiny minority of non-food producers. They
lived within a predominantly rural landscape
and were at first entirely dependent for foodstuffs on their immediate environment. The
extent of the hinterland tributary to a city was
limited partly by the military power of its
ruling élite, but mainly by the primitive
means of transport available to bring in food
from the countryside. Human and animal
porterage, ox-drawn carts and river barges
remained the main methods of moving commodities until late medieval times. Most early
cities thus remained small. Estimates of their
total population can be made based on the
number of dwellings revealed by archaeo-
logical excavations, but exact figures are impossible to ascertain due to the lack of reliable
statistics. It seems likely that very few of them
exceeded 20 000. Furthermore the urban proportion of a population probably kept below
2% because no less than 50–90 farmers were
needed to support each city dweller. Early
cities stayed small, too, because they were un-
hygienic, unhealthy and afflicted by high
death rates. Inward migration from the
countryside was a mere trickle, partly because
the feudal peasantry were rooted to the land
by tradition, sentiment and obligation and
also because there were few opportunities for
employment in the cities' varied but small-
scale craft industries.

For three millenia urban growth was confined to irrigated regions in the sub-tropics.
Only the certain sunshine and heat of such
regions made it possible for primitive farmers
to grow enough cereals to feed growing town
populations. The dry climate of Egypt,
Mesopotamia and the Indus Valley also
minimized soil leaching, so that plant nutrients
deposited by an annual flood stayed in the
topsoil throughout the ensuing year.* The art
of irrigation gradually spread from the Near
East to the islands and coastlands of the
eastern Mediterranean. Among the many
urban communities which consequently grew
up there were those of Levant (Phoenicia),

*P. Wheatley, 'Proleptic observations on the origins of
urbanism', *Liverpool Essays in Geography* (Ed. Steel &
Lawton), p. 316, Longman.

Crete (Minoa) and Greece. Mediterranean town growth was particularly prolific during the Greco-Roman period, i.e. from *c.* 800 B.C.– *c.* A.D. 400, for both the Greeks and the Romans solved the problem of urban food supply by colonial expansion and the development of trade.

The relevance of irrigation, annual flooding, a benign climate and indeed of all physical 'controls' has recently been re-examined by several distinguished geographers. Professor Wheatley, for example, emphasizes the role of ceremonial centres in initiating permanent settlements. Sacred tribal shrines are discerned in the ruins of most early societies. These sacred enclaves were administered, guarded and maintained by a non-cultivating élite of priests, scribes, warriors and craftsmen. 'Specialized priests were probably the first persons to be released from the daily round of subsistence labour.'* The priests, by virtue of their religious authority, eventually gained total social and political power. This they did via their consultative role relating to matters of crop and animal fertility: payments (and later taxes) in grain went into central granaries controlled by the priests, who therefore took charge of redistribution. In Mesopotamia, for example, agricultural labour was often under the centralized management of the temple and '. . . the centralization of control over labour and land, as well as over the produce of the earth, whether plant, animal or mineral, was an invariable concomitant of the rise of ceremonial centres. . . . There is overwhelming evidence that the earliest urban forms were the preconceived undertakings of priestly élites rather than haphazard aggregations of people responding to a human desire for economic gain.'*

On this argument the earliest urban centres arose as a direct consequence of magico-religious practices. Technological changes in agriculture then made it possible, by increasing yields, for priests to acquire greater power and allowed their settlements to grow in size: these technological changes did not in themselves, however, necessitate urban growth. Moreover, the precise location of a proto-urban sacred site was largely fortuitous and was not directly related to any favourable circumstance in the physical environment. The fact remains, however, that many prehistoric ceremonial centres did *not* become nuclei of urban growth. Examples include Avebury, Stonehenge, Bomlitz (Lüneburg Heath) and Carnac (Brittany). This may have been due to an unfavourable climate and a terrain which did not generally encourage farming and the redistribution of farm

Op.cit. p. 341.

Photo 14
Megalithic stone circle, Avebury, Wiltshire. Several prehistoric trackways converge on this part of southern England and Avebury appears to have been a site of considerable magico-religious significance, yet no permanent settlement evolved there. The present village dates from Saxon times.

products. Yet such reasoning cannot explain the absence of early cities on the very fertile loess belt of the Central European börde, a zone which has been relatively densely settled by farming communities for two millenia. The exact relationships between urban growth and the nature of the physical landscape remain tantalizingly obscure.

Greek city-states grew up, isolated from one another, on fragments of fertile coastal plains in an otherwise mountainous and barren environment. To the Greeks a city was essentially a political community, and its size was influenced by this viewpoint. According to Aristotle 'the city (or *polis*) must have a population which is self-sufficient for the purpose of living the good life after the manner of a political community. But it must not be so unwieldy that the members cannot maintain personal contact with one another.'* In fact most Greek city-states contained less than 10 000 inhabitants, the number which Hippo-damus the town-planner of Miletus thought ideal. That most Greek cities remained relatively small was due as much to the

limitations imposed by the physical landscape as to ideals of democratic self-government. At first the cities were intended to be self-sufficing in foodstuffs, so that numbers were restricted by a scarcity of agricultural land and of water for irrigation and domestic purposes. The urban nucleus of a state, moreover, housed many persons who owned and tilled land outside the city walls: thus a state remained small enough for its citizens to walk to and from their cultivated plots. 'In their formative period the Greek cities never lost their connections with their countryside or their villages: there was a tidal drifting in and out of the city with the seasons. As late as 400 B.C. . . . three quarters of the Athenian burghers owned some land in Attica . . . the roots of village life were so deep that even the displaced victims of a savage conquest could sometimes survive the destruction of the city. When the Spartans, for example, compelled the inhabitants of Mantinea to destroy their own city . . . these miserable people retired to their rural *demes*, from which they had never been completely severed.'†

†Lewis Mumford, *The City in History*, pp. 151, 153, Pelican.

*Aristotle, *Politics*, ii, 5.2.

Figure 9
Greek cities in the fifth century B.C.

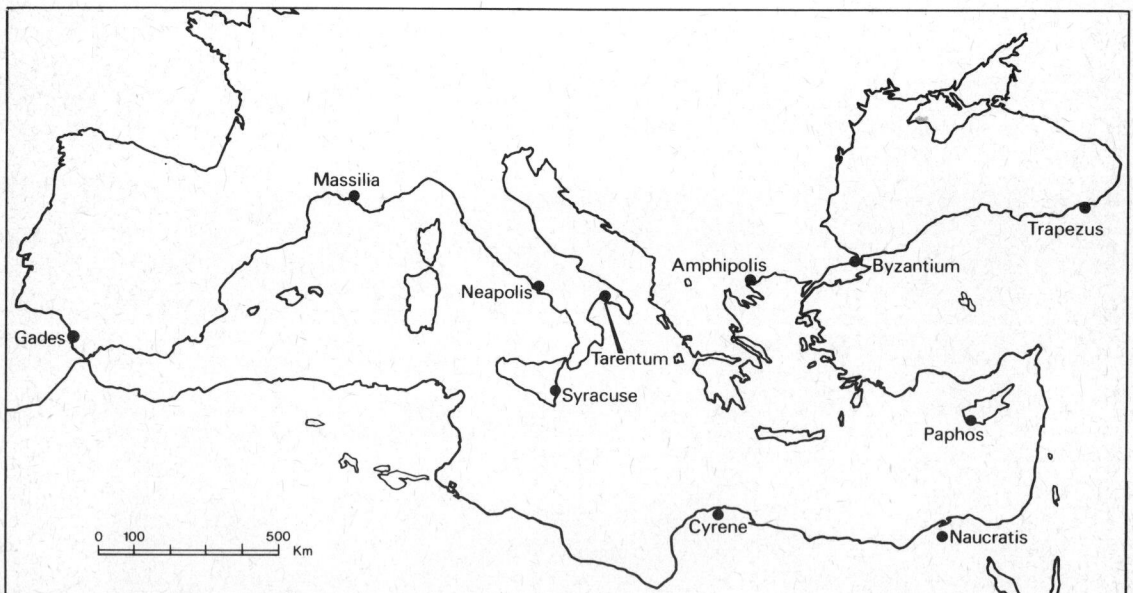

Photo 15

Paestum was an important Greek colonial city (Poseidonia) founded c. 600 B.C. It lies near the coast 35 kilometres south of the modern Italian port of Salerno. Paestum was laid out with a grid-iron pattern of paved streets. It contains three remarkably well preserved Greek temples, including the Temple of Neptune seen here. With the gradual silting up of the nearby River Sele the city became malarial and its prosperity waned. It was finally abandoned after being sacked by Saracen Invaders in A.D. 871. The present ruins were rediscovered in the eighteenth century, after lying hidden by swamp vegetation and *macchia* scrub.

As their populations gradually increased, creating serious problems of food and water supply, most Greek city-states deliberately chose to remain relatively small and self-contained. This they did by sending out their 'surplus' persons to found daughter colonial cities as far apart as Gades, Massilia, Naucratis and Trapezus. *(See figure 9.)* This photograph shows the remains of the Greek colonial city of Paestum: note the typical 'grid-iron' arrangement of its streets, a pattern which was later incorporated into Roman urban planning. *(See overleaf.)* Colonizing cities such as Miletus and Rhodes eventually became important centres of commerce, with the result that their numbers grew somewhat due to the presence of many merchants and slaves: even so, no Greek city is thought to have exceeded 100 000. This smallness—part deliberate, part the result of a cramping physical environment—eventually proved fatal, for despite the formation of political leagues the Greeks could not indefinitely ward off an attack by stronger outside enemies.

Roman cities were the product of an Empire which, at its apex, imposed a common

Figure 10
The Roman Empire from Augustus to its greatest extent under Trajan. (*Source:* Cambridge Ancient History)

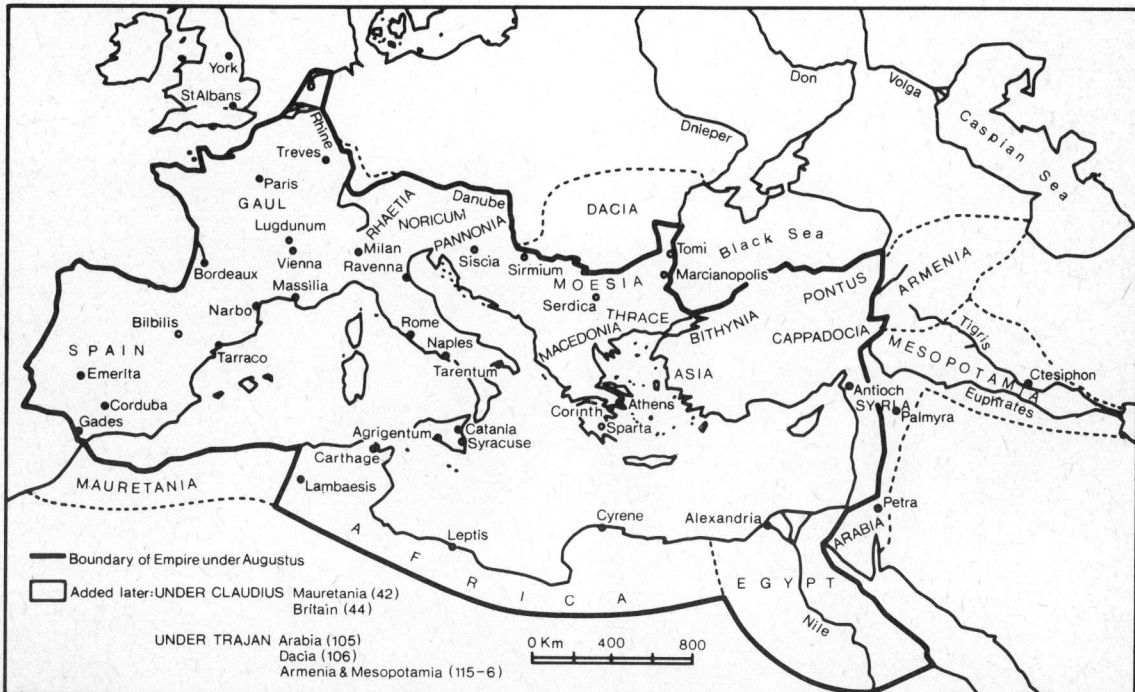

political authority from Carlisle to Cairo and from Gibraltar to the Caspian Sea. (*See figure 10.*) Sited and built with military precision and thoroughness, these cities and the famous paved roads which linked them to one another and to Rome had permanent effects on the human geography of Europe. Many present-day cities occupy Roman sites, and some modern roads still follow the alignment chosen by Roman constructors. Roman cities had both garrison and administrative functions and formed nerve-centres of what was essentially an urban culture: even country dwellers were 'attributed' as non-citizens to the nearest town. Thus the Roman Empire bestowed upon Western Europe a concept of urban living which, due to the solidity and strategic siting of its cities, survived a thousand years of barbarian invasion and medieval chaos. More directly Roman urbanism survived in the Byzantine and Islamic territories of Asia Minor and North Africa.

The most obvious legacy of Roman urbanism is the grid-iron pattern of streets within the walls of its former settlements. (*See figures 11 (a) and 11 (b).*) This rectilinear pattern was probably copied from the Etruscans, a people who migrated from Asia Minor to peninsular Italy in the eighth century B.C., but similar layouts characterized many Greek colonial towns in the Italian South and in Sicily. The Roman emphasis on the construction of defensive walls, aligned whenever the terrain would allow in the form of a rectangle, made the grid-iron street plan commonplace throughout the Empire. The main roads within a Roman fortress were deliberately orientated north–south and east–west and were named the *carde* and the *decumanus* respectively. These roads entered the walls at four symmetrically sited gates and intersected in the city centre at the *forum*. Like the Greeks whom they conquered, the Romans located their temples and sacred relics in or close to the *forum*, the open space of which made it a gathering place for political discussion and social gossip. Around the *forum* the land within the walls was subdivided by other roads into blocks, each of which was approximately 80 metres square. To what extent is

Photos 16 and 17
Pompeii, Italy. This Roman city was completely destroyed and submerged beneath volcanic ash and mud during a violent eruption of Vesuvius in 79 A.D. These photographs show (*below*) a paved street gouged by chariot wheels, pavements and stepping stones: Mount Vesuvius looms in the background; (*right*) a view looking south to the ancient forum.

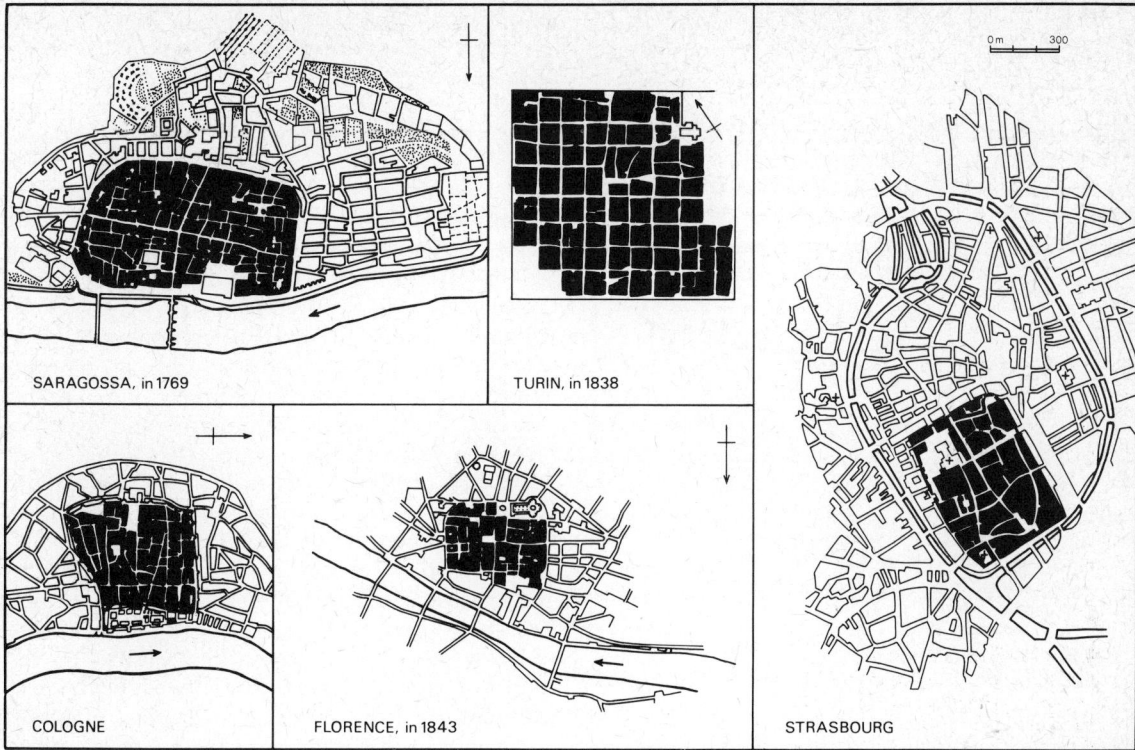

Figure 11 (a)
Roman town plans. Areas in black indicate Roman site. (*After* J. M. Houston)

Figure 11 (b)
Roman Silchester (Calleva Atrebatum). This Roman town north of Basingstoke, Hampshire, has not survived in a modern form. From an air photograph it is possible to identify the former grid system of roads and the central forum. The relative lack of buildings within the walls suggests that Silchester was never a flourishing district capital. (Based on a map in the *Town and Country Planning Textbook*)

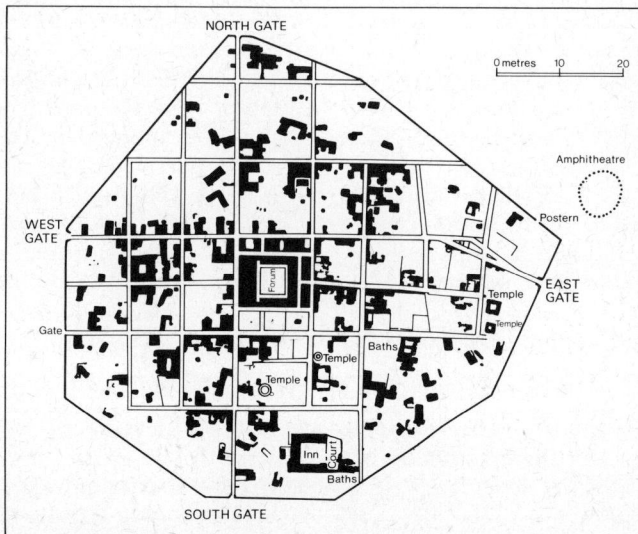

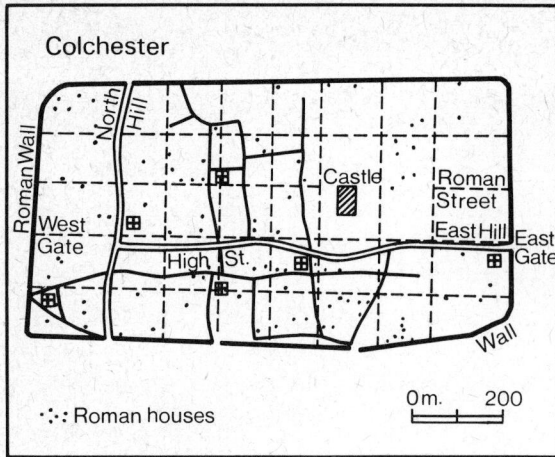

Figure 12
A reconstruction of Roman Colchester, in which the ancient streets appear as broken lines. The modern roads are curved heavy lines. Modern churches are inserted. (*After* T. Adams)

this pattern still discernible in the modern street plan of Colchester? Roman towns were remarkable for their street paving, aqueducts and sewers and especially for their elaborate public baths and oversized arenas. 'The regular chequerboard layout within a rectangular boundary, the arcaded walks, the forum, the theatre, the arena, the baths, the public lavatories (over-costly, over-decorated) were standard equipment. All these are to be found in Timgad. Similar forms were repeated from one end of the empire to the other: from Chester in western England, which still has an elevated and covered 'Roman' shopping street, to Antioch and Ephesus in Asia Minor. The new market-places at Coventry and Harlow, with their upper tiers and offices, are, no less than the early nineteenth-century shopping arcade at Providence, Rhode Island, only a recovery of the admirable Roman multi-level plan.'*

The great paradox of Roman urbanism was Rome itself. This city, to which all roads led and to which all tribute was due, never achieved the ordered elegance which might have been expected as the focal point of an

essentially urban civilization, and which was in fact sometimes approached in Roman colonial settlements. This failure was due partly to the city's great size (at its zenith it possibly contained nearly a million inhabitants) and partly to the parasitic role which Rome's rulers and citizens chose to adopt within the Empire. Because it was so big Rome faced problems of congestion and pollution which its engineers and planners never managed to solve. Thus the city's much-lauded aqueducts and sewers served only certain buildings, and those only at ground-floor level. Public buildings, e.g. baths, arenas, lavatories, monuments and temples were massive and ornate, but the great majority of Rome's citizens lived in squalid barrack-like blocks, sub-divided into dark insanitary hovels for which they paid exorbitant rents, and which were so badly built that they were liable to collapse without warning. Most human ordure was piled up in the narrow streets or dumped in open pits on the edge of the city. In consequence Rome was afflicted by all manner of diseases and was scourged by the plague in 23 B.C. and again in A.D. 65, 79 and 162.

In addition to sickness and material squalor, Rome was besmirched with a moral decay attributable to a lack of purpose of its parasitic population. Loot flowed into Rome daily from the length and breadth of the Empire: corn, wine, oil, slaves, metals, timber, fruit, fabrics, all arrived in an ever-increasing torrent. The inflow of food made possible the growth of the city, but, because it was handed out as a dole, the Roman proletariat had little incentive to work. To fill in the vacuous hours of enforced idleness the Romans thus attended endless shows and spectacles laid on in the arenas by wealthy patriarchs. By A.D. 359 there were no less than 200 public holidays each year, including 175 days of 'games': the latter included public sex-orgies and a continuous slaughter of tens of thousands of men, women and animals in gladitorial combat in the infamous Colosseum. Rome was grandiose but corrupt and its citizens were condemned to non-creative and passive roles in a dictatorial society. The Romans never solved the problem of the devolution of power and their city suffered pathological overgrowth. Some scholars draw a parallel between the material

*Lewis Mumford, *op. cit.*, p. 242.

and social excesses, vices and ultimate collapse of Rome and the problems of present day conurbations.

The collapse of the Roman Empire brought about a withering of urban life in the former Roman territories to the north of the Alps, but though many cities fell into decay the traditions of urbanism did not die out completely. Groups of people continued to live inside the Roman walls, for these afforded some protection against the wandering Eurasian tribes which scourged the countryside. In some cities, e.g. Nîmes and Arles, former amphitheatres were sealed off and converted into fortresses, but it was not until the eleventh century that there was any general attempt to rebuild Roman defences.

The concepts of collective living also survived the Dark Ages in the various monastic orders of the early Christian Church. The Church, moreover, was the only institution in early medieval Europe which was organized at more than a local level. In an era of almost universal distress the Church provided a faith and a unique unifying discipline: people who looked to the Church for guidance also rallied to its defence, and so Church buildings became focal points in urban reconstruction.

Photo 18
The ruins of the Colosseum, central Rome. The Palatine Hill lies beyond and the Roman Forum is to the top right.

Photo 19
The Roman Forum, heart of ancient Rome. In the background is the Arch of Titus and the Colosseum.

The gradual reawakening of city life owed much, too, to the growth of trade. Merchants sought the relative security of walled encampments within which they could assemble their markets or fairs and conduct transactions in peace and quiet. Cities like Mainz, for example, where the Roman walls were restored after A.D. 500, attracted a motley collection of tradesmen, merchants, craftsmen, nobles and clerks, as well as priests, monks and scholars. Mercantile urban communities multiplied especially in the thirteenth and fourteenth centuries, a period of growing political stability during which many towns were granted charters and a degree of self-government. Persons who lived in a town for a year and a day became free men. As the rural population increased, putting pressures on land resources, living conditions in the countryside deteriorated and the towns attracted peasants eager to shed their feudal obligations. Once free, a town dweller could buy and sell urban land, conduct trade and enjoy many other legal and political privileges.

The fastest growing towns in the Middle Ages were located at strategic points on trans-continental trade routes, the most important of which ran from northern Italy to Flanders via the Rhineland, and from the Baltic coast to the Paris Basin. Fortified river-crossings were especially important: see, for example, this map of the German portion of the trans-Alpine routes. Medieval trading cities such as Ulm, Augsburg and Mainz had much in common: their populations were mainly involved in trade or craft industries; they were legally constituted and virtually self-governing; and they were regional centres

Figure 13
Southern Germany. Main cities and trade routes in the Middle Ages. All towns on this map were formerly Roman and were later occupied by German-speaking peoples.

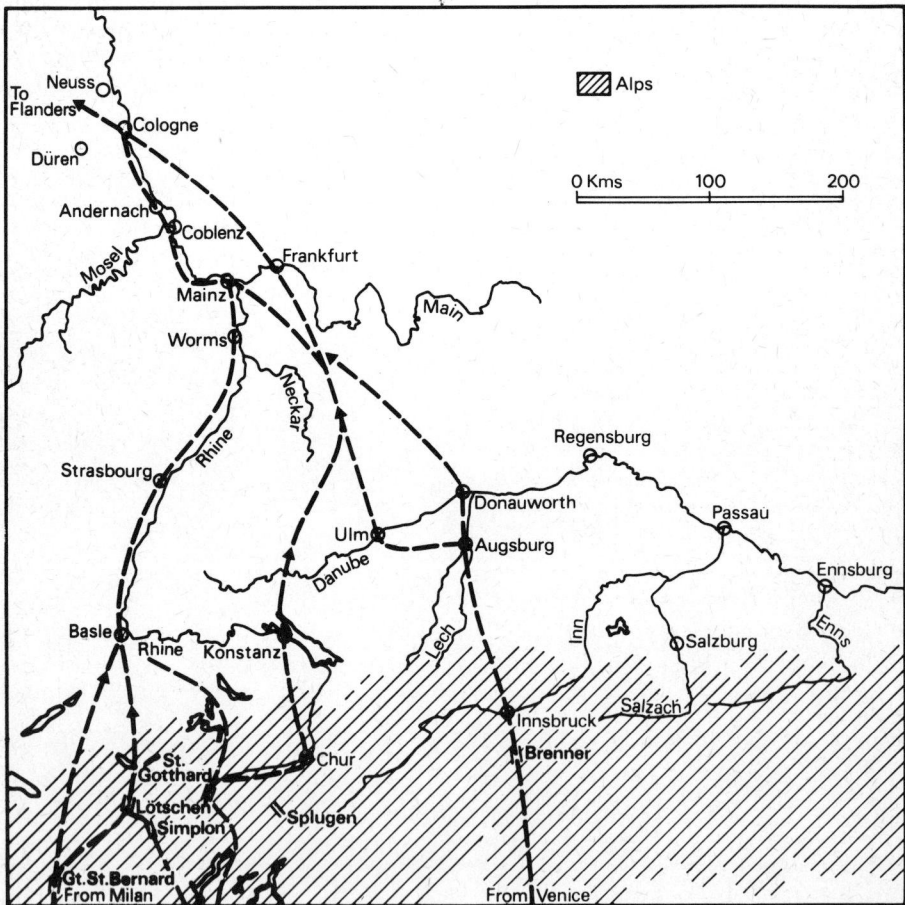

22

of administration, religion, culture and the arts. The most famous of these cities became commercial and industrial emporiums—city states like Genoa and Venice, and Hanseatic ports such as Hamburg, Lübeck and Cologne.

A variety of other urban settlements appeared in the Middle Ages in addition to those concerned mainly with the Church and trade. The twelfth and thirteenth centuries, for example, saw the establishment of universities at Bologna, Oxford, Cambridge and Salamanca. These centres of learning, with their collegiate system, pursued a concept of communal living and studying akin to that of monastic foundations. Like many monasteries the universities also tended to be located in remote rural settings where they became natural foci for traders, merchants and craftsmen, thus acquiring functions additional to those of an academic nature. Other settlements were established by pioneer farmers. The Middle Ages was an era of reclamation of fen, heath and forested land in many parts of Europe, notably in the east where there was a remarkable colonising drive by German-speaking peoples. Throughout the newly-won territories fortified market towns were built, many of which have retained distinctively rural functions. Examples include Villeneuve (a *bastide* town in south-west France), Magdeburg, Posen and Regensburg.

Although there were notable exceptions, most medieval cities lacked symmetry. The term 'shambles' accurately conveys the lack of overall plan, the twists and turns of narrow alleyways and the maze of various buildings and open spaces which characterized such cities. It is a mistake, however, to think that a medieval shambles was necessarily congested, for most cities included gardens, courtyards, orchards, greens and even cultivated fields within their walls. The congestion came later when town populations grew and the former open spaces were used as building plots: by the early eighteenth century overcrowding, noise, squalor and traffic chaos had become commonplace.

It was against this background of mounting urban congestion that the Baroque planners tore down the shambles of many European cities. Broad, straight avenues were built to establish formal order to provide open vistas of the palaces and monuments of the wealthy

Photo 20
The Palace of Versailles: a typical example of 'asterisk' planning.

Figure 14
Street plans of Karlsruhe (*above*) and Versailles (*below*). (*After* Gallion & Eisner)

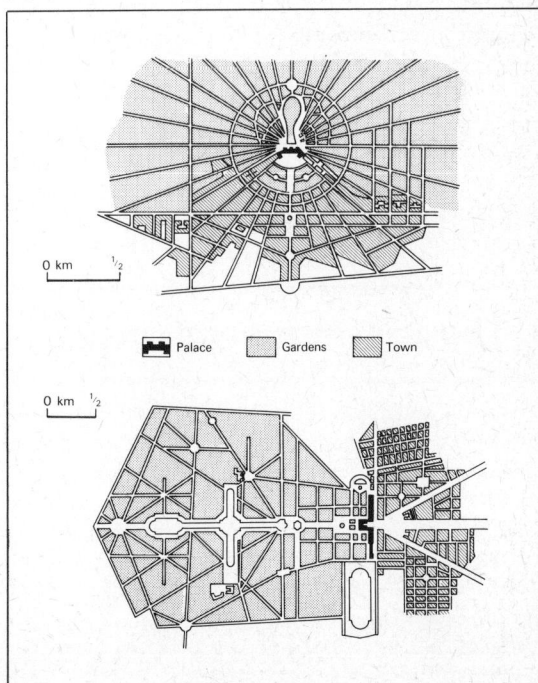

0 km   1/2

Palace   Gardens   Town

0 km   1/2

patrons who commissioned their work. Monarchs in many European capitals undertook grandiose schemes of city reconstruction. Such schemes were used to inspire awe in a populace by displaying the material trappings of royal power. A new street pattern was employed—the asterisk. A palace or fortress placed at its centre could be seen from all quarters and was a constant reminder of the wealth, strength and dominance of the political authority. The most remarkable example of asterisk planning is at Versailles, but similar patterns were used at the princely residences of Karlsruhe and Potsdam as well as in various garrison towns such as Glück-stadt and Palma Nuova.

Another factor which increasingly affected urban morphology in the Baroque era was military strategy. By the seventeenth century artillery had become so powerful that complex fortifications were needed for a city to withstand siege. Capital cities, in particular, were given special protection because of the royal residences, courts, departments of state, arsenals and military headquarters which they contained. Cities were therefore encircled by elaborate walls and ditches, a defensive girdle which restricted urban expansion at a time of increasingly rapid population growth. The resulting congestion was partly relieved by building on traditional open spaces within the walls or, as in Edinburgh, by constructing tenement blocks up to ten storeys high.

3 The pre-industrial city

Urban growth has now been traced through some fifty centuries, from pre-historic origins in Mesopotamia to the pre-industrial era in north-west Europe. It has been possible to highlight only the main trends in city building through such a vast period of time, and special attention has been paid to Europe. One hypothesis, however, places into a single category *all* cities which grew up before the Industrial Revolution, together with all present-day cities which are not substantially affected by Western technology. Professor Sjoberg, for example, considers '. . . that in their structure or form, pre-industrial cities— whether in medieval Europe, traditional China, India or elsewhere—resemble one another closely and in turn differ markedly from modern industrial-urban centres.'* This viewpoint does not ignore the great diversity of pre-industrial cities—Göttingen, Ghent, Mecca and Mandalay clearly differ from one another in many particulars—but these differences are held to be less fundamental than the dissimilarity of all of these cities from, say, Pittsburgh, Port Talbot or Perm.

Most pre-industrial cities have or had all or some of the following characteristics:

(i) they are surrounded by a defensive wall through which access is controlled via a small number of fortified gates;

(ii) they are unplanned, in the sense that the street pattern is irregular and there is no overall symmetry or specified layout for roads or buildings. The latter are packed closely together in a disorderly jumble, the spaces between them becoming alleyways for pedestrians and vehicles. Population densities are high, often very high, and there is a constant sense of congestion

*Professor Sjoberg, *The Pre-Industrial City*.

Photo 21
Market wares in the pre-industrial city of Kano.

24

Photo 22
Agades, Niger: a typical West African pre-industrial 'cellular' city.

and turmoil. This congestion has worsened in recent decades as modern medicines have become increasingly available and city death rates have fallen. (*See also page 4, para. 3.*)

(iii) There is little evidence of conscious functional zoning: houses, work premises, public buildings, shops, street markets and temples are found intermingled in all parts of the city. A degree of zoning may arise, however, when workers in a particular craft e.g. coppersmiths, goldsmiths, jewellers, potters, weavers and so on, group together. Furthermore, the wealthier and more powerful citizens live and work in the central part of the city, whilst the very poor congregate in shanty towns around the perimeter. Zoning may also result from the grouping together of people of different ethnic, linguistic, religious and caste affinities. Such groupings, however, tend to be haphazard and make the city's structure kaleidescopic rather than regular.

(iv) The city may serve many functions, but those concerned with commerce, marketing, craft industries and religion are dominant. There is no large-scale factory production and no separate industrial quarter.

(v) Public administration is inefficient and corrupt. Public services such as electri-

Photo 23
The great majority of buildings in West African pre-industrial cities are single-storied. An exception is this Moslem temple in Mali. All the buildings and walls are constructed of adobe.

city, gas, mains drainage, refuse collection, fire and police protection and transport are rudimentary or absent. Pre-industrial cities therefore tend to be chaotic, unhealthy and violent.

(vi) With the exception of temples or palaces, the great majority of buildings are of one or at most two storeys, crudely and sometimes flimsily built of stones and bricks and plastered with wattle and daub.

Cities showing these characteristics may be found in many cultures. The very early cities of Mesopotamia and of the Nile and Indus Valleys, for example, were theocracies in which élite priesthoods dwelt in sacred buildings in the city centres. Around these religious nucleii were the dwellings and shops of various artisans and merchants, whilst towards the urban fringe lived very poor part-time farmers. Both in structure and function there are obvious similarities between these very early settlements, those of Greco-Roman times and the cities of medieval Europe. Life in the latter was moulded by the Christian Church, in much the same way that Athens, Paestum, Marsala and early Rome were geared to the worship of pagan gods. Yet the unique Christian injunction of charity led to the appearance of a new function—that of caring for the sick, the old, the orphaned and

the poor, as witness the building of hospitals, isolation wards, alms-houses and asylums. Thirteenth-century Firenze (Florence), for example, had no less than thirty hospitals to cater for its 90 000 inhabitants, and during the fearful bubonic plagues it was members of religious orders who led in caring for the sick and burying the dead.*

The dominant role of specialist artisans and merchants in medieval European cities was indicated by the power of trade and craft guilds. Town halls often served as market halls, and guildhalls were amongst the largest and most ornate buildings in the cities. Yet medieval craftsmen worked in the humble surroundings of their homes in much the same manner as did the inhabitants of Pompeii some fourteen centuries earlier, or of Ur twenty centuries before that. Residential and craft activities coalesced in all cities up to the appearance of mass production factory methods in the eighteenth century: in Timbuctu, Kano and Kabul—cities largely untouched by Western technology—they still do.

The grouping of artisans according to their crafts gave to the pre-industrial cities of Europe a cellular structure which is sometimes still discernible in their street names. A similar cell-like structure may be seen in many present-day cities in Africa and south-east Asia. Calcutta, for example, has many occupational groupings derived mainly from the various castes but also from the different languages, religions and historical traditions of its cosmopolitan population of more than seven millions. The Hindu caste system is rooted in India's ancient economy of agriculture and handicrafts, within which each caste fulfilled a role akin to that of a craft guild in medieval Europe. The survival of a recognizable form of this system in a port and commercial city the size of Calcutta indicates the strength of Oriental influences, despite the fact that the city was founded in 1690 by the British East India Company. Notable caste occupational groups include Subarnabanik bankers and Brahman merchants in the old native quarter, Kansari brassworkers in a ward in the northern part of the city and Rajasthan and Gujaratis in commerce in the

*A point made with dramatic intensity in Manzoni's great work *I Promessi Sposi*.

south. Low caste fishermen and gardeners live on very low land to the east and north of Calcutta, but for generations their offspring have provided unskilled and semi-skilled labour in all parts of the city. Religious groupings include Sikhs, mainly in transport jobs in the south, Christian clerks to the east and south of the maidan *(see figures 15 (a) and 15 (b))* and wealthier Moslem traders in the centre.

These occupational groupings are neither absolute nor legally enforceable, but are sustained by tradition and preference. If members of a caste move away from ancient tasks it is usually into analogous occupations. The Kansari brassworkers, for example, have traditionally supplied Calcutta with water jugs and eating bowls. Recently, in the face of competition from workers in glass and porcelain, many Kansari have become silversmiths and goldsmiths.* Occupational rigidity such

*See Nirmal Kumar Bose, 'Calcutta: a premature metropolis', *Scientific American*, Vol. 213, No. 3.

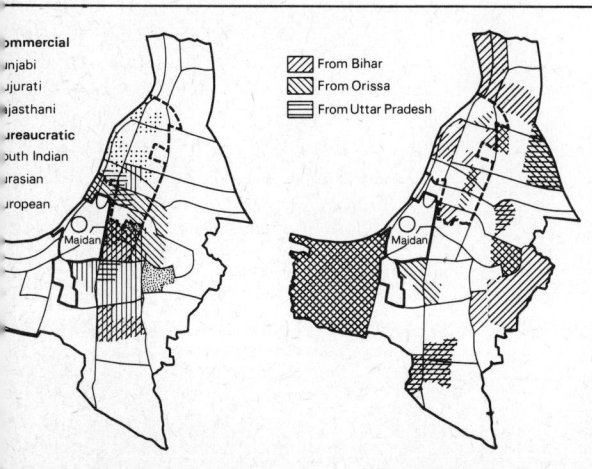

Figure 15 (a)
Calcutta: differentation of the population by caste and occupation. *Bengali-speaking Hindus* of upper, middle and artisan classes were the earliest settlers of Calcutta and still make up 50% of the city's population. At first concentrated in the 'native quarter' north of the maidan, many of them have moved to less congested neighbourhoods in the southern portion of the city. *Bengali poor*, who also include not only hereditary farmers and former 'untouchables' but also 700,000 Hindu refugees from East Pakistan, are widely scattered, but the main concentrations are in slum districts in the extreme north and south and along the eastern outskirts. They total three-quarters of the city's unemployed. (*After* N. K. Bose)

Figure 15 (b)
Calcutta: differentation of the population by caste and occupation. *Non-Bengalis* of the commercial and bureaucratic classes were also once concentrated (Europeans excepted) in the native quarter. Many have since moved to former European neighbourhoods and other southern parts of the city. Gujaratis have effectively replaced the original Bengali residents of one such southern neighbourhood. *Non-Bengali poor*, like their Bengali counterparts, mainly live in peripheral slums. But unlike the Bengalis, most of those immigrant coolies and factory hands are single men whose numbers swell the male population of Calcutta to 60% of the whole. They send savings home, thereby leaving the city's economy poorer. (*After N. K. Bose*)

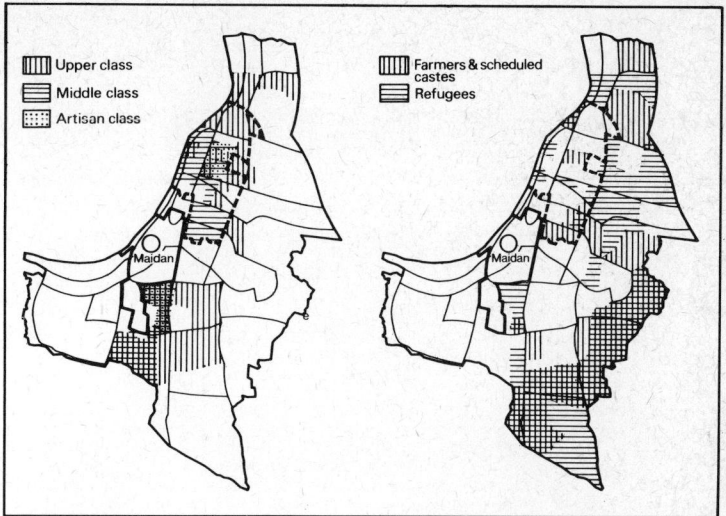

as this makes it virtually impossible for cities to evolve along Western industrial lines. The great majority of jobs in Calcutta, for example, are scattered throughout the city in small family workshops in bustee (slum) buildings. In this and other ways Calcutta has become a metropolis without the apparatus of Western technology which would allow it to function effectively. Conditions there epitomise the ills faced by many overgrown pre-industrial cities. Three in four of Calcutta's population live in overcrowded slum quarters, two-thirds of them in flimsy dwellings made of unbaked bricks. On average there is one water tap for twenty-eight persons and one latrine for twenty-two. The principal supply of washing, cooking and drinking water for the city comes from contaminated hydrants *(see photo 63, p. 118)*; uncovered surface drains carry the bulk of the city's sewage; mounds of refuse accumulate in the streets because of infre-

Photo 24
A refugee family in Calcutta.

quent garbage collections—little wonder that Calcutta is a permanent plague-spot for cholera. Calcutta's traffic congestion is appalling: the great majority of its workers walk to work, no less than 500 000 of them crossing the Howrah bridge each day. Streets are clogged by tens of thousands of rickshaws and by carts drawn by oxen, water buffaloes and men. Crime and violence go largely undetected and human squalor and misery is ever present. Three hundred thousand of Calcutta's inhabitants have no houses. During the cold season men, women and children fight for sleeping places in the city's gutters where, covered by scraps of newspaper, they can avoid freezing to death.

A cellular structure similar to that of Calcutta is discernible in certain indigenous African cities. In West Africa, for example, some large settlements consist of a great number of compounds, each of which contains a family group. Compounds vary greatly in size and shape and are jumbled together in a jigsaw fashion reminiscent of a medieval European shambles. Spaces between compounds form narrow alleyways and the entire mass of compounds is surrounded by a protective wall. With improved security in modern times the walls have been allowed to fall into decay and remnants of older walls within the settlements indicate various stages of past urban growth. These 'compound cities' originated when several village communities joined together for common defence and in some of them the former village 'cells' can be identified by the location of tribal groups.

Cities like Kano, Kumasi and Timbuktu are primarily market centres. In each of them the principal market lies at the city centre, adjacent to the ruler's compound; lesser markets are located in various parts of the city and have tribal affinities. In Timbuktu there are also clearly defined ethnic and caste occupational groups within the city's cosmopolitan population of Arabs, Tuaregs and Songhai. In keeping with pre-industrial cities elsewhere those of West Africa have the dominant social groups at the centre and poorer people at the urban fringe. Although craft and merchant functions are often well developed, a sizeable proportion of the inhabitants are peasant farmers. In this respect they resemble the cities of classical Greece *(page 16)*, medieval Europe *(page 22)* and Monsoon Asia. Other similarities include their ubiquitous single storey adobe dwellings and a general lack of basic public services. West African cities are rapidly changing, however, and most of them now show some visible signs of Western influence—roads, vehicles, electric light and even supermarkets and office blocks.

Section 3 **The impact of technology**

4 The factory system

Since the early eighteenth century a whole series of technological innovations in industry, transport and communications has made possible far-reaching alterations in the rate and nature of urban growth and in the quality of urban life, changes which had profound effects on city size, function and structure.

The nineteenth century, especially its latter decades, saw a mushroom growth of towns both in Britain and in other countries such as Germany, Belgium, France and the USA which were undergoing industrial development. In all these countries the forces impelling society towards urbanization were essentially similar. The new techniques in industry, especially the use of steam power to operate machinery, the organization of production in centralized factories, the use of coke to smelt iron ore and the growth of steel-using engineering trades, all favoured coalfield location for industrial expansion. At the same time the traditional subsistence agriculture of Western countries was giving way to mechanized cash-cropping. The use of farm machinery in such labour-demanding jobs as drilling, weeding and reaping released a flood of agricultural labourers for migration into the growing towns. Evictions of peasants and tenant-farmers also took place, so that landowners could gain the use of more land on which to grow saleable commodities. The movement of hundreds of thousands of dispossessed and jobless farm workers and their families into the growing towns was the most significant characteristic of nineteenth-century urbanization. Rural-urban migration is in places still very important, in Italy for example more than ten million peasants have left the land and moved into Italian and other towns since 1945. Paradoxically the 'flight from the land' is now giving rise to serious shortages of agricultural labour in such traditionally farming countries as Denmark and Greece.

Urbanization thus occurs mainly because industrial and commercial activities tend to cluster together at specially favourable sites. The advantages of a site may be its easy access to raw materials, its transport facilities, the availability of skilled labour and so on. There are also benefits to be gained by locating offices near to financial institutions such as banks and insurance houses. During the age of steam-power the obvious advantages of coalfield locations gave rise to bleak black-country landscapes like those of the German Ruhr, the Russian Donbas, Pittsburgh in the USA and the Birmingham area in the English West Midlands. 'One gets a superb view of this industrial concentration . . . from the higher ground on which Dudley stands. Below this ridge, formed of ancient rocks, the landscape forms a plateau, and one sees it

Photo 25
This woodcut, dated 1859, emphasizes the importance of railway and canal transport for industrial development in the nineteenth century. Note the rural setting of this small colliery village near Barnsley.

stretching away level beneath its canopy of smoke unbroken to the horizon: factory-chimneys and cooling towers, gasometers and pylons, naked roads with trolley-bus wires everywhere, canals and railway tracks, greyhound racecourses and gigantic cinemas; wide stretches of cindery waste-land, or a thin grass where the hawthorns bloom in May or June—the only touch of the natural world in the whole vast scene; plumes of steam rising all over the dark waste; and the gaunt Victorian church-spires rising above the general level, or completely blackened towers receding into the smoky distance. This is the Black Country, well and truly named.'*

In recent years some of the smoke and grime of such regions has lifted, for 'clean-air' legislation enforces the use of smokeless fuels and there has been a continual switch towards electricity as a source of industrial power. In fact it has been possible for modern industries to develop in locations far removed from coalfield congestion ever since the late nineteenth century when important discoveries were made in the generation, transmission and application of electrical energy. Access to cheap supplies of hydro-electricity favoured industrial expansion in cities such as Munich, Zurich and Milan: other centres, especially those like London and Paris which were located on navigable waterways, generated thermal-electricity using imported coal (and later petroleum). At the same time a rapid expansion of international trade, aided by the invention of steamships, resulted in a feverish growth of ports such as New York, London, Hamburg and Rotterdam. Some industries therefore became more 'footloose' and the possibilities of industrial dispersal were accentuated by revolutions in transport and communications made feasible by inventions like those listed on the next page. It seemed possible that industry, once it became fully electrified, would decentralize to such an extent that urban blight might vanish. Such

Chilterns to Black Country (Ed. Grisson) Collins.

Photo 26
The Fiat car factory, Turin, northern Italy. In the distance lie the Alps from which the city obtains hydro-electric power.

Telephone (Bell, 1876)
Petrol motor (Daimler, 1883)
Carburettor (Banki, 1893)
Radio (Marconi, 1896)

5 The metropolitan expansion

optimism proved mistaken, however, for the most significant trend in recent decades has been a faster than average urbanization of old-established cities, especially metropolitan centres like London, Paris, Moscow and New York.

Figures 16 and 17 show the general trend of the world's population towards urbanization, the recent increase in the numbers of really large cities and the dominance of certain metropolitan centres in many advanced societies. The metropolitan expansion had its origins in the development of joint-stock banks with limited liability. In the early stages of Western

Figure 16
Million cities of the world. (The information for the decades up to the early 1960s is derived from a diagram by Alan B. Mountjoy. That for the early 1970s is derived from UN Statistics)

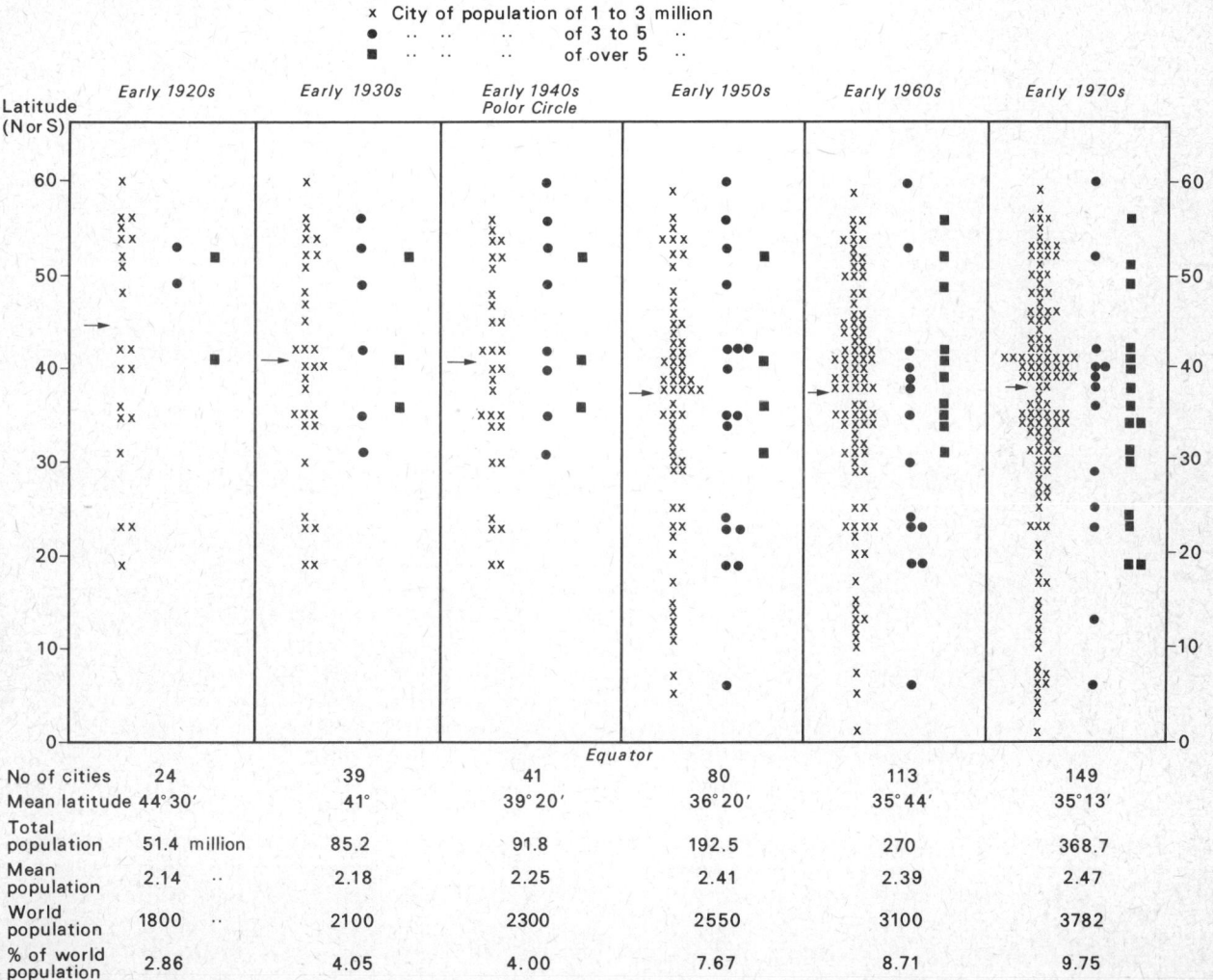

x   City of population of 1 to 3 million
●   ..   ..   ..   of 3 to 5   ..
■   ..   ..   ..   of over 5   ..

Latitude (N or S)

	Early 1920s	Early 1930s	Early 1940s Polar Circle	Early 1950s	Early 1960s	Early 1970s

Equator

	Early 1920s	Early 1930s	Early 1940s	Early 1950s	Early 1960s	Early 1970s
No of cities	24	39	41	80	113	149
Mean latitude	44°30'	41°	39°20'	36°20'	35°44'	35°13'
Total population	51.4 million	85.2	91.8	192.5	270	368.7
Mean population	2.14 ..	2.18	2.25	2.41	2.39	2.47
World population	1800 ..	2100	2300	2550	3100	3782
% of world population	2.86	4.05	4.00	7.67	8.71	9.75

31

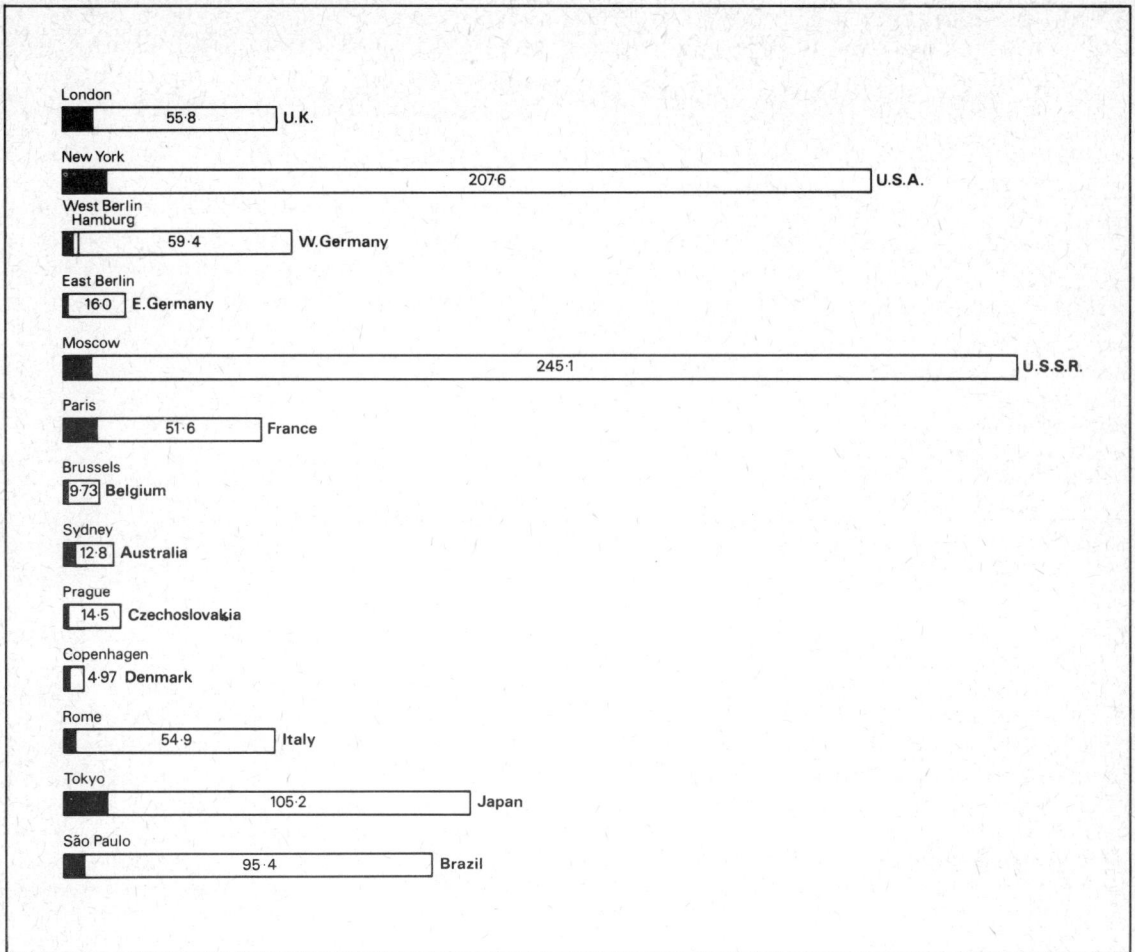

Figure 17
Size of metropolitan cities in certain countries. Figures indicate total population
of countries in millions. (*Source:* UN Statistics)

industrialization most businesses were small family concerns or partnerships. Capital was raised from local banks or by the ploughing in of profits, and both managerial and financial control was exercised on the spot by the same person or persons. By contrast modern businesses tend to be very large-scale corporate enterprises which raise capital on a national and even international scale via the money markets which characterizes finance capitalism. In such concerns those who control finance and dictate policy are not the people involved in day-to-day factory administration. This separation of executive functions—with a shift of emphasis away from the factory towards problems of finance and marketing— marked the birth of the modern administrative office. At the same time it became an advantage for business managers to be in close touch with finance houses, commodity markets, trading agencies, insurance brokers, large banks and so on, many of which were located in metropolitan centres. The headquarters of many firms were therefore deliberately transferred from provincial factories to specially-built office blocks in capital and other large cities. This change of location was given an added impetus with the decline of *laissez-faire*, for the State's role in industry and commerce steadily increased and it became important for management to have easy access to the world of government and politics.

The provision of office accommodation in cities was made necessary not only by the hiving off of management but also by an enormous increase in the number of 'white collar' and service occupations. Clerks, secretaries, telephone operators, typists, lawyers, advertising agents, management and market research consultants, trade union officials, technicians, journalists . . . a host of such jobs, mostly new and many of them filled by women, characterize modern societies. The multiplication of tertiary employment provides the main reason why metropolitan centres have grown so quickly during the past century, for the new jobs attract a flood of aspiring migrants to the town and create a virtually insatiable demand for office space and housing. In the United States, for example, total white collar employment rose from 5·1 million in 1900 to 48·2 million in 1971, or from 17% to 61% of the country's total labour force.

Yet another reason for urbanization in an advanced society is the proliferation of light industries. Examples include the production of (i) *durable consumer goods* like refrigerators, vacuum cleaners, television sets and furniture, (ii) *office equipment* like typewriters, computers and duplicating machines and (iii) *expendable household requirements* such as processed foods and toilet goods. Unlike heavy industries the choice of location of light engineering and food processing firms is little influenced by the distribution of coalfields or the sources of basic commodities. In fact they are largely market orientated, i.e. located as close as possible to their potential customers. This minimizes marketing costs and allows manufacturers to be in constant touch with changing tastes and fashions, an all important consideration in high-pressure competitive selling. The most desirable consumer markets are those in big cities, especially metropolitan centres such as London and Paris where per capita incomes are usually above the average. Large cities therefore act as magnets for consumer goods industries, most of which locate themselves in the city outskirts where land prices are relatively cheap. In London, for example, there has been a mushroom growth of light industries in an arc around the north-ern and western edge of the metropolis, particularly along the main road and rail arteries leading into the capital. Such sites give immediate access to a city's huge buying public and also facilitate the distribution of products to more distant provincial markets.

6 The transport revolution

The factory system created an unprecedented demand for labour in the growing industrial cities. Row upon row of tiny terraced houses were built by factory owners to house the tens of thousands of labourers who, with their families, moved in from the surrounding countryside. A typical dwelling consisted of two bedrooms and two downstairs rooms and had neither garden nor indoor sanitation. At the time of their construction the houses compared favourably with the small farm cottages recently vacated by their new occupants. Set within a growing urban environment of factories, collieries and slag-heaps, however, and beneath a permanent pall of smoke and poisonous fumes, these closely packed 'Coronation Streets' were destined to become squalid slums. In Britain many of the worst of the slums were cleared in the 1920s and 1930s, but thousands of houses in working-class

Photo 27
Nineteenth-century terrace housing, Sheffield.

districts still lack such basic amenities as bathrooms. Photo 47 *(p. 57)* shows a 1970s slum tenement in Liverpool.

As the original workers' houses fell into decay and were demolished their valuable central sites were used to build new factories and, increasingly, for administrative buildings and offices. This change in function was made possible by a long-continued movement of residents outward from the city centres, as new means of transport permitted people to live at increasing distances from their place of employment. The first to move out were wealthier people, including employers who formerly resided in some style in large family houses near their factory premises. Such houses were sometimes detached residences but they also included terraced dwellings of four or more storeys. The basements and top floor contained kitchens and servants' quarters and the families occupied the rooms in between. As they were abandoned these large

Photo 28
Formerly elegant town houses now subdivided into flats, off the Harrow Road, London.

town houses were put to other uses. Some become offices for solicitors, accountants, insurance brokers, small businesses, political rooms and so on, but the majority were divided and sub-divided into rented accommodation. Today they form a 'twilight' zone towards the centre of many industrial cities, including buildings which are decayed, damp, dirty and without proper sanitation, water or other amenities. These 'Rachman' areas tend to become centres of vice and provide desperately overcrowded housing for the poorest strata in society. Coloured immigrants in Britain are drawn to such districts through a process of social ostracism combined with a lack of funds.

Having established the first residential suburbs on the fringe of the adjoining countryside the wealthier classes became the first commuters, travelling to and from work by means of horse-drawn cabs. They were followed in their search for pleasanter places to live by poorer working people as soon as horse-drawn omnibuses came into use. This revolutionary form of public transport first appeared on the streets of Paris during the 1820s and came to London a decade later. Ever since that date technological developments in public and private transport have made it feasible for ever-increasing numbers of people to live at constantly increasing distances from their places of work. The principal innovations have been horse-drawn trams (1875–1900), electric trams and trolley buses, motor-buses, railways, bicycles, motorcycles and private cars.

The very widespread ownership of private motor vehicles is a very recent phenomenon, a result in Britain of improved living standards since the late 1950s. Prior to that it was the buses and railways which made possible the most dramatic expansion of suburban sprawl. In some metropolitan centres like New York, Moscow and London the electric underground railway system and suburban branch lines moulded the pattern of urban growth. In the case of London new lines constructed by the Underground and Southern Railways between 1918 and 1939 were largely responsible for the growth of a suburban residential zone approximately 8–24 kilometres from the centre. New stations were opened, for example at Edgware, Hendon and Harrow to the north

Photo 29
Typical 'twilight' tenements, Peckham, London.

UNDERGROUND

BY
**DISTRICT
RAILWAY.**

**RIGHT INTO THE
HEART OF THE COUNTRY.**

BOOK TO HARROW, SUDBURY OR PERIVALE.

and Bexley, Bromley and Croydon to the south, all places which at that time stood in open countryside. These stations became the foci of residential estates built within walking distance of frequent train services to the City. As the stations were strung out at frequent intervals along the railway lines, elongated 'fingers' of built-up land soon protruded from London into the surrounding country, giving the growing capital the appearance of a complex asterisk. These urban corridors were at first quite narrow, but they rapidly widened as bus services provided access to the railways; thus whole segments of green land disappeared beneath bricks and mortar.

More recently the commuting range has been greatly increased by the spread of car ownership, the building of motorways and improvements to existing road and rail arteries leading into large cities. It is not uncommon for a person to travel daily more than

Photo 30
Advertisement for the London Underground, 1922.

35

is capable of sub-division—has given rise to a considerable and sometimes controversial literature. What follows is an outline of the more generally accepted hypotheses.

Photo 31
Urban motorway, Essen, West Germany.

130 kilometres to work, using private car, main-line railway, underground and taxi en route. In the case of very large cities, however, relatively few long-distance commuters drive all of the way into the centre because of traffic congestion and delays. In London only 9% of persons entering the central area between 0800–1000 do so in private cars. The establishment of new factory areas in the suburbs has also complicated the daily traffic pattern. It has led to much lateral travel within cities and also to some *outward* commuting from inner residential areas. The significance of such trends for urban structural evolution is referred to on pages 40 and 56.

The centrifugal movement of urban populations has been accompanied by the emergence of more or less distinctive functional zones within industrial cities. The principal zones discernible are (i) a central business district, (ii) industrial areas and (iii) residential areas. The exact definition, location and interrelationships between these zones—each of which

Section 4 Modern urbanism

7 The city centre

The Central Zone of an industrial city is in many ways distinctive. It is here that one finds the greatest intensity of urban land-use and certain characteristic functions mainly related to retailing, office work, entertainment and public administration. It is also the focus of city road and rail routes and therefore the area of greatest pedestrian and vehicular traffic. The unique quality of central zones is common knowledge, yet it has not proved easy to distinguish and delimit them precisely. One difficulty arises from terminology and it is particularly important to differentiate between Central Business District (CBD) and Central Area. The CBD concept originated in America and seeks to identify the business 'centre of gravity' of a city: it is therefore more restrictive than the British concept of a Central Area, for the latter may include non-business land-use functions such as government and municipal offices, public libraries, parks and museums.

The CBD contains, above all, establishments concerned with retailing certain specialized goods and services for profit. Here are the city's largest department and variety stores, e.g. Selfridges, Marks and Spencers and Littlewoods. Here, too, are specialist bookshops, art dealers, furniture and clothing shops, jewellers and furriers, as well as nightclubs, theatres, opera-houses and premier-performance cinemas. All of these establishments have one thing in common—they need to attract *many* customers if they are to be economically viable. (In the jargon of Central Place Theory they all have *high threshold values : see pages 83, 102.*) Such enterprises are located at the centre of a city because that is the zone most easily reached by potential customers from all over the city and from the surrounding countryside. Other profit-making concerns in the CBD which are directly dependent on the zone's optimal accessibility include advertising firms and travel agents. In addition many firms locate their head offices in a city centre primarily for reasons of prestige but also find that this centrality minimizes staff travel problems, both to and from work and on business trips farther afield.

The fact that big businesses are located within the CBD also explains the assembly there of many ancillary services such as large and specialized banks, finance houses, stock-brokers, insurance firms, lawyers and accountants. Into this bracket one can also place more humble retail establishments such as newsagents, tobacconists, pubs, barbers and restaurants: these are drawn to the centre not because that is the only place where they can flourish, but because the 'true' CBD work-people and their customers create a demand for their services.

The unique advantages of a city-centre location causes great competition for sites. This has led to the construction of multi-storey buildings which allow the most intensive usage of relatively small plots. Vertical construction originated in Chicago in the 1880s when iron girders were used to build the first skyscrapers. Iron- and later steel-girder frames proved far stronger than conventional building materials, making it possible to erect very tall blocks without the use of massive and space-consuming supports at ground level. At the same time lifts and new methods of fire-proofing were invented, so that rooms high above street level could be reached quickly and occupied safely by large numbers of people. In New York there are as many kilometres of lift shafts as underground track and it would be impossible for all occupants of the city's skyscrapers to find pavement space at the same time. Skyscrapers, for long a characteristic feature of American cities, are less common elsewhere mainly because of building restrictions based on amenity, health

Photo 32
The Barbican housing development project, central London.

Photo 33
New York: high-rise buildings on Manhattan Island.

Photo 34
The Central Business District of São Paulo, Brazil.

Photo 35
The Central Business District of Sydney, Australia.

and aesthetic grounds. In the face of mounting urban land-use pressures, however, such regulations are being relaxed and high-rise central blocks are becoming familiar landmarks in industrial cities the world over. (See photos 32–35.)

The uses to which multi-storey CBD blocks are put varies according to height above the ground. Street-level premises are mainly engaged in retailing, but at higher storeys offices predominate. Also in the city centre are a city's largest hotels, with kitchens, store rooms, dining and reception rooms at lower levels and bedrooms higher up. A more recent addition to CBD buildings is the multi-storey car park, the need for which draws attention to possibly a fatal flaw in cities of conventional structure. The whole *raison-d'être* of a CBD is its alleged optimal accessibility, but in recent decades the centre of a city has become increasingly *in*accessible due to a massive increase in vehicular traffic of all kinds. The resulting congestion is causing serious worry to existing CBD entrepreneurs who fear that their premises will become uneconomic as frustrated customers take their business elsewhere. Functions traditionally located in a city centre are now being deliberately placed, for convenience of access, on the city fringe or even at hypermarkets in the open countryside.

The alternative is to make the CBD more accessible for those who work or do business there. This can be achieved either by redesigning the city's transport system so that commuters travel to and from the centre at very high speeds, or by providing accommodation within the centre so that travelling becomes unnecessary. This latter method is as yet largely untried, although luxury flats for wealthier CBD executives have recently appeared in parts of central London. Some planners suggest that the entire problem could be solved by the construction of vertical 'core cities', with buildings up to two kilometres high and sixty square kilometres in area. A labyrinth of vertical and diagonal lifts would interlace this central 'core', enabling very large numbers of residents to live literally on top of their places of work. This would replace the city centre as it is now known but would require most people to live and work out of sight of the sky in the human equivalent of an

Photo 36
A motorway junction at Pomona, California. Pomona lies on the eastern edge of the Los Angeles metropolitan area. Elaborate urban highways such as these make possible a widespread distribution of CBD-type functions.

ant-heap. Even conventional attempts to make the centre more accessible may lead to its obliteration. Los Angeles, for example, has such an elaborate complex of urban motorways and multi-storey car parks (see photos) that virtually all parts of the city are equally accessible. In such a case the functions traditionally located in the centre can be dispersed to a variety of transport nodes. San Francisco, by contrast, has a revolutionary Bay Area Rapid Transit system (see p. 135) which tends to reinforce the importance of the existing CBD.

Photo 37
Urban motorway interchange, Los Angeles.

40

Access to and movement within a CBD would be greatly improved if heavy goods vehicles were banned in cities, at least from central areas. This concept is not entirely far-fetched, for successful experiments have been conducted into the movement of goods in underground tubes—cargoes are loaded in containers which are propelled through the tunnels by means of compressed air. Traffic flow in a city might also be improved if all vehicles within it were moved automatically by a central electronic control: this again is technically feasible but extremely expensive and so unlikely to be adopted in the foreseeable future.

Delimiting the Central Business District

The central part of an industrial city has obviously become very much a problem zone. As such it has attracted the attention of urban planners as well as that of geographers seeking to understand its characteristics and spatial distribution. Many attempts have been made to delimit the CBD of cities in both North America and Europe, but methods have varied so much that comparative studies of the results are of limited value. Valid generalizations must therefore await the widespread use of a standard method of analysis.

The principal criteria used to delimit a CBD are indicated below. These may be

---

Table F

Some criteria commonly used to delimit a CBD

Shop rent
Business turnover
Building height
Traffic flow
Pedestrian count
Population distribution
Value of building
Value of building land
Land use

---

employed separately or jointly, but many of them have serious disadvantages. To identify the 'central shopping district' of Stockholm Olssen* used a *shop rent index* obtained as follows:

SRI (Shop Rent Index) =

$$\frac{\text{Total shop rents of a building}}{\text{Length of frontage of building}}$$

The results were plotted on a large-scale map, each building being represented by a rectangle. The base of the rectangle showed the building's frontage and its height was proportional to its shop rent index. Olsson then delimited the 'central shopping district' by drawing a boundary around those contiguous buildings with index numbers above a certain size. Sund and Isachsen† prepared similar maps for Oslo, using each building's total annual turnover instead of its rent to prepare a *shop trade index*. Both of these methods are of limited use for CBD delimitation because (i) they do not take into account non-retail functions such as banks and offices and (ii) details of shop rent and turnover are difficult and often impossible to obtain. Building heights at first seem a plausible means of CBD identification, for central zones almost invariably contain buildings appreciably higher than most others in a city. (*Photos 32–35.*) Such an index, however, is too inexact because building heights rarely diminish evenly as one moves out from the centre and non-CBD buildings such as factories, warehouses, rooming houses, power-stations and barracks would be included.

Vehicular and pedestrian traffic flows are usually very high in a city centre but attempts to correlate them with the location of CBD buildings may break down because a large proportion of the vehicles and people involved may be un-related to CBD functions. City centres are frequently the focus of a regional road network so that many vehicles are simply passing through. Pedestrians, on the other hand, frequently travel to and from their place of work outside a CBD via bus or railway stations in the centre. Only those vehicles and pedestrians travelling to or from a CBD on business are relevant to its delimitation, and such information may be very difficult to obtain. Even so, most if not all CBDs are grouped around a city's busiest traffic intersection.

*W. William-Olsson, 'Stockholm: its structure and development', *Geographical Review*, Vol. 30, pp. 420–33.

†Tore Sund and Fridtjov Isachsen. *Bosteder og arbeidssteder i Oslo*, Oslo kommune, Oslo.

As regards population distribution some analyses are based on the fact that CBDs have very few residents. This approach fails because it cannot distinguish between those parts of a city which are empty of residents because they contain CBD buildings and other parts which are parks, derelict plots, museums, zoological gardens, factories and so on.

By far the most fruitful approach to CBD delimitation is that which considers land values and/or land use. The land valuation method was pioneered in the United States by Charles M. Downe, the town planning officer of Worcester city. Downe's *front-foot valuation index* was obtained for each plot as follows:

FFVI (Front-foot valuation index) =

$$\frac{\text{Value of plot from street frontage to a depth of 100 feet}}{\text{Frontage of plot in feet}}$$

A boundary to show the CBD was then drawn around those contiguous plots with values of $300 or more. Another boundary around plots with values of $2000 or more delimited the CBD's 'hard core'. *(See figure 18(a).)* This method assumes that the great competition for plots within the CBD pushes up land values there to such an extent that the

Figure 18 (a)
Worcester's central business district and hard core as delimited by Charles Dorone about 1950. He worked with lots basing his boundaries on front-foot land values reduced to a uniform 100-foot depth. (*After* Murphy & Vance)

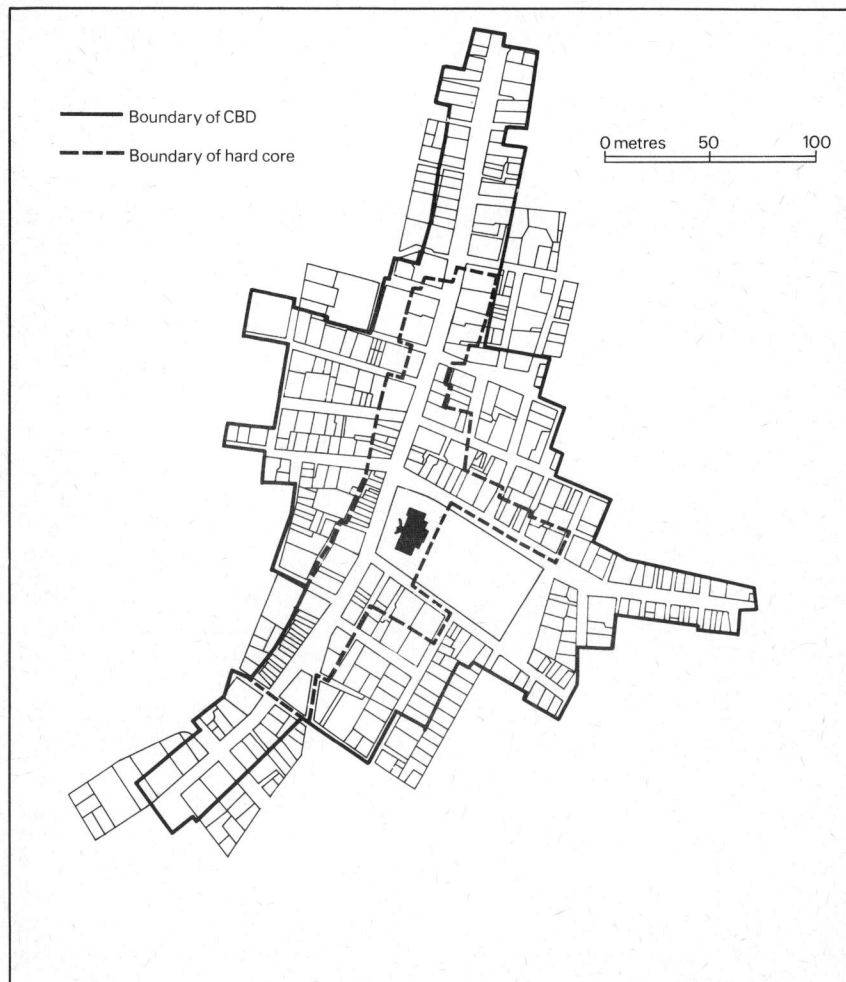

- —— Boundary of CBD
- --- Boundary of hard core

0 metres   50   100

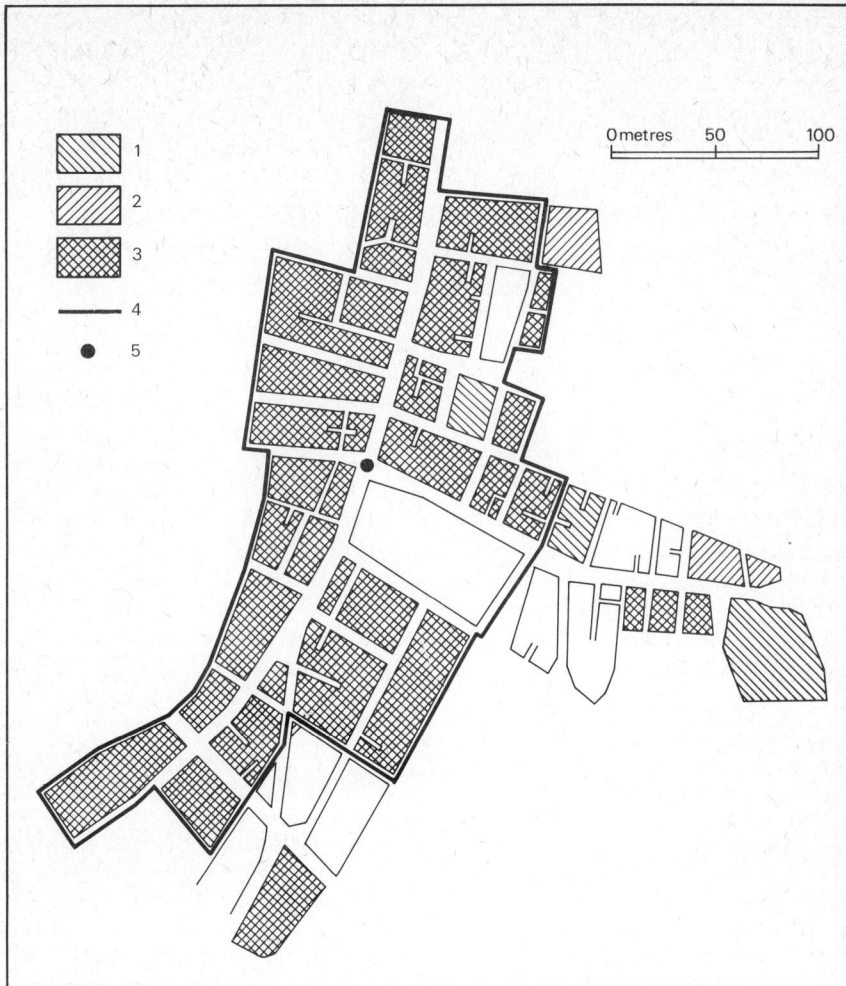

Figure 18 (b) [*For explanation see p. 45*]
Worcester's central business district is elongated in a roughly north-south direction along its axis, Main Street. A relatively steep upward slope to the west, particularly north of the centre, and the presence of railway tracks to the east help to account for its shape. The peak land value intersection is at the point where Pleasant Street reaches Main Street from the west and continues south-eastwards as Front Street. The delimitation problem was complicated by a great range of block sizes in central Worcester. *Key:* 1: Central Business Height Index of 1 or more; 2: Central Business Intensity Index of 50 or more; 3: Central Business Height Index of 1 or more and Central Business Intensity Index of 50 or more; 4: Central business district boundary as determined by Central Business Index Method; 5: Peak land value intersection. (*After* Murphy & Vance)

district can readily be identified. It has the advantage that little field work is required, the data being obtained from assessors' records in city offices and large-scale maps. In the USA a problem arises because land values are assessed differently in various parts of the country, but this can be resolved for purposes of comparison by using percentages instead of actual values. Let the front-foot valuation of the highest-valued plot be 100% and the value of each other plot be calculated as a percentage of this peak value plot. A line is then drawn enclosing all contiguous plots with a value of 5% or more.

For British cities a very similar technique uses the gross rateable values obtainable from municipal offices. These values are assessed objectively by rating officers for local taxation purposes. As methods of valuation are virtually uniform throughout the country the CBD maps derived from rateable values can be compared for cities throughout Britain. The CBD delimited in this map of Hanley was identified by D. T. Herbert using a *rate index* obtained as follows:

$$RI \text{ (rate index)} = \frac{\text{Gross rateable value}}{\text{Gross floor area}}$$

The ground-floor area was obtained by means of a planimeter from the relevant 1:1250 plans.

The rate index is an expression of the value of a building in terms of the total ground-floor space. Once these indices were derived, the range of values was divided into classes for mapping purposes.

Figure 19

Hanley. Location of Central Business Functions. (*After* Davies, Giggs & Herbert)

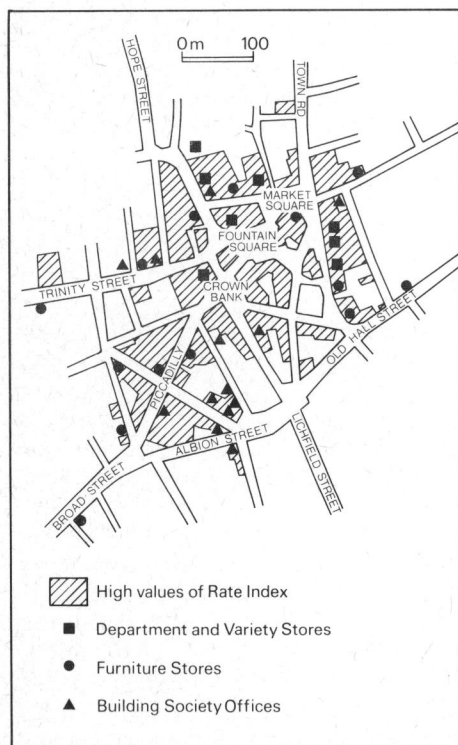

Legend:
- High values of Rate Index
- ■ Department and Variety Stores
- ● Furniture Stores
- ▲ Building Society Offices

Figure 19 below demonstrates the way the rate index was used in the study of the CBD of Hanley. The area of high rate index values in Hanley is centred around Market Square, Fountain Square and Crown Bank with extensions down Piccadilly and along Parliament Row. It can be seen that the rate index might be used as a means of delimiting the CBD since this area of high values corresponds with the effective core area of Hanley's CBD. A number of investigations were undertaken in Hanley to help understand the character of this delimited area of high values. It was found that the area corresponded with the greatest intensity of land use by central business functions and in particular had a virtual monopoly of the location of those functions which require high threshold populations. Stores with low threshold populations, such as food stores and confectioners, were found to be much less typical of this core area. Office functions were clustered in a group around Albion Street but this was peripheral to the high-value area. Other criteria, apart from land use, were applied to the area. It was found, for example, that this high-value area was characterized by the highest intensity of pedestrian flow within the town; counts decreased from the peak-value area towards the CBD periphery.

The map also shows that the rate index allows the locational characteristics of individual central businesses to be studied. Department and variety stores, besides showing a tendency to cluster, are also seen to be highly central in their locations. Furniture stores, although demanding on floor space, still require access, but are more peripheral in their locations within the CBD. On the other hand, building society offices require limited access but seek central locations more for prestige and advertising purposes. Some are found in reasonably central locations within the CBD, but the main cluster is near Albion Street. A great deal more could, of course, be said about CBD structure and the location of individual functions, but it is sufficient in this study to demonstrate the way in which gross rateable values may be used. The rate index is one simple adaptation of the actual value and this, taken in conjunction with the other standard techniques of land use, such as pedestrian flows, allows a meaningful analysis of the commercial area of the town to be made.*

The land value approach to CBD delimitation has considerable merit, provided its data has been evaluated objectively. Its main defects are that it ignores building height as a criterion and tends to include factories and other non-CBD users within the zone finally designated. The latter problem is most likely to arise, however, on the outer edge of the CBD where clear-cut differentiation is seldom possible whatever criteria are employed.

Perhaps the most satisfactory technique is that developed in the USA by Murphy and Vance†. This uses a combination of land-use, building height and land-value analyses. A survey records the uses of all floors of all buildings surrounding the city's *peak land-value intersection*. Both built-up land and open spaces are included in the survey, with a vacant lot or an open space being charted in the same way as a single-storey building. The only differentiation made is between land being used or not being used for CBD functions. Non-CBD functions, according to Murphy and Vance are listed on the right. A synopsis of the actual survey method is given in figure 20. From collected data two indices are prepared for each city block. These are: (i) *the Central Business Height Index* (CBHI), where

$$CBHI = \frac{\text{Total floor area of all CBD functions}}{\text{Total ground floor area}}; \text{ and}$$

(ii) *the Central Business Intensity Index* (CBII), where

$$CBII = \frac{\text{Total floor area devoted to CBD functions}}{\text{Total floor area}} \times \frac{100}{1}$$

(The floor area may be calculated from relevant large-scale maps.)

*W. K. D. Davies, J. A. Giggs and D. T. Herbert, 'Directories, rate books and the commercial structure of towns'. *Geography* No. 238, pp. 51–2.
†Raymond E. Murphy and J. E. Vance Jr, 'Delimiting the CBD', contained in *Readings in Urban Geography* (Ed. Mayer and Kohn) Section 13, pp. 418–46. The University of Chicago Press.

Table G

General types of land occupance considered to be non-central business in character

Permanent residences (including apartment houses and rooming houses)

Governmental and public parks and schools as well as establishments carrying out city, state, and federal government functions

Organizational establishments (churches, fraternal orders, colleges, etc)

Wholesaling

Vacant buildings or stores

Vacant lots

Commercial storage

These two indexes are both taken into account in deciding whether a city block is to be included in the CBD, only *contiguous* blocks with a CBHI of 1 or more *and* a CBII of 50% being eligible. Voids within an otherwise contiguous area are given CBD status, together with government or municipal buildings if they are adjacent to or contiguous with *bona fide* CBD blocks. *(See figure 18(b).)*

Experience suggests that the Central Business Index mapping technique of Murphy and Vance produces as valid a boundary of the CBD as is practicable. No line, however drawn, can represent the CBD with complete precision, '. . . but the area delimited does include the major part of the CBD . . . and the boundary is believed to be as fair an approximation of the zone as a single line can be.'‡ The only obvious problem arises because the shape and size of urban blocks tends to vary from city to city. The exact nature of the finalized maps, furthermore, hinges on the method adopted to differentiate CBD from non-CBD functions. Thus some planners argue that, for practical purposes, municipal and other central parks, cathedrals, museums, art galleries, big company offices, embassies and so on should be included to delimit a Central Area. This may be so but it does not invalidate the method, rather it modifies the technique so as to obtain a different result.

‡Murphy and Vance, *op. cit.*, p. 446.

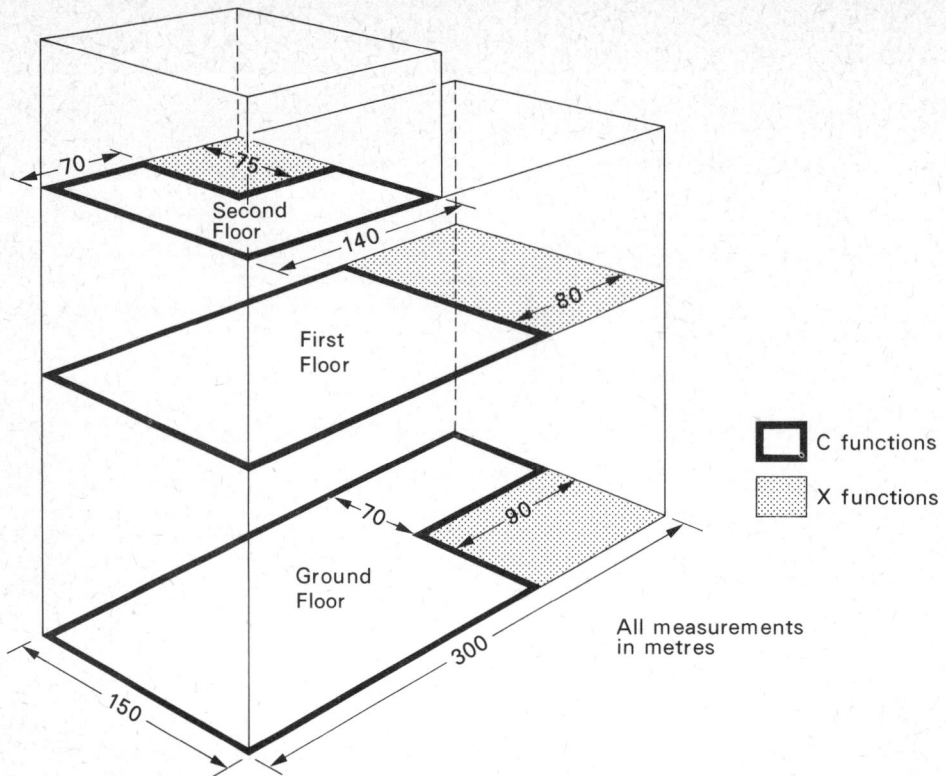

	Ground Floor	1st Floor	2nd Floor	Total for building
C function (i.e. Central Place)	150 × 210 + 70 × 90 37 800	150 × 220 33 000	140 × 75 + 75 × 70 15 750	86 550
X function (i.e. non-Central Place)	90 × 80 7200	80 × 150 12 000	75 × 70 5250	24 450
Total area	45 000	45 000	21 000	111 000

$$\text{C.B.H.I.} \quad \frac{\text{Total C area}}{\text{Total ground floor area}} = \frac{86\,550}{45\,000} = 1.92$$

$$\text{C.B.I.I.} \quad \frac{\text{Total C area}}{\text{Total floor area}} \times \frac{100}{1} = \frac{86\,550}{111\,000} \times \frac{100}{1} = 78\%$$

Figure 20
Delimitation of a Central Business District. Method of designating a building (hypothetical). All areas are in square metres.

The practical value of CBD delimitation clearly lies in the field of urban planning. In this respect a vital consideration is the extent to which a CBD is undergoing change. Surveys indicate that CBDs tend to grow in some directions and fall into limbo elsewhere. Advancement is indicated by recent intensification of CBD retail functions: decline is revealed by a growth of low turnover retail outlets such as pawnshops, low grade cafés and by vacant buildings. To highlight changes of this nature surveys must be taken at successive intervals of time and must record the quality of CBD functions as well as their quantity. One significant point which emerges from the few existent surveys of this type is that the peak land-value intersection tends to move as a CBD migrates.

8 The location of industry

The Industrial Structure of cities has, paradoxically, received less research attention than has the nature and functions of their central zones. This may be due in part to the complexity of industrial distribution—because there is no obvious pattern there is no self-evident problem calling for urgent solution. The complexity arises because most industrial cities contain a variety of industries, each of which tends to be located in a particular part of the city for different reasons. The factors which influence industrial location are mainly concerned with accessibility—access to water, power, raw materials, skilled labour, markets, port facilities and so on—and the relative importance of these factors varies from industry to industry and even from firm to firm in the same industry. For many industries access to consumer markets is the prime locating factor: proximity to markets minimizes transport costs and keeps selling prices competitive. This helps to explain why most industry is located in or close to large cities, but does not go very far in explaining why an individual firm chooses a particular site in an industrial area. Many factors influence such a decision, including economic history and pure chance.

The Central Zone often contains old-established industries including those which made the city's commercial name. The precise location of these 'relic' industries depends upon local economic history. If the city existed prior to industrial development they tend to be grouped in a partial ring around the ancient core; if on the other hand the industries themselves initiated urban growth they are found right at the city centre. The former case is well illustrated by London, where in the early nineteenth century a crescent-shaped manufacturing belt grew up to the north and north-west of the ancient city. *(See figure 21.)* This inner and older industrial zone contains many relatively small firms with single workshops and a handful of employees. They include large numbers of garment manufacturers, both in the East End at Shoreditch and Bethnal Green and in a maze of West End streets to the north of Oxford Circus. Small firms of this type rely for success on their expertise in design and technology. Because they are adjacent to the central showrooms and big shops which buy the bulk of their products they are immediately aware of trends in fashions and can change their line of production at very short notice.

In Birmingham there is a similar group of 'relic' workshop industries in an area to the north-west of the city centre which includes Vyse Street and Warstone Lane. The main

Figure 21
Areas of specialized industrial function in Central London (*After* Jones)

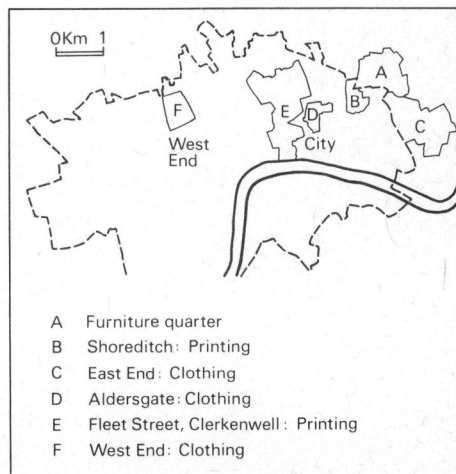

A   Furniture quarter
B   Shoreditch: Printing
C   East End: Clothing
D   Aldersgate: Clothing
E   Fleet Street, Clerkenwell: Printing
F   West End: Clothing

products are jewellery and brass-, gold- and silver-wear. Nearby, around St Mary's Church, other old craft industries are now mostly concerned with the production of sporting guns. Other cases of early, centrally located industries are found in Paris. There is, for example, a group of small workshops devoted to the production of exclusive and expensive clothing *(haute couture)* in the Rue de la Paix and in the 2nd and 3rd arrondissements. Many of these firms are in the upper floors of commercial or residential buildings and so are not apparent from street level. Most are in old converted premises in side streets off major shopping thoroughfares, i.e. within the zone of urban blight on the edge of the CBD *(See also pages 56, 57.)* Similar firms

make quality furniture in the district of Saint Antoine, and many others make furs, jewellery and toilet preparations *(articles de Paris)* in the inner arrondissements.

During this century the growing congestion in industrial city centres led to a dispersal of industry analogous to the outward movement of residents discussed on page 34. Lines of factories were built along arterial railways and roads, especially suburban ring-roads, and this eventually brought about a grouping of newer industries in the suburbs. Industries were attracted to the suburbs mainly because land prices there were markedly lower than elsewhere in the city. A suburban location also gave good access to transport routes both into and away from the city and was thus

Figure 22
Birmingham. Modern industrial pattern. (*After* Smailes)

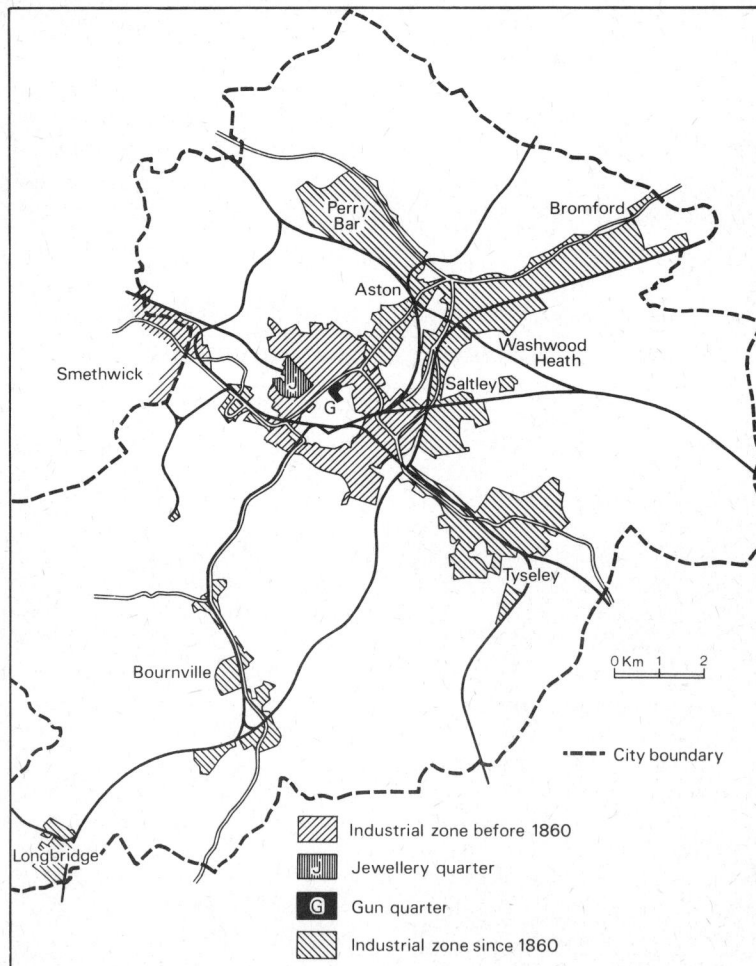

Key:
- Industrial zone before 1860
- Jewellery quarter
- G Gun quarter
- Industrial zone since 1860
- — · — City boundary

0 Km 1 2

Photo 38
Factories, research establishments and houses form a Science Park in the New Town of Peterlee, County Durham.

particularly favourable for labour- and market-orientated assembly industries, the classic example of which is vehicle manufacture. Assembly industries need a great deal of space, for their entire plant is laid out in single-storey buildings and there must be plenty of room for expansion. Skilled labour is recruited from the adjacent city and because most employees drive to work there must be adequate car-parks. The modern trend, too, is to locate factories in landscaped industrial 'parks' which include, in addition to the basic factory buildings, such facilities as canteens,

Photo 39
Industrial development alongside the Great West Road at Brentford.

clubrooms and sportsfields. Even more room is needed for off-street lorry loading bays, railway freight sidings, storage sheds and auxilliary workshops of painters, cleaners, fitters and other maintenance engineers. Industrial demand for space has increased as machinery has become larger and more sophisticated: giant presses and extruders may, for example, each occupy 300 square metres of workshop floor.

Suburban industries are virtually all 'new', the goods which they mass-produce by modern techniques having mostly appeared on the market only during the past half-century. Typical products include TV sets, computers, domestic electrical appliances, baby-foods, razor-blades, cosmetics and breakfast cereals. By providing direct access to consumer markets almost any suburban location favours such industries. In Britain, however, a recent trend is for consumer goods industries to cluster in the vicinity of suburban motorway junctions. Photo 40 *(overleaf)* shows factories adjacent to the M6–A38(M) junction at Gravelly Hill, Birmingham.

The tendency for older, smaller, industries to be located centrally and for newer, larger, industries to be widespread in the suburbs provides a broad basis for classifying urban industries, but there are many other complications. Tidewater sites, for example, attract industries which use bulky raw materials, including metal smelting, chemicals, petroleum and vegetable oil refining, and flour,

49

Photo 40
Industrial development alongside a motorway junction at Gravelly Hill, Birmingham.

wood-pulp and paper milling. On tidal estuaries such industries may at first be located well outside the nearest city's boundaries, but with continued growth the two tend to fuse together. Some industries which depend on a city for their labour supply are nevertheless deliberately located in remote and isolated settings because they emit noxious fumes or

are very noisy or are potentially dangerous: examples include petro-chemicals, explosives, some heavy metal-working and aeronautical research establishments. In Britain noxious industries are frequently located on the eastern side of a city, i.e. in such a position that the prevailing westerlies blow fumes and smoke away from residential districts.

The complexity of urban industrial distribution is reflected in these diagrams of selected American cities. The areas in black denote manufacturing land-use. The five concentric circles in each diagram have as their centre the city's main CBD intersection. The outermost ring marks the mean limit of the metropolitan area. The radius of this outer ring is divided into four to give the circles shown. Clearly there are marked variations in the patterns of each city, although central, lineal and suburban clusters can be discerned in most of them. Figure 24 *(p. 52)* is Hamilton's model of the industrial distribution of a metropolis based on a map of industrial areas in London. The four categories of industries shown are (A) central location; (B) port locations; (C) radial or ring transport artery location and (D) suburban locations. Professor Harold Carter* has proposed a more elaborate classification of

*Harold Carter, *The Study of Urban Geography*, p. 307. Edward Arnold.

Photo 41
A coal-fired electricity generating station located beside the River Trent. River water is used for cooling and is re-cycled through these huge towers.

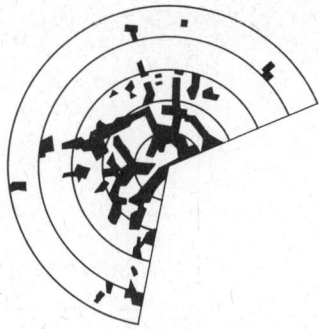
Detroit

Easton

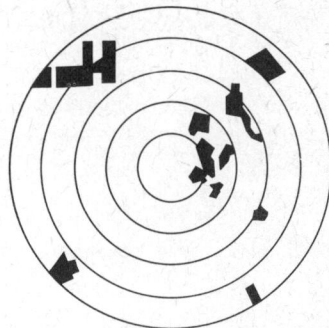
Elkhart

Flint

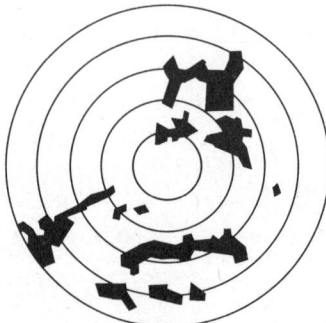
Saginaw

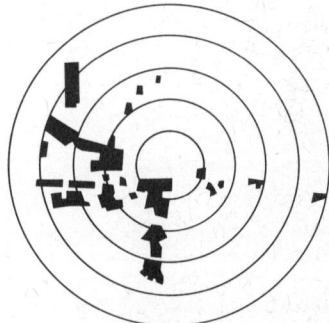
South bend

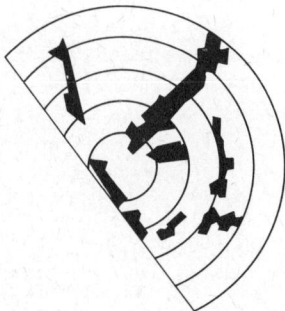
Springfield Mass.

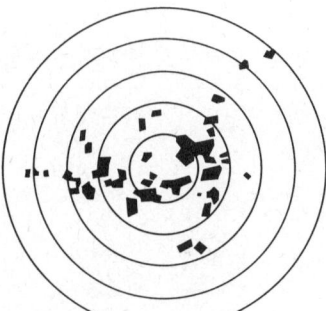
Thomasville

Youngstown

Figure 23
The distribution of manufacturing in selected American cities. The areas in black denote manufacturing land-use. Five distance rings are superimposed in each case by taking the major CBD intersection as centre and drawing an outer ring at the mean limit of the metropolitan area. The radius of this outer ring is divided into four to give the circles shown. (*After* L. K. Loewenstein)

51

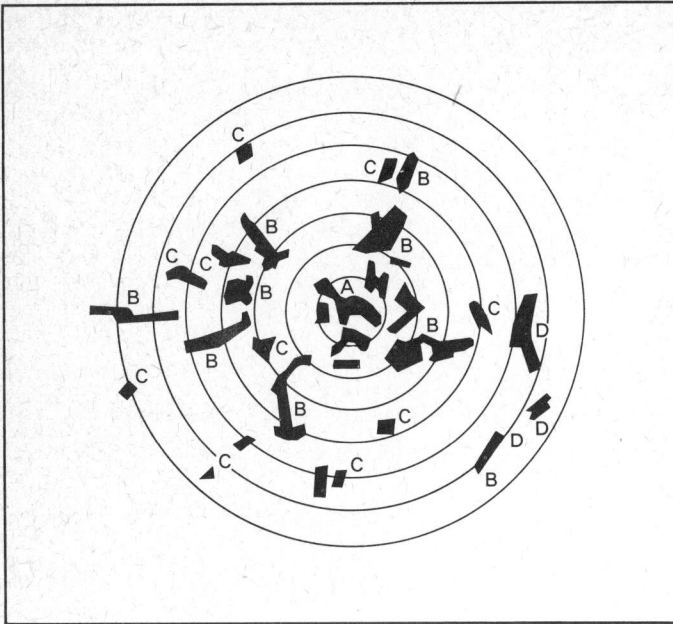

Figure 24
A model of the spatial industrial structure of a metropolis. This is based on a map of industrial areas in London. The four categories shown are: A—Central Locations; B—Port Locations; C—Radial or Ring Transport Artery Locations; D—Suburban Locations. (*After* Ian Hamilton)

urban industries as follows:

(1) *Centrally located industries* which are either labour- or market- or CBD-orientated and which mainly serve the whole metropolis.

(2) *Randomly located high-value industries*. These serve national or export markets greater than the metropolis and produce goods with a high value-to-weight ratio. Transport costs are relatively unimportant and so a random location pattern can result. A typical example is the manufacture of calculating machines.

(3) *Large basic processing industries*, e.g. chemicals and metallurgical industries, which serve a national market. Ideally these are best located in the suburbs where there are advantages of transport and space and where noise and pollution risks can be minimized. They are often found, however, in central areas where they have long been established and from where it may be very costly to move.

(4) *Waterfront or port ('tidewater') industries* using raw materials imported in bulk.

(5) *Route-orientated industries* which cluster along lines of communications. These include highly technical engineering industries which need to cluster together to keep abreast of technological innovations. 'Science-park' industries are of this type (*see photo 38, p. 49*).

(6) *Suburban industries*: the product of the process of decentralization mentioned on page 48.

This classification emphasizes that industry can be found in every zone of the city from CBD to outer suburbs.

9 Residential areas

Residential areas cover more land in industrial cities than any other type of district, even though such cities are essentially dependent on business and marketing activities. Table H shows the percentage land uses or urban areas in Britain. In American cities residences also constitute the largest single use of land, varying between 30% and 40% from city to city.*

*Raymond E. Murphy, *The American City*, p. 369. McGraw-Hill.

Table H
Percentage land use of total urban area for all British Settlements of over 100 000 population
(Source: R. H. Best and J. T. Coppock, *The Changing Use of Land in Britain*, Faber.)

Urban category	Residential	Industry	Open space	Other uses
London	42·0	5·0	15·0	38·0
All settlements over 10 000 population	42·6	6·2	20·0	31·2

Geographers are concerned with residences primarily from the viewpoint of their *distribution*, and maps to show this have been prepared for a great many cities. Such maps are usually made, however, according to two different, though comparable and overlapping criteria, *viz.* (i) house types and (ii) socio-economic status of residents. This has tended to give rise to confusion because type of residence (classified by mode of construction, roofing material, size, age and so on) is sometimes assumed to correlate directly with type of residence (labourer, clerical workers, executive etc). In fact house types are sometimes described in such terms as 'older working-class', 'middle-class semi-detached', 'executive mock-Tudor'. The confusion arises mainly because of a 'filtering-down' process

Photo 43
Typical inter-war suburban semi-detached dwellings.

Photo 42
Edwardian terrace houses, York.

Photo 44 (a)
Inter-war detached 'stockbroker Tudor'. Large dwellings of this type often had no intergral garage nor garage space. Although occupied by commuters the residents travelled to work by bus or train. Such houses had to be within walking distance of bus or train services.

Photo 44 (b)
Modern detached. Integral double garage or car-port is now commonplace. Note the landscape setting much favoured by British planners. Relatively remote suburban sites pose no problems to car-owning commuters.

Photo 44 (c) and (d)
(c) Inter-war terrace. (d) Modern terrace. The similarities in style are obvious. Note the trend towards large 'picture' windows and the unfenced garden plots.

Photo 44 (e) and (f)
Contrasts in modern housing. The detached bungalows in their rural settings are very costly in land. The three storey terrace houses permit a much higher density of residents per hectare but there are problems from street parking despite the provision of integrated garages.

whereby houses are passed down to successively lower-income groups as new-style dwellings are built for upper-income clientele. This is a never-ending process which can evolve at different rates in separate parts of the same city, so that at any given moment there is an overlap between house-type and the socio-economic status of residents.

Further complexity arises because a person's choice of residence alters according to such factors as age and marital and family status. For example, a student from a high-income family background may well take 'digs' in a dilapidated central 'twilight' Victorian rooming-house, but a few years later when he becomes a married professional man he will seek a suburban detached house. Attempts to link house-type and occupational and/or class groupings also fail when, as in Britain, persons can readily climb—or slip down—the social ladder. This does not mean that residential classifications by house type are invalid, but to be meaningful they must use a nomenclature which avoids reference to the supposed socio-economic status of residents. Similarly, surveys of the distribution of socio-economic groups should not use house-type names as a basis for classification.

Photo 45
Edwardian semi-detached town houses, now used for rented accommodation.

Table I
Liverpool: constitution of population by social class (%)

Social class	Inner Zone	Middle Zone	Outer Zone
I & II (administrative, professional, shopkeepers and small employers)	6	13	19
III (clerical service workers, firemen and skilled workers)	39	52	55
IV & V (semi-skilled and unskilled workers)	55	35	26

Source: Emrys Jones. *Towns and Cities*, p. 122. Oxford University Press.

Socio-economic studies reveal the paradoxical situation that the richest people in cities mostly live on the cheapest land and *vice versa. (See, for example, the Table above.)* This is because of the centrifugal movement of the better-off referred to on page 34. Wealthier people abandon outmoded dwellings in the congested city centre, preferring low-density residential estates in the suburbs. Detached houses on spacious plots, surrounded by gardens to give privacy and the illusion of rural charm, are particularly sought after by the English upper classes, and grandiose properties of this calibre can only be economic where land is comparatively cheap, i.e. on the city's fringe. This assumes that suburban residents can afford and are willing to commute daily into the CBD. Very recently this assumption has been challenged, for some wealthier suburbanites have chosen to live in newly-developed luxury accommodation in the city centre, so as to avoid long and tiresome commuter journeys. The central accommodation is frequently made available by property developers who modernize dwellings such as terrace houses which have fallen into decay and which have ceased to be fashionable with the lower social groups. Urban fashions in house types thus tend to be cyclic. An interesting question is whether the wealthy occupants of rejuvenated central terraces, mews flats and the like will move farther out as their restored property begins to age and lose its newly acquired fashionable appeal. Will there eventually be a repetition of the flight of residents to the suburbs such as that which characterized the first half of the twentieth century?

The parts of a city most likely to contain old decayed properties ripe for redevelopment lie in the 'twilight' zone on the outer edge of the CBD. Slums arise there because new building takes place at ever-increasing distances from the city centre. In time the earlier residential areas fall into disarray, an inevitable consequence of age and neglect. Antiquated dwellings are neglected because they are wasting assets: further investment in them can bring little or no return. Owners of tenement blocks in central areas therefore spend a minimum on maintenence and try to maximize rent returns by subdividing their property into very small dwelling units. Central residential areas thus form a high-density zone, inhabited mainly by (i) poorer workers who cannot afford to commute and so must

Photo 46
The outer edge of the Central Business District in Brussels. This is the 'twilight' zone in which poorer class housing is being displaced by new Office blocks and large retail stores.

Photo 47
A slum dwelling in a 'twilight' district of Liverpool.

live close to their place of employment, (ii) young persons, such as students, who choose to live close to their place of study or are attracted by the 'bright lights' and (iii) immigrants. The latter gravitate to slum areas because they have relatively poorly paid jobs and little money and because they face ostracism in pleasanter residential areas. They may also yearn for social coherence with people of their own ethnic, linguistic, religious and cultural background.

The redevelopment of obsolescent 'twilight' zones for housing is so costly that private entrepreneurs must build luxury high-rent accommodation if they are to make a profit on their capital outlay. Houses for lower-income groups can only be built by municipal authorities who are prepared to spend vast sums of public money on social grounds and who may charge nominal or subsidised rents. The most extensive scheme of central urban renewal in Britain has been undertaken by the city of Birmingham during the past two decades. Birmingham's structure is concentric, with three main zones at increasing

distances from the CBD: firstly a 'twilight' zone of obsolescent houses and industrial buildings, mostly dating from the mid-nineteenth century; next a middle zone of late Victorian 'bye-law houses', rows of drab terraces surrounding large industrial premises; then an outer zone built since 1918, consisting of large municipal and private housing estates intermingled with, but segregated from, suburban industrial firms. The main areas of redevelopment have been the CBD and the inner zone of obsolescence, but future schemes will affect the late Victorian districts which are also falling into decay.

In 1946 393 hectares of land in the city centre were acquired by compulsory purchase. The purchased land included 32 000 dwellings (inhabited by 103 000 people), 4000 shops, 2300 industrial and commercial buildings and 330 'special' buildings such as churches and schools. Many of the houses lacked basic amenities—some even had no water supply— and 77% were considered unfit for habitation. A massive slum clearance programme was thus put under way, with the purchased land

Photo 48
Part of the Lee Bank district of Birmingham which was demolished to build a Central Development Area.

Photo 49
Part of the Central Development Area at Lee Bank, Birmingham.

Photo 50
The Gravelly district of Birmingham prior to redevelopment.

Photo 51
The Gravelly district of Birmingham after redevelopment. The urban scene has changed almost beyond recognition. The modern church with a domed roof (*top, right*) stands on the site of the church shown in the bottom right of the photograph on the left.

being divided into five Comprehensive Development Areas, (CDAs). Within each CDA land uses have been segregated to produce neighbourhood 'groupings' of dwellings, shops, schools, community centres, churches and pubs. Through traffic has been re-routed to a Ring Road at some 2·5 kilometres radius from the city centre and new open spaces incorporated into the CDAs on the basis of 1·6 hectares per 1000 population. Within the redeveloped area the average residential density per hectare has fallen from 474 to 298 and houses have been deliberately built overlooking the parks so as to reduce still further any sense of congested living. (*See figure 25(b) overleaf.*)

Table J
Principle land uses in the CDAs before and after development

Percentages of total areas: (i) 1952 (ii) 1972

	Newtown (i)	(ii)	Nechells Green (i)	(ii)	Ladywood (i)	(ii)	Lee Bank (i)	(ii)	Highgate (i)	(ii)
Residential	41	26	44	30	48	30	45	24	43	29
Industrial	30	30	24	24	21	21	24	21	22	21
Open space	2	16	1	16	1	17	0	13	4	17
Schools	3	10	3	10	2	2	2	7	3	14
Others (Public buildings, roads, etc.)	24	18	28	20	28	23	29	35	28	19

The massive increase in the proportion of land given over to open space following redevelopment is shown in Table J. To achieve this dilution of population density it has been necessary for 46 000 people to be re-housed outside the CDAs, many of them in 'overspill' locations outside Birmingham itself. A similar problem arose through the need to relocate some 1600 industrial firms disturbed by redevelopment. All existing large industrial concerns were left in place but many smaller firms were relocated within the CDAs, some of them in specially built 'flatted factories'. Examples of these establishments at Nechells Green and Lee Bank *(see figure 25(a))* contain 46 and 42 factory units respectively. Other firms have been relocated with municipal help elsewhere in the city and many have left Birmingham, encouraged to some extent by the 'overspill' policy pursued by the West Midlands authorities. More than 100 firms went out of business as a direct result of redevelopment, but most of these were very small, depending for their survival on the cheap rents of old, decayed workshops in the former slums. A survey showed that after two years the firms resettled in 'flatted factories' had increased their productivity per worker by an average of 21%, and firms relocated elsewhere by an average of 15%. About 40% of the new industrial premises built in the CDAs have been occupied by firms from outside the slum-clearance area. This is because the city's policy has been to give preference in central areas to labour intensive *manufacturing* industries such as metal goods, paper and printing, plastics and engineering.

Although the Birmingham scheme has proved largely successful it highlights the

Figure 25 (a)
Redevelopment projects in inner Birmingham. Based on information supplied by Birmingham Corporation. (*After Stedman & Wood*)

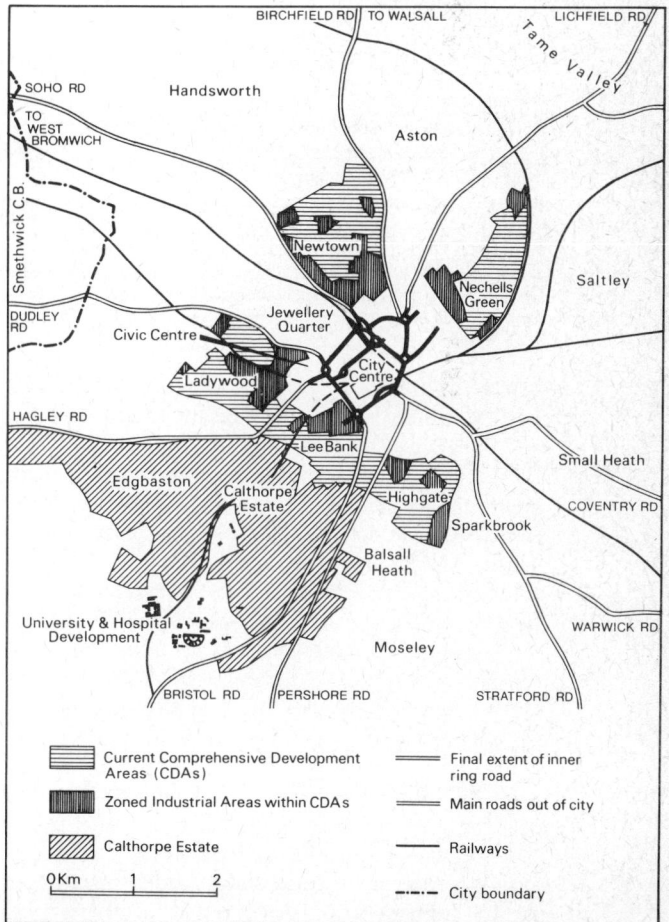

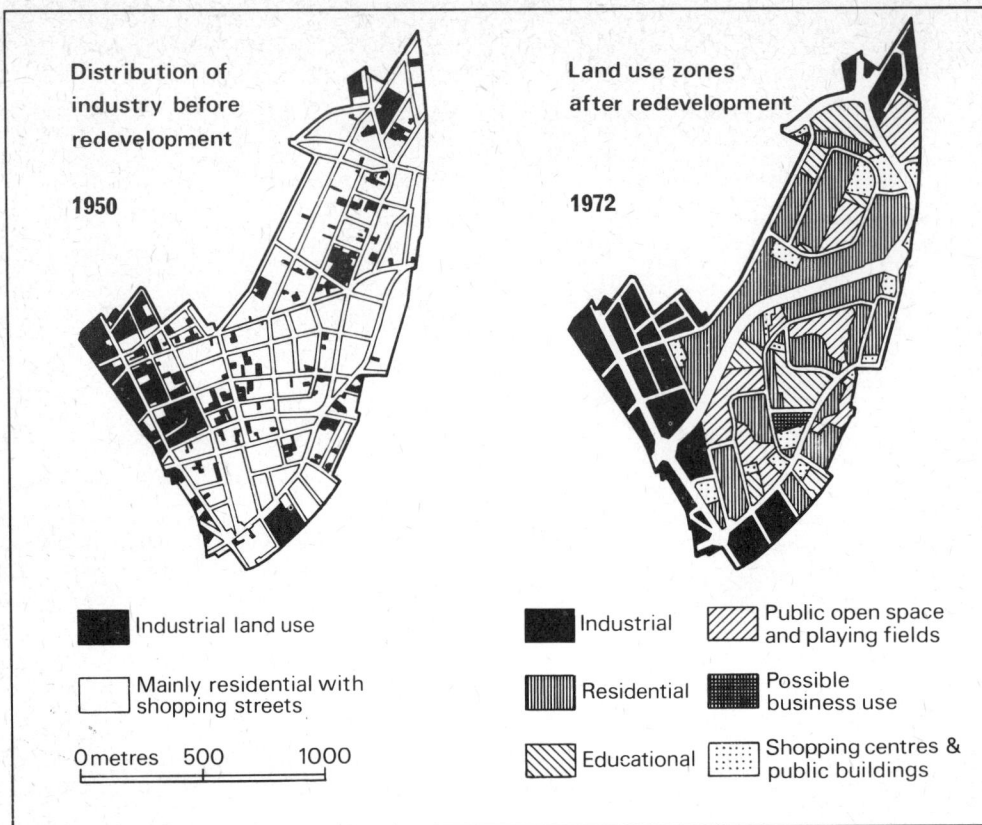

Distribution of industry before redevelopment

1950

Land use zones after redevelopment

1972

■ Industrial land use

□ Mainly residential with shopping streets

0 metres 500 1000

■ Industrial

▥ Residential

▨ Educational

▧ Public open space and playing fields

▦ Possible business use

▒ Shopping centres & public buildings

Figure 25 (b)
The Nechells Green Comprehensive Development area. Based on information supplied by Birmingham Corporation and on field work by Stedman & Wood.

problems of redeveloping inner city zones with high densities of residential population and large numbers of small industrial firms. In particular it emphasizes that large slum clearance schemes, through 'overspill' programmes and so on, necessarily affect communities far removed from the slums themselves. A large majority of slum dwellers belong to clearly defined and lowly regarded socio-economic classes such as labourers and service workers. Experience in British cities shows that the resettlement of these people in or close to districts already occupied by professional men, managers and other members of high-status groups causes burning resentment and hostility. This hostility tends to be mutual, for class antipathy and segregation is greatest, both socially and by distance, at the highest and lowest ends of the socio-

economic scale. This fact was first demonstrated quantitatively by O. D. and B. Duncan* who measured social segregation by means of two indices. The first is the index of dissimilarity:

$$\sum_{i=1}^{n} \frac{(x_i/\Sigma x_i) - (y_i/\Sigma y_i)}{2} \cdot 100$$

Where x_i represents one occupation and y_i represents another occupation residing in zone i. Essentially it measures the percentage of an occasional group (x) which would have to move to make its distribution identical with another occupational group (y). If this is computed between one occupation group and all others combined it gives the second measure, an *index of segregation*. Tables K and L show these two indices for the city of Chicago.

In American cities these antipathies be-

*O. D. and B. Duncan, 'Residential distribution and occupational stratification', *American Journal of Sociology*, Vol. 60, pp. 493–503.

Table K
Indices of dissimilarity in residential distribution for major occupational groups, employed males, Chicago.

	1	2	3	4	5	6	7	8
1	—	13	15	28	35	44	41	54
2	8	—	13	28	33	41	40	52
3	11	7	—	27	35	42	38	54
4	20	18	17	—	16	21	24	38
5	26	23	25	12	—	17	35	35
6	31	29	30	16	14	—	26	25
7	31	31	30	19	25	19	—	28
8	42	41	42	32	30	21	24	—

Table L
Index of residential segregation of each major occupation group, employed males, Chicago.
O. D. and B. Duncan (1955).

Occupation group

1 Professional, technical and kindred workers	30
2 Managers, officials and proprietors, except farm	29
3 Sales workers	29
4 Clerical and kindred workers	13
5 Craftsmen, foremen and kindred workers	19
6 Operatives and kindred workers	22
7 Service workers, except private households	24
8 Labourers, except farm and mine	35

tween social groups have given rise to well-established *ghettoes,* i.e. areas of a city which are exclusively dominated by one cultural group, e.g. Italians, Chinese, Puerto Rican or Negroes. Ghettoes may be 'slums of hope' or 'slums of despair', according to whether their occupants may or may not look forward to the ultimate possibility of moving out. Those ghettoes which contain immigrant groups usually fall into the former category, providing non-English-speaking newcomers with a familiar and safe environment within which they may become adjusted to the American way of life. Although at first such immigrants will find jobs only at the bottom of the socio-economic ladder there is a chance of self-improvement and of moving out into the general body of American society, even if only for one's children. For Negroes and other coloured minorities, however, the ghetto is virtually a citadel of despair: movement to other parts of the city where there are better houses, schools, amenities and jobs is almost impossible due to the workings of the colour bar. The bitterness bred in such stagnant, inward-looking ghetto slums lies at the root of much American violence. No true American style ghetto exists as yet in Britain, even in areas of high coloured immigration. Birmingham, for example, has several separate clusters of immigrants *(see map)* where blacks form 14%–19% of the total population. In Cleveland, by contrast, 80% of the city's Negroes live in a single 'black collar' around the CBD, a 'collar' in which 75% of the inhabitants are Negroes. *(See also photo overleaf.)*

Figure 26
Coloured immigrant areas in Birmingham. (*After* P. N. Jones (1967))

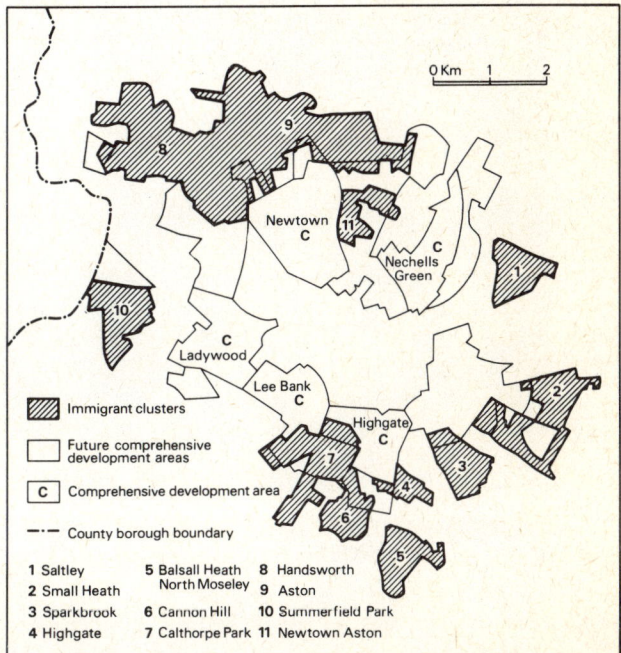

Immigrant clusters
Future comprehensive development areas
C Comprehensive development area
County borough boundary

1 Saltley
2 Small Heath
3 Sparkbrook
4 Highgate
5 Balsall Heath North Moseley
6 Cannon Hill
7 Calthorpe Park
8 Handsworth
9 Aston
10 Summerfield Park
11 Newtown Aston

Photo 52
A play street in Haarlem, the Negro ghetto of New York.

Section 5 **Urban patterns**

10 Theories of urban structure

Even a cursory glance at maps of industrial cities reveals that they have many structural similarities. The question therefore arises whether these similarities result from the operation of common processes and whether it is possible to generalize about the pattern of land use regions within a typical city. The three main theories of urban structure—concentric, sectoral and multiple nuclei—all assume that variations of urban land use primarily reflect differences of urban land values. In this view the various activities locate themselves according to whether or not they can afford the economic rents commanded by sites in different parts of the city. Generally speaking, urban land values are highest at those points which are most easily accessible, and early theorists assumed that the city centre was especially sought after because of its optimal accessibility.

The Concentric Theory was first expounded by E. W. Burgess in 1924 to throw light on the growth and structure of Chicago and other American cities. Burgess stated that 'in the absence of opposing factors' a city grows outwards from its centre to form a pattern of five concentric zones. *(See figure 27.)* As the city expands there is a tendency for each of the inner zones to increase its area by encroaching upon the zone next farthest out. Burgess did not explain why such zones develop but the concentric theory, both as originally put forward and as modified by later workers, makes the following basic assumptions:

Figure 27
Concentric theory of urban structure. (*After* E. W. Burgess)

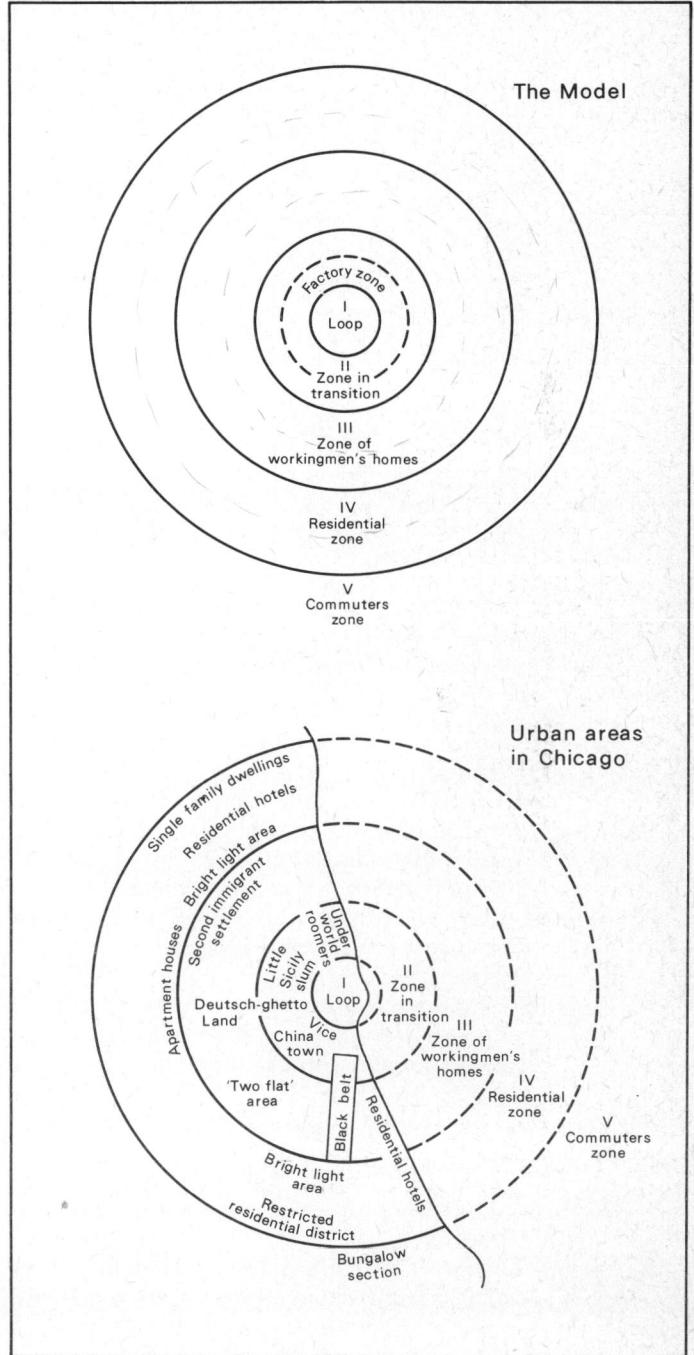

The Model

I Loop
Factory zone
II Zone in transition
III Zone of workingmen's homes
IV Residential zone
V Commuters zone

Urban areas in Chicago

Single family dwellings
Residential hotels
Bright light area
Second immigrant settlement
Apartment houses
Little Sicily slum
Under worlds roomers
Deutsch-ghetto
Land
China town
Vice
I Loop
II Zone in transition
III Zone of workingmen's homes
IV Residential zone
V Commuters zone
'Two flat' area
Black belt
Residential hotels
Bright light area
Restricted residential district
Bungalow section

(1) Land values, and hence economic rents, are highest at the city centre and fall off steadily as one moves out towards the periphery. This brings about the zoning of urban functions according to their capacity to meet the economic rent. *(See figure 28.)*

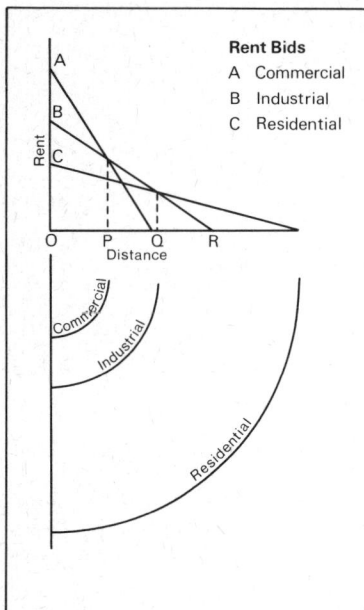

Figure 28
Hypothetical rent-distance relationships within a city.

(2) Space is in greater supply towards the city fringe.
(3) Central areas are more accessible and therefore more desirable for commercial and industrial usage.
(4) City populations are heterogeneous, i.e. they contain a variety of well-defined socio-economic, ethnic and possibly racial groups.
(5) The poorer classes cannot afford to travel long distances to and from work and must therefore live towards the inner part of the city.
(6) The wealthier classes will always prefer to move out to the city's edge where land values are relatively low and where large suburban properties can be bought economically.

Critics of Burgess maintain that in reality clearcut concentric zones are rarely met with, for each land-use region merges gradually into its neighbours. Zones are also much more varied than Burgess suggests, with very few parts of a city being used for only one specific purpose.

M. R. Davie*, who studied New Haven and other American cities, found little evidence of concentricity and pointed out that CBDs, for example, are more usually rectangular or square than circular. Davie also found that areas of commercial land extended outwards from the centre along radial routes. This latter point is, however, consistent with the concentric theory if one assumes that economic rents fall off in proportion to *time*-distance and not to *actual* distance from the city centre. Zonal boundaries then become star-shaped as explained in figure 29. The greater the number of radial streets the closer the zonal periphery approximates to a true circle. P. H. Mann†, who attempted to apply Burgess's concentric model to three British cities (Huddersfield, Nottingham and Sheffield) noted that the transition or 'twilight' zone *(see page 56)* is *not* concentric but is most clearly developed on the sides of the CBD which lead to the more salubrious residential areas. Mann also observes that what Burgess calls the 'working-class' housing zone is better defined as the zone of older housing, adding that this zone, intermixed with heavy industry, tends to coalesce in wedge-shaped patches along transportation lines such as roads, railways and waterways.

The Sheffield Black Belt which begins on the edge of the Central Business District goes in a north-easterly direction to Rotherham, the boundary between the two towns being of no significance industrially at all. Around this vast area of steel works and engineering works are to be found many of the poorest quality houses remaining in the cities; street upon street of small terraced houses. Moving in an arc on both sides of this to the north and east, are to be found older houses of better quality (the larger bye-law type with semi-detached villas) and

*M. R. Davie, 'The pattern of urban growth', *Studies in the Science of Society*, (Ed. G. P. Murdock), Yale University Press.
†P. H. Mann, *An Approach to Urban Society*, London, Routledge and Kegan Paul.

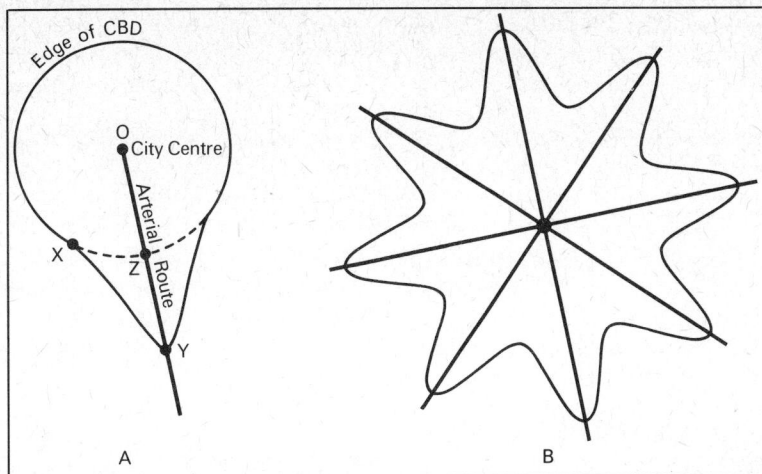

Figure 29

The distortion of the CBD boundary by an arterial route. In Diagram A point X is the same *absolute* distance from O, the city centre, as is point Z. In terms of travel time and cost, however, point X is as far from O as is point Y. This is because Y lies on a main arterial route leading directly to the city centre. A person wishing to reach O from X must either negotiate a maze of side streets or go via Z.

Thus the city centre is equally accessible from X and Y. The *friction of distance* between places along the arterial route and the city centre is less than that for other places equidistant from the centre.

Where there are many arterial routes the CBD is distorted to become star-shaped as in Diagram B. With an infinite number of arterial routes the CBD becomes circular.

older council estates. Moving yet farther around the circle the areas become more middle-class, so that on the south-west side of the city centre, there are the most desirable suburbs in the city, all placed within easy access to the Peak District and Derbyshire, and all to the windward of the Black Belt since the prevailing wind is from the west. The extreme hilliness of Sheffield results in numerous exceptions to this general plan, with streets of terraced houses in the middle distance range of middle-class suburbs, but it is worthy of note that an area described by John Betjeman as being one of the finer suburbs in England is less than three miles as the crow flies from the heart of the Black Belt, but this three miles is almost exactly on the other side of the city centre from the industry.

The lack of concentricity in Sheffield's housing pattern would be explained by Burgess as due to the operation of 'opposing factors', in this case the variety of terrain within the city and its desirability as a location for housing. Critics of Burgess' model complain that these 'opposing factors' apply so frequently that concentricity rarely, if ever, occurs and so his theory is invalid. Such criticisms are unfair in so far as they attempt to apply Burgess' ideas to present day cities where conditions differ greatly from those which appertained when the concentric model was first put forward. In particular Burgess could not have for seen the impact of almost universal motoring, which has so reduced the friction of distance within cities that residences, factories, retail shops and wholesale markets can all be much more widely distributed than formerly. Such phenomena as suburban factories and office blocks, intercity motels and hypermarkets, central highrise flats and planned community shopping arcades cannot be fitted into Burgess' scheme, but he never intended that they should. The concentric theory was designed as a rough guide to the structure of American cities in the 1920s; today it is no longer generally applicable.

The Sector Theory was first put forward in 1939 by Homer Hoyt and in its initial form was designed to explain the distribution of housing. Hoyt's ideas confirmed those of Burgess in so far as housing zones expand on the side facing away from the city centre, but Hoyt maintained that they are not concentric. The pattern of residential areas was seen by Hoyt to be a function of rent and

. . . Rent areas in American cities tend to conform to a pattern of sectors rather than of concentric circles. The highest rent areas of a city tend to be located in one or more sectors of the city. There is a gradation of rentals downward from these high rental areas in all directions. Intermediate rental areas . . . adjoin the high rent area on one or more sides and tend to be located in the

same sectors as the high rental areas. Low rent areas occupy other entire sectors of the city from the centre to the periphery.*

(See figure 30.) According to the sector theory housing zones originate, adjacent to areas of other land use, near the city centre. Thereafter the zones grow outwards to form elongated wedges *(see figure 31)* as newer houses are added at the suburban fringe.

Figure 30
Theoretical pattern of distribution of rent areas in six American cities. (*Source:* US Federal Housing Administration)

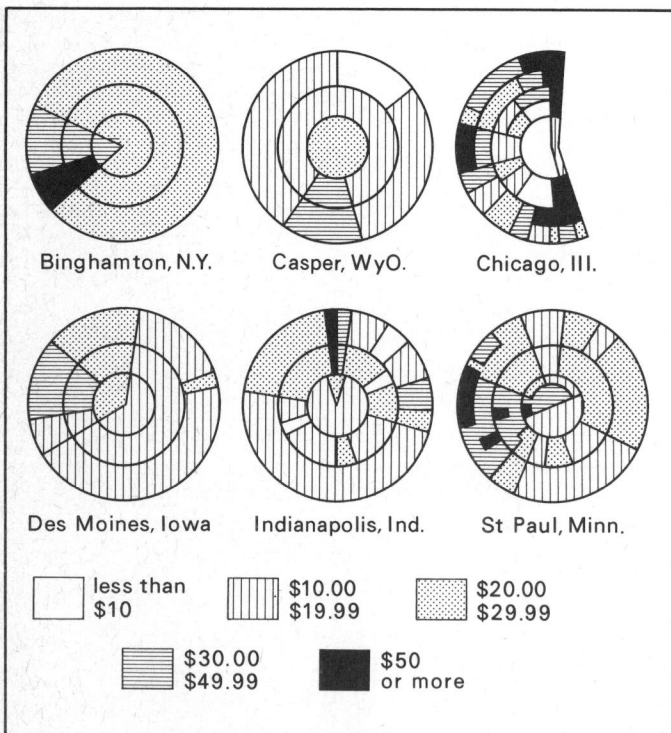

Figure 31
Sector theory. (*After* Harris and Ullman)

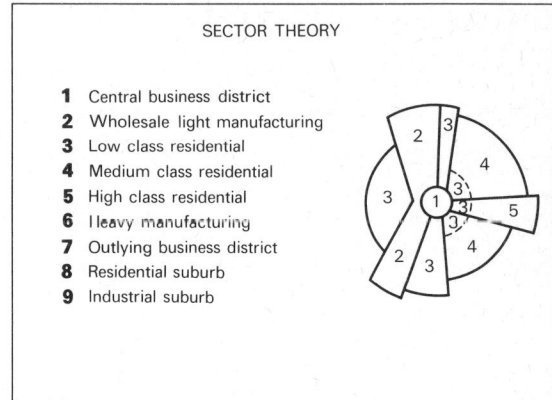

A striking feature of the sector theory is the way it highlights the outward migration of high-class housing districts as the city evolves. This point is well illustrated by figure 32 which shows the changing pattern in several American cities over a period of thirty-six years. It will be seen that the sector theory retains a degree of concentricity, for the various housing sectors spread out laterally as they expand. The inner parts of a housing sector form zones of older housing and may include 'twilight' districts of material and social decay. It is also clear that the sector theory may be extended to include all types of urban land use, with each of the principal functions—commercial, industrial and residential—occupying adjacent sectors of terrain. Sectors of industrial land, for instance, tend to develop along major road, rail or water routes leading out from the city centre. Figure 32 also shows that newer high-class residential districts may appear on the periphery of a city in a location unrelated

The Structure and Growth of Residential Neighbourhoods in American Cities, U.S. Federal Housing Administration, Washington, D.C., p. 76.

66

to the main existing housing sectors. This may be explained partly in terms of the greater mobility afforded by private transport in modern times, and partly because of the 'irrational' influence of successful land promoters and speculative builders. These newer housing districts often originate as commuter estates lying at first within open countryside but later joined to the city as the latter expands.

The exact pattern of the various sectors in a city obviously owes much to the initial location of land-use districts within the city centre. With old-established settlements the precise reasons for these original locations may be impossible to determine and may well have been due largely to chance. Yet ultimately the pattern of sectors is similar for all cities, for they are all moulded by forces which have general application. This point is made by B. T. Robson* who suggests that his model of urban development for Sunderland is valid for other river-based British and American cities with a common cultural and 'commercial–industrial' base. Robson argues that two principal factors—attraction to the Central Business District and repulsion from industrial areas—are the mechanisms which bring about these common sector patterns.

The resolution of the balance of these forces in a river-based town gives rise to the juxtaposition of sectors and zones arranged in the manner that has been noted. (See figure 33.) The focus around which the residential areas of a medium-sized town are orientated is the Central Business District. This is the retail and entertainment centre which exerts much of the centripetal force which is responsible for the creation and maintenance of towns. In the case of the professional workers, the Central Business District is also usually the place of work. We can thus see that the object of selecting a residential location within a town is to achieve maximum accessibility to this point while at the same time meeting other requirements such as a good site, open land, access to the sea, of high social value. Thus accessibility is the first of the two considerations. The second prime factor is

*B. T. Robson, *Urban Analysis*, pp. 130–1, Cambridge, Cambridge University Press.

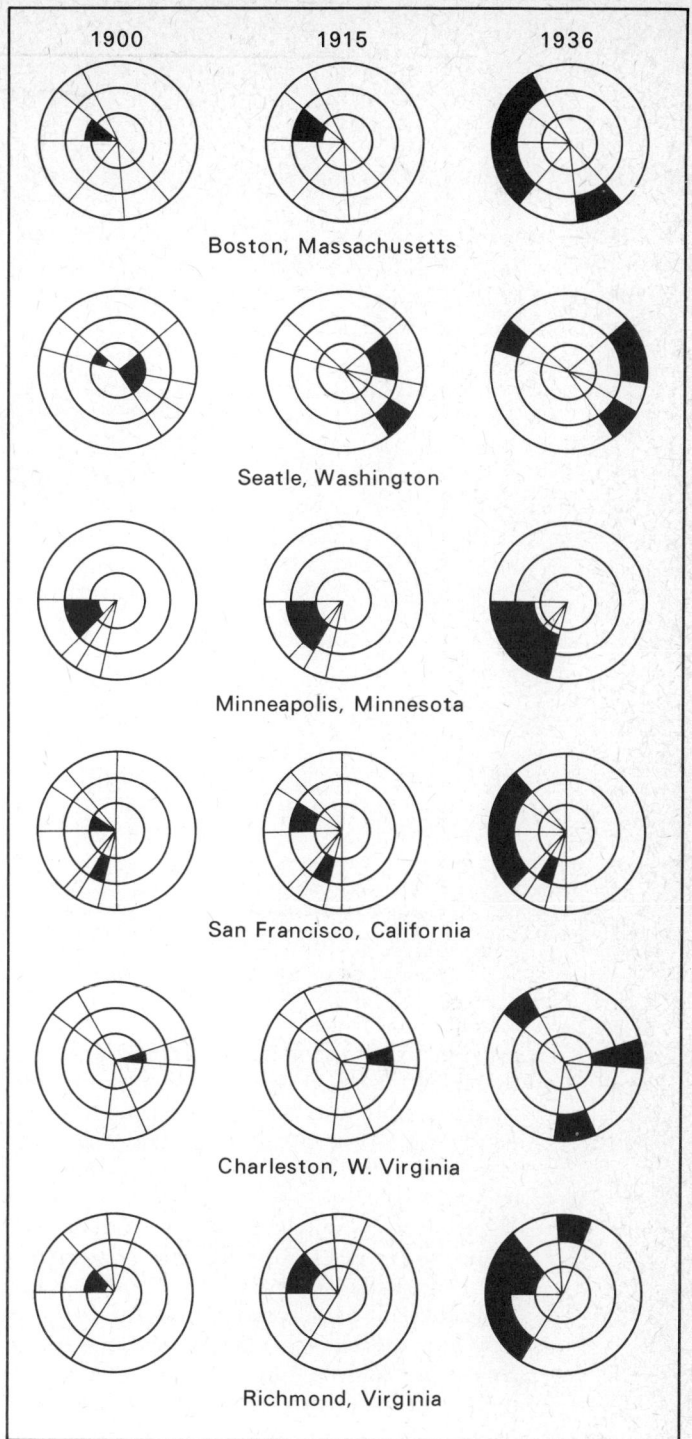

Figure 32
Shifts in location of fashionable residential areas in six American cities. Fashionable residential areas indicated by solid black. (*Source:* US Federal Housing Administration)

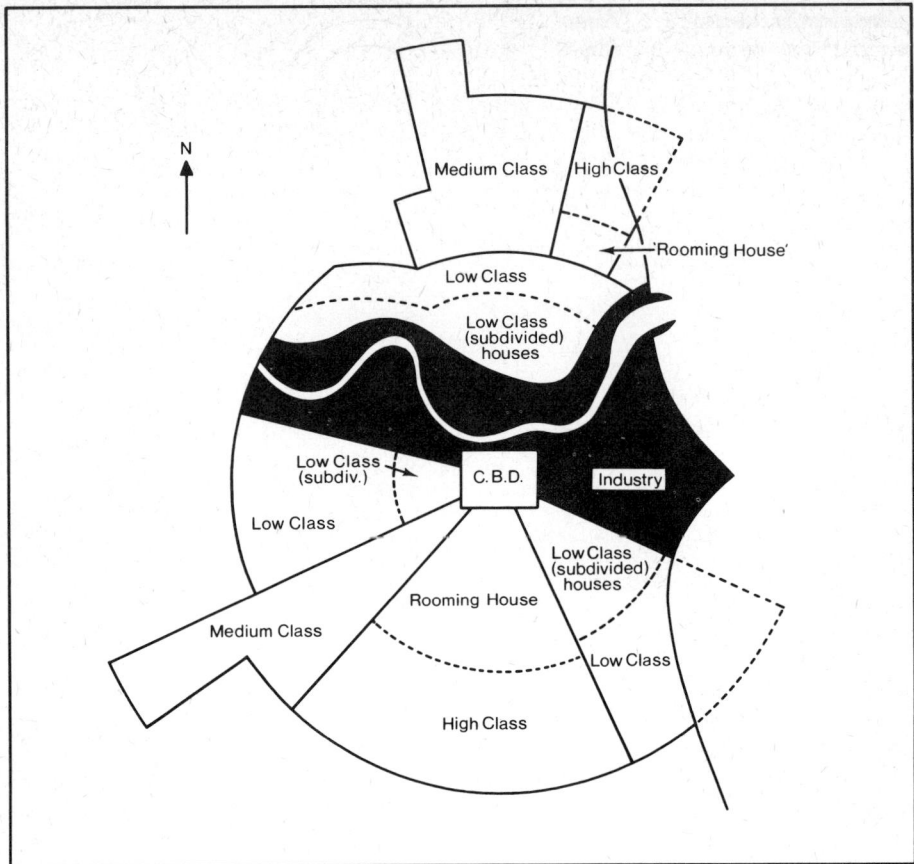

Figure 33
Sunderland—Land use model. (*After* B. T. Robson)

avoidance of industrial areas. . . . Especially in industrial towns like Sunderland (or Belfast, or New Haven, or Chicago) where industry is largely heavy and noxious, the patterning of the residential areas has to be viewed in terms of the location of industrial uses.

The interplay of these two forces can therefore be held to be primary in determining residential patterns. The highly-rated area will tend to be located in such a position that it is at once accessible to the Central Business District and yet not adjacent to industrial areas. And indeed this offers an explanation for the juxtaposition of sectors and concentric zones on opposite sides of the river. On that side of the river on which the Central Business District has developed, access to it can be achieved directly without contact with the industrial areas of the river

banks, whereas on the opposite side of the river, direct access between the highly-rated area and the Central Business District would involve building highly-rated houses adjacent to the riverside industrial areas. To avoid this a low-rated concentric zone is, as it were, allowed to interpose itself between the highly-rated zone and the industrial area, so that a concentric pattern develops which permits the maximum possible access between the highly-rated area and the Central Business District, without there being physical contact between highly-rated housing and industrial areas. Thus, for the highly-rated areas on both sides of the river the two objectives have been achieved; in one case by interposing the Central Business District itself between the highly-rated area and industry; in the other, by using an intervening low-rated area as a buffer. The

Photo 53
View looking west up the River Wear at Sunderland. Heavy industry lines both banks. The houses (*top*) form part of a concentric residential area. For details, see text and figure 33.

resolution of the balance of these two forces of attraction to the centre and repulsion from industry, thus produces the juxtaposition of sectors and concentric zones on opposite sides of the industrial belt, which, in the case of Sunderland and the other towns cited, forms along the line of the river. The highly-rated area forming a concentric ring on the opposite side of the river to the Central Business District might be expected to develop at a later date than the sector-wedge highly-rated area, as indeed was the case in Sunderland.*

Hoyt based his sector theory on such a wealth of evidence that little testing has subsequently taken place. Walter Firey†, however, claimed that the land use pattern of central

*B. T. Robson, *op. cit.*
†W. Firey, *Land Use in Central Boston*, Cambridge, Mass., Harvard University Press.

Boston was not sectoral. Firey also thought it unsatisfactory to make generalizations about urban land use patterns when cities differ so markedly in such matters as their relief, location on a waterfront and so on. He added that Hoyt paid too little attention to cultural and social factors such as fashion, colour, class and creed, all of which may influence land use. But these criticisms do not really invalidate the sector theory, rather they limit its applicability in particular circumstances.

The Multiple Nuclei Theory was first propounded in 1945 by C. D. Harris and E. L. Ullmann. It differs from the concentric and sector theories in that it considers a city to contain not one but a number of growth points or nuclei. Around each nucleus an urban cell develops, with each cell containing a distinctive variety of urban land uses. These cells merge to form a complex cellular structure

69

which is much more in accord with reality than are the relatively simple models of Burgess and Hoyt. Reasons for the existence of multiple nuclei include:

(1) Certain specialized functions can only operate where particular facilities are available. For example a Central Business District locates at the point of maximum accessibility; a port area grows along a navigable waterway; factories and wholesale premises require large areas of flat land and high-class housing is drawn to higher parts of a city commanding fresh air and fine views.

(2) Some activities group together because close contact brings mutual advantages. In Lancashire, for example, textile engineering works frequently lie adjacent to the mills they serve, whilst banks, insurance brokers, research establishments, exchanges and merchants involved in the textile trade are also close at hand. Similarly by-product industries are located close to the works from which they obtain raw materials—hence the close association, in Chicago for instance, of slaughter houses, meat-packing factories and firms making glue, buttons, leather and furs.

(3) Activities which are detrimental one to the other must be kept apart. Heavy industry, for example, especially if it is noxious, noisy or dangerous must not lie adjacent to high-class housing, luxury hotels or recreational parkland. Then again wholesalers try to avoid busy shopping districts where street congestion interferes with loading and blocks access to warehouses and freight yards.

(4) Some functions cannot be located ideally because rents are too high. Thus professional people such as dentists, solicitors or accountants may be obliged to set up premises some distance away from their potential customers. For the same reason warehouses may be placed in remote suburban districts where land is relatively cheap.

(5) Sometimes the existence of separate nuclei is traceable to historical causes. In central London, for example, the ancient City became the focus of financial and business activities whereas administration

became centred in and around the Palace of Westminster. In some coalfield cities such as Roubaix-Tourcoing multiple nuclei were provided by separate collieries; the industries, houses and shops which grew up around each pit-head eventually fused to form an industrial city. Merthyr-Tydfil had similar origins.

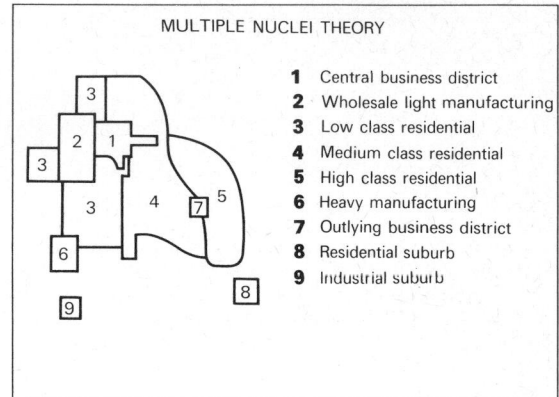

MULTIPLE NUCLEI THEORY

1 Central business district
2 Wholesale light manufacturing
3 Low class residential
4 Medium class residential
5 High class residential
6 Heavy manufacturing
7 Outlying business district
8 Residential suburb
9 Industrial suburb

Figure 34
Multiple-nuclei theory. (*After* Harris and Ullman)

It is clear that this theory makes it possible to construct an elaborate model of urban structure which is far more widely applicable than either the concentric or the sector models. In particular the multiple nuclei theory is in accord with the dispersal of urban functions made possible by mass car ownership and other modern transport facilities. It can explain, for instance, the growth of retail sub-centres—'mini-CBDs'—which are such a characteristic feature of modern industrial cities. These shopping and service precincts cater for whole communities within the urban area which find the traditional central CBD no longer readily accessible. Other nuclei are provided in suburban districts by industrial estates, slum-clearance 'overspill' and high-class 'dormitory' housing, and in some cases by airports. At Heathrow, for example, a large hotel has recently been added to the district's industrial and service functions. This suburban hotel, moreover, advertises its ready accessibility as an attraction for business conventions—a function traditionally associated with hotels in central London. The multiple nuclei theory is able to accommodate changes of urban structure such as this whilst at the

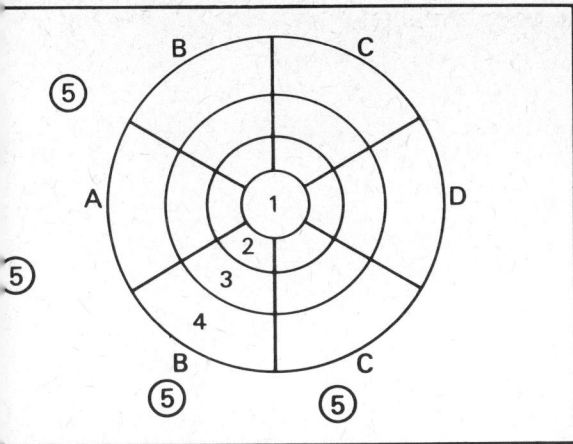

Figure 35
The structure of a hypothetical British city. This diagram assumes a prevailing wind from the west. Features of the model include: 1, the city centre; 2, transitional zone; zone of small terraced houses in sectors C and D, larger bye-law houses in sector B, large old houses in sector A; 4, post-1918 residential areas, with post-1945 development mainly on the periphery; 5, commuting-distance 'villages'. A, the middle-class sector; B, the lower-middle-class sector; C, the working-class sector (and main municipal housing areas); D, industry and lowest-working-class sector. (*After* P. Mann)

same time retaining elements of the concentric and sectoral models. It is argued, however, that the construction of high-rise buildings for occupation by a multiplicity of functions makes nonsense of *all* theories of urban land use. This view is rather unfair because most high-rise blocks are used predominantly as office accommodation.

Photo 54
Peak-hour traffic heading for London.

Photo 55
A new hotel built alongside the Hammersmith Flyover, London. Large hotels are traditionally located within a city's Central Business District, but traffic congestion in central areas is leading to their more widespread dispersal.

Gradient analysis

All three of the theories outlined above assume that urban land-use patterns reflect the distribution of urban land-values, and via those values the distribution of economic rents. It is instructive, therefore, to make a re-appraisal of the concentric, sectoral and multiple-nuclei hypotheses by means of rent-gradient analysis. This approach assumes that all decisions on location, whether made by financiers, industrialists, retailers, house owners or whoever, are regulated by the economic processes of supply and demand which operate in society. Each activity (or function) has the ability to derive *utility* from every site in a city, the degree of that utility being measured by the rent which that activity is willing to pay to secure any particular site. The entire range of functions bidding against one another for sites may conveniently be classified into three categories, *viz.* commercial, industrial and residential. For all three categories it is assumed that access to the city centre is a

71

Photo 56(a) and (b)
The centre of Guildford. This photograph shows the Central Business District and portions of the city devoted mainly to either industrial or residential use. The main shopping street, High Street, runs west-east across the middle of the picture. Typical Central Business District buildings on or adjacent to this street include the office block *(left)*, large department store *(left, centre)*, new shopping precinct and multi-story car-park *(right, centre)* and theatre *(middle, foreground)*. A linear industrial zone runs northwards, left, adjacent to the River Wey. The background, right, contains mainly a sector of nineteenth-century terrace housing. Newer suburban estates and some factories are shown in the photograph below.

vital consideration. Each function, by bidding for sites as close in as is economically feasible, can thus reduce to a minimum its *friction of distance* from the city centre.

But the need and ability to bid for very high value central sites varies from function to function. CBD retail activities, for example, have an overriding necessity to be as close as possible to the city centre, for only there is turnover and sales potential high enough to make their operations profitable. Industries, by contrast, may be profitably located farther out, provided they have access to transport facilities and public utilities. Residents can rarely, if ever, afford to bid sufficiently high to obtain central sites and so can enter the market effectively only towards the city's outer edge. Figure 28 *(p. 64)* shows the typical rent-bid gradients which may be expected from the three main categories of urban land users.

It is apparent from this figure that, providing rents diminish evenly in all directions outwards from the city centre, the urban land-use pattern will be in accord with Burgess' concentric theory. In figure 36 this concentric distribution of rents and land-usage is represented in three-dimensional form. It may be argued, however, that rents are unlikely to fall away evenly in this manner. In particular land astride arterial transport routes will command higher utility and hence

higher economic rents than other land equidistant from the city centre. The land-use pattern thus becomes distorted as shown in figure 37. This distortion is more in accord with Hoyt's sector theory, especially if one assumes that the 'ridges' of higher value land are likely to broaden towards the city's edge, i.e. where wider patches of rural land become available for industrial expansion. *(See point S on figure 37.)* Further sophistication of the urban transport network will arise from the construction of radial ringroads, and those points where radial and arterial routes intersect will become especially valued by virtue of their optimal accessibility. The areas surrounding such intersections therefore command high economic rents—see the 'cones' on figure 38—and the land-use pattern acquires added complexity. Industrial and even CBD functions will be attracted to these very accessible localities and so the model has evolved to accord with the multiple nuclei concepts of Harris and Ullman.

The various high-economic-rent areas shown on the more complex diagram may be explained as follows:
(1) Convergence of routes: hence high rent bids by CBD-type functions. Note that such functions may themselves become differentiated. According to Horwood and Boyce the CBD comprises two parts, *viz.*

Figure 36
Predicted land-use pattern where economic vents fall off evenly from the city centre.

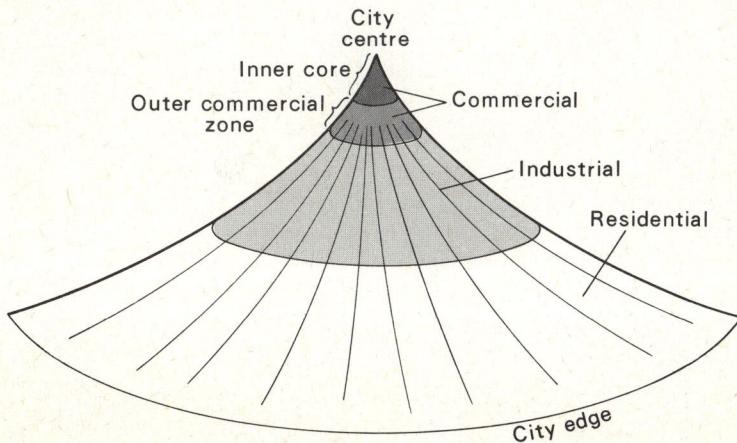

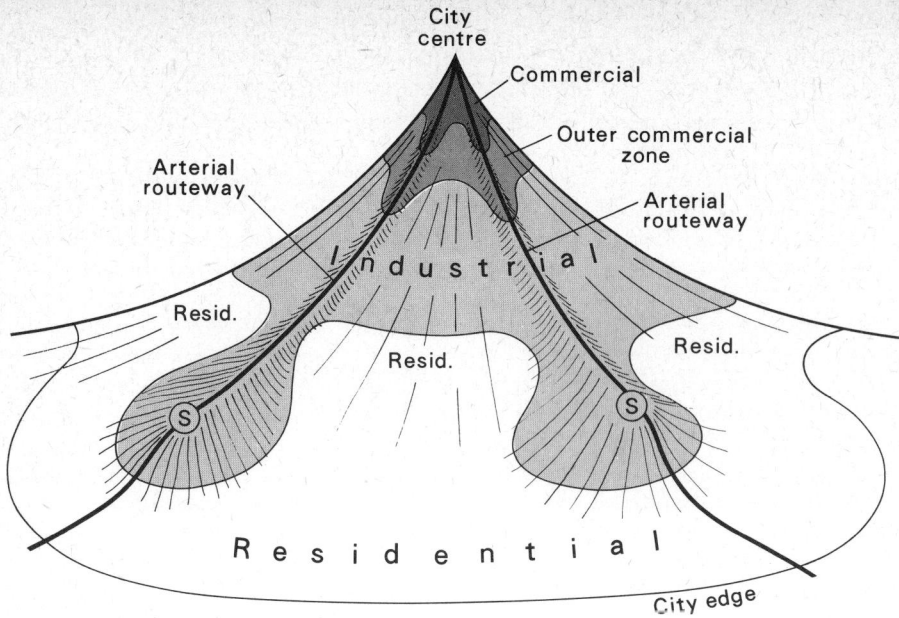

Figure 37
Predicted land-use pattern where economic rents are distorted by arterial routeways.

Figure 38
Predicted land-use pattern where economic rents are distorted by intersecting routes and a favoured residential area.

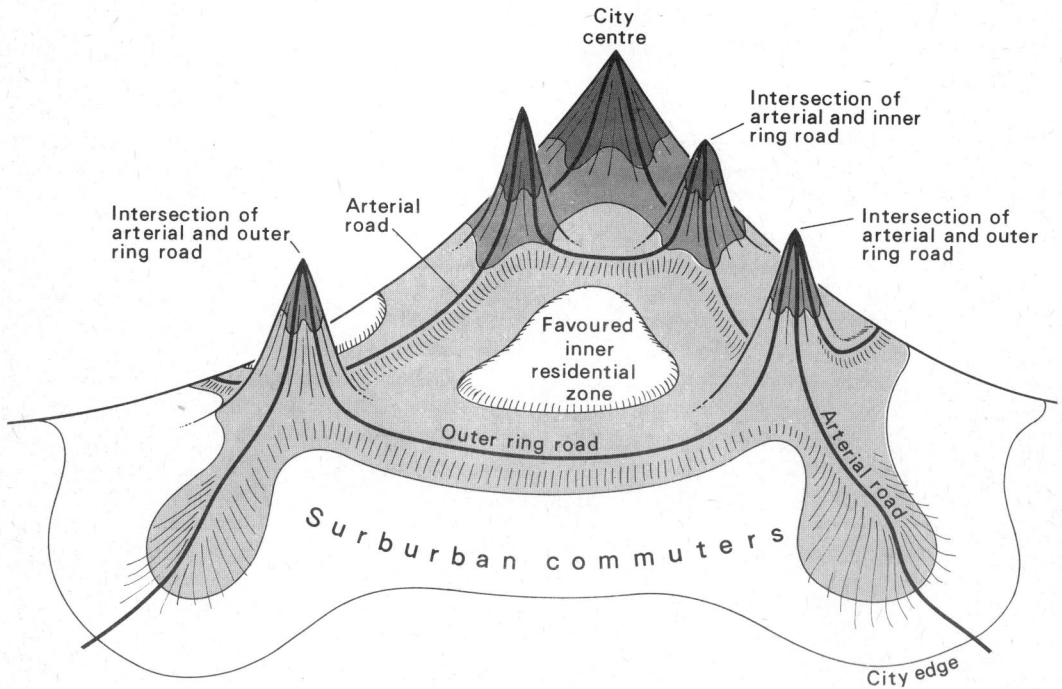

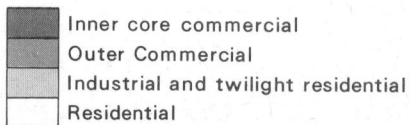

Photo 57 (a)

The Hampshire Centre, Bournemouth. This is a shopping complex deliberately located on the edge of Bournemouth, to avoid traffic congestion. It attracts customers with cars both from the city and from a wide area of the adjoining countryside.

Photo 57 (b)

A hypermarket at Permus, New Jersey, USA. Note the rural location alongside a motorway junction, the vast car parks and the varied retail stores and service buildings.

(i) an *inner core*—where intensive use of very high-value land results in marked vertical (i.e. 'skyscraper') expansion and where there are strong functional links between shops and between various offices; and (ii) a less intensively developed *outer zone* where land values and economic rents are lower and where functions have very little in common except location. This differentiation may repeat itself within the secondary CBDs at suburban traffic intersections. Note, too, that such centres may lack *inner core* functions; a descending hierarchy of CBD activities locate themselves at transport nodes successively farther out from the city centre. *(See also figure 38.)*

(2) Arterial routes: hence high rent bids from wholesalers and light manufacturing industries anxious to obtain good transport links to places outside the city.

(3) Areas of hills, lakes, woodland and open space within the city: hence high rent bids from residents anxious to obtain 'better' accommodation.

(4) Remote rural locations: hence relatively high residential bids from suburban commuters.

Such a model can, of course, be made even more complex by adding high-rent 'plateaux' around hypothetical airports, estuaries, canals, 'up-wind' residential districts and so on.

Gradient analysis also provides a valuable method of studying the distribution of population density within a city. Colin Clark has shown that, for a wide range of cities throughout the world, residential population densities decline with increasing distance from the city centre. This situation holds good irrespective of any variations in land *use* patterns between cities, and is valid for both Western and non-Western cities. *(See, for example, figure 39.)* There are, however, considerable variations in the *rates* at which population densities decrease in different types of city. Studies to explain these variations have focused attention on the interrelation of such factors as *per capita* car ownership, the proportion of manufacturing jobs available, the extent of 'twilight' zones, the cost of public transport and the age and extent of the urban area. Tentative conclusions suggest (i) that larger cities with low transport costs, extensive inner areas of decay and dispersed centres of manufacturing employment are less compact than other cities; and (ii) that older industrial cities tend to have the highest overall population densities.

The prime factor influencing the urban

Figure 39

Population density-distance relationships for (a) Hyderabad, India and (b) Chicago, USA. (*Source:* Haggett, *after* Berry, Simmons and Tennant)

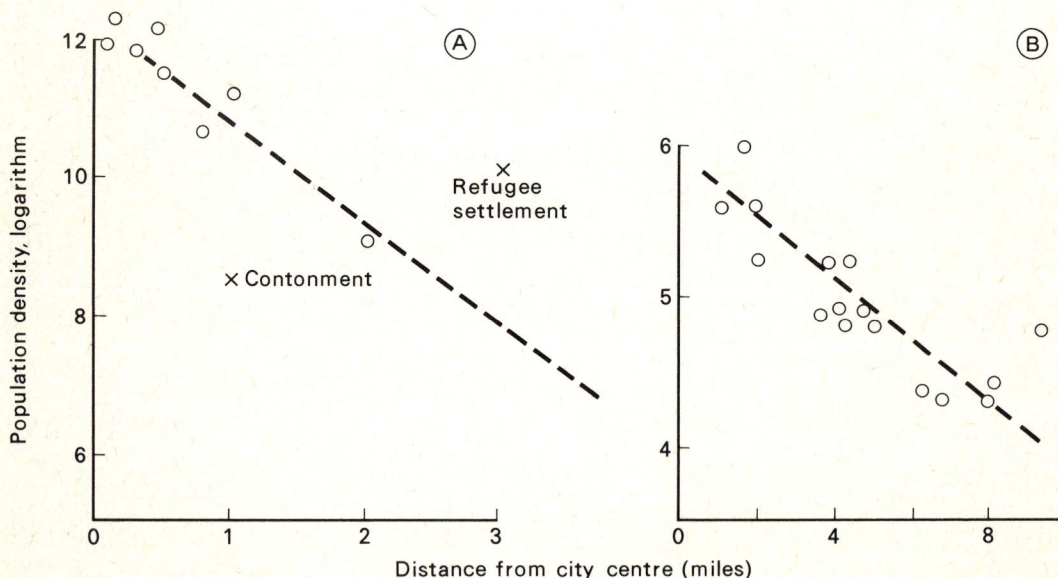

population gradient is transport. Assuming that employment opportunities predominate towards the city centre a person's need to live close to the centre will depend upon his income. For the poor the marginal impact of transport costs is higher than for the rich. Poorer people are therefore likely to forgo ideas of living in suburban locations, preferring to use the money saved on transport to pay relatively high rents for congested accommodation in 'twilight' areas. Their rent-bid curves are therefore likely to be steep.* *(See figure 40.)* Richer people who prefer low-density living and who can afford the transport costs involved in commuting will locate towards the city fringe–their rent bid curves have a gentler gradient. On this analysis there is a substitution on the part of poorer households of rents for transport costs and urban population densities are explained in terms of the urban land market.

If density-decay curves of Western and non-Western cities are compared certain interesting contrasts become apparent. Figure 41(a) shows typical curves for Western cities at three points in time. In the early stage of growth residential densities are very high towards the centre but fall off rapidly at increasing distance from the city centre. This reflects the early central location of factories and the absence of effective means of public transport. Through time, however, there is a centrifugal movement of residential population made possible by increasingly sophisticated transport links with the city's periphery; densities decline sharply in the centre (where commercial and

*The collective payments which poorer tenants are prepared to make to property owners for their accommodation in congested tenement blocks or terraced houses off-set the very high economic rents which the owners must pay to secure the sites on which such accommodation is built. In effect the tenants of crowded tenements are paying a high economic rent to share the use of very high value central sites.

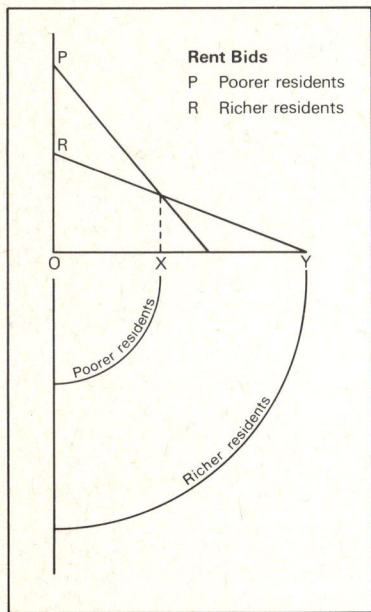

Figure 40
Hypothetical rent-distance relationships of poorer and richer residents within a city.

Figure 41 (a)
Comparative diagrams of density-distance relationships in 'Western' and 'non-Western' cities. (*After* Berry, Simmons and Tennant)

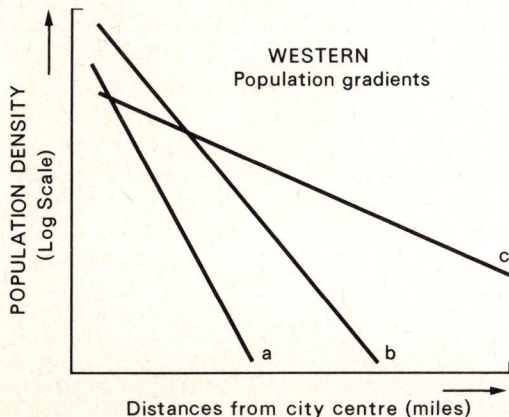

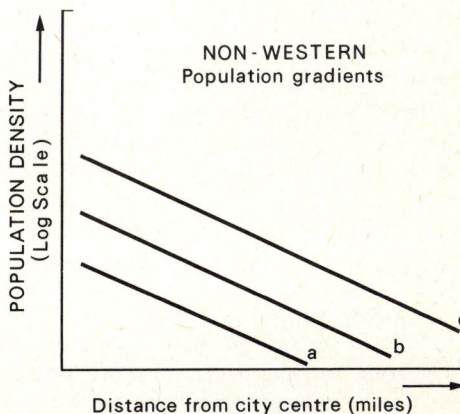

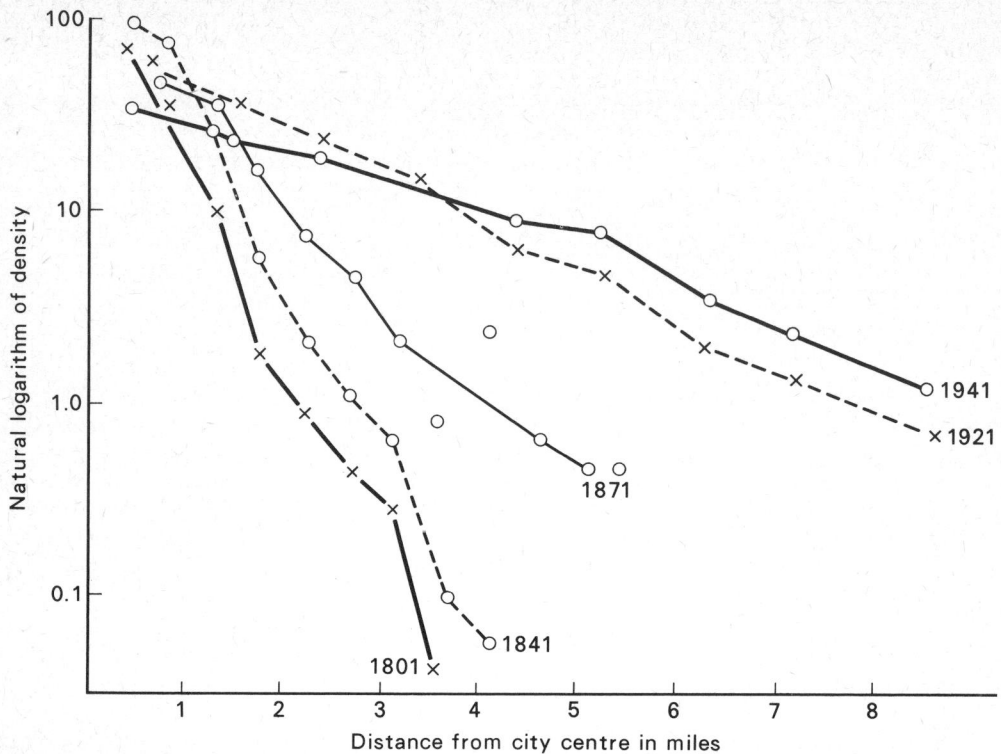

Figure 41 (b)
London: population density and distance from city centre. (*After* Clark)

industrial functions displace former residents) but increase and reach further out into the suburbs with the growth of commuting. The changing density patterns also reflect the impact of planning, which aims at achieving lower residential densities, thus the density gradient becomes more gradual. (*See also figure 41(b)*.)

In non-Western cities there is a continual increase of densities throughout the whole urban area. Congestion increases in the centre as it becomes the target of those persons moving up the socio-economic ladder (*see also page 25*). At the same time the periphery becomes crowded with migrants from the surrounding countryside. Non-Western cities, because they have less sophisticated systems of transport, push outwards more slowly than Western cities of similar total populations. They therefore tend to be more compact and have greater overall population densities.

The evolutionary changes that occur in urban population densities are a useful reminder that the urban land-use pattern is itself dynamic. Any factor which alters the relative utility of urban sites for commercial, industrial or residential occupation will inevitably trigger off changes in land-use. Most important in this respect are developments in transport, for these affect accessibility throughout the urban area. Other relevant factors include changes in the functions of a city and in the availability of public utilities such as gas, electricity and water supply. Recent changes in the Canadian city of Calgary have been analysed by P. J. Smith.[*]

The maps of Calgary (*figure 42*) clearly suggest a sectoral pattern of growth. Since

[*]*Economic Geography*, Vol. 38, pp. 326–9; P. J. Smith, *A Study of Calgary's Past and Probable Future Growth*, Calgary, 1969.

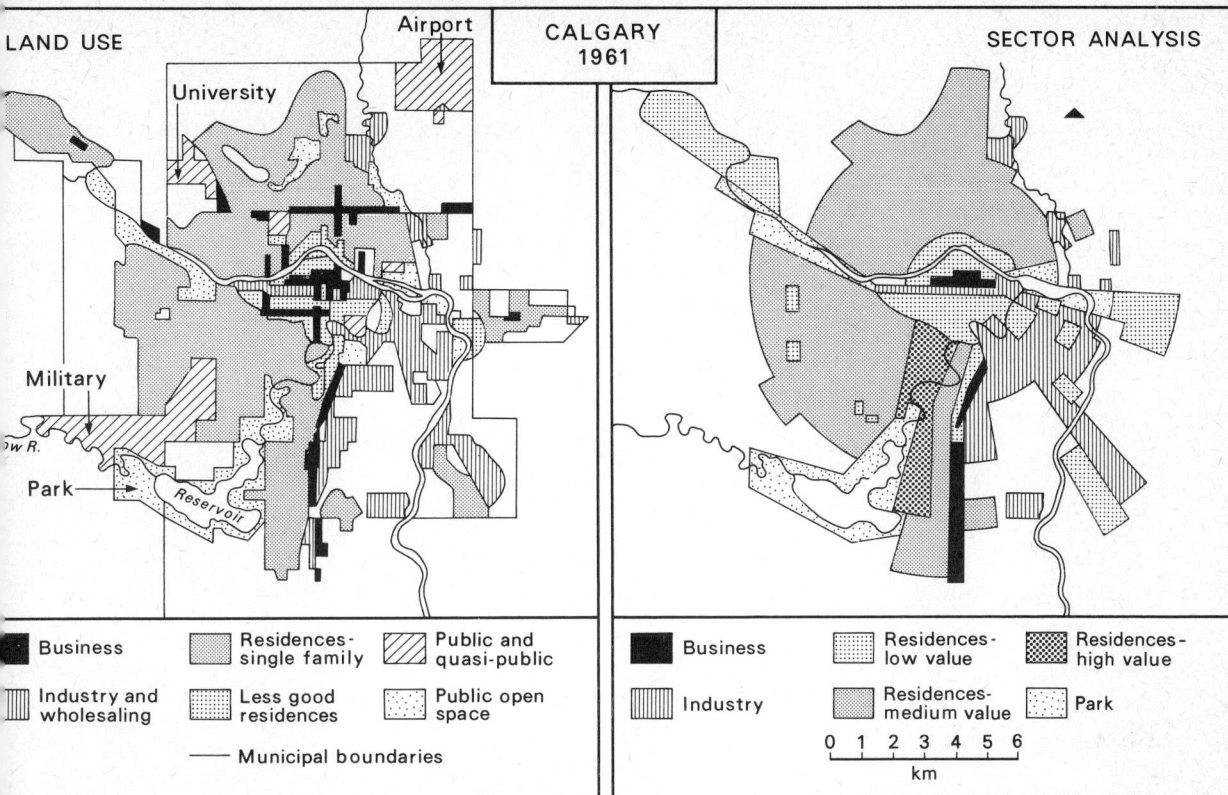

Figure 42
Calgary, 1961: land-use and its interpretation by sectors. (*After* P. J. Smith)

1950, however, this pattern has begun to break down due to inefficiencies in land-use brought about by a rapid period of growth. Symptomatic of these inefficiencies are:

(1) *The inability of the CBD to maintain its role as the sole retail and service centre.* Between 1950 and 1961 the radius of Calgary's built-up area increased from 4 to 8 kilometres and its population from 120 000 to 265 000. During that period the number of commercial nuclei outside the CBD shot up from 6 to 60, the latter number including two regional centres each with a department store and some fifty smaller stores, offices and services facilities. At the same time two other commercial activities formerly confined almost exclusively within the CBD—the hotel trade and car sales—have spread into outlying areas. Motels are now found along all the main arterial routes leading out of Calgary and both new and used car

agencies are located along the main road to Lethbridge.

(2) *The diminishing utility of central, railway-orientated sites for the city's older wholesale and industrial firms.* With the growth of road transport the wholesale premises, with narrow congested approach roads and no off-street loading facilities, are ill-adapted to modern techniques of mass-handling of commodities. A central location, furthermore, has largely lost its advantages for wholesalers now that so many retail outlets have grown up in the suburbs. The old industrial zone along the Bow River has also become increasingly congested, not least because traffic moving along its narrow streets is frequently held up at level crossings. To avoid such difficulties two planned industrial estates were opened in 1955 on municipal land between the Bow Valley and the main road south to Lethbridge. These estates, each with excellent

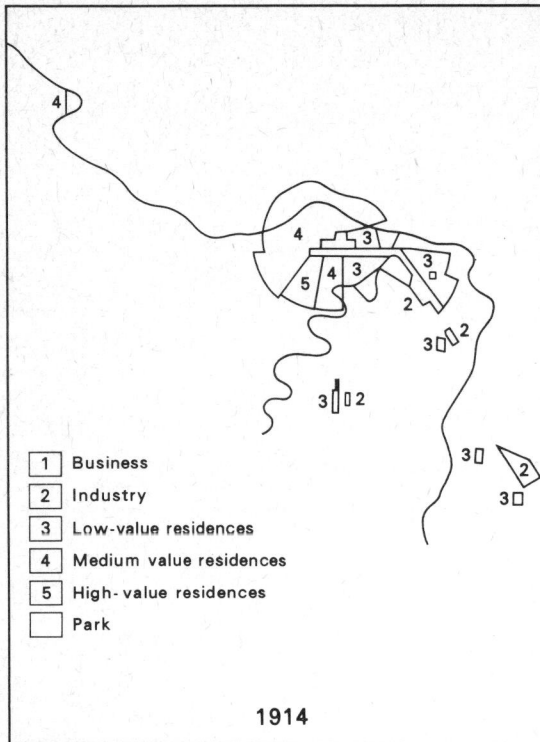

Figure 43 (a)
Hoyt's sector theory applied to Calgary's land-use pattern, 1914, when the city population was approximately 50,000. (*Source:* Assessment records, city of Calgary *after* P. J. Smith)

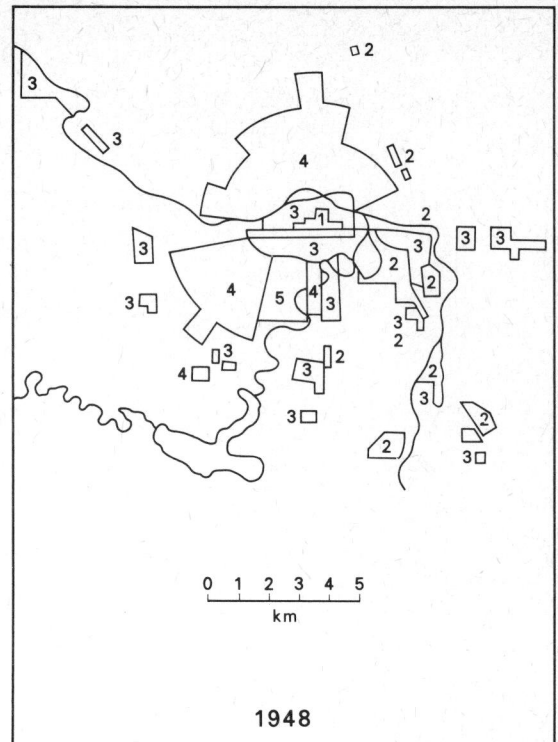

Figure 43 (b)
Hoyt's sector theory applied to Calgary, 1948, when the metropolitan population was approximately 105,000. (*Source:* National Topographic Map Series *after* P. J. Smith)

road and rail facilities, soon became magnets for new and relocated businesses. They are now well-established and their success has led to the building of more private industrial estates in the suburbs.

(3) *The extreme shortage of land available within Calgary for cheap housing.* This shortage, coupled with the ready availability of cheap cars, has resulted in a mushroom growth of three suburban towns, with a collective population exceeding 25 000.

The overall effects of these changes in Calgary have been to create many new growth points, e.g. municipal and private industrial estates, dispersed clusters of shops and service facilities, commercial enterprises along the arterial routes and residential 'dormitory' towns with low-cost housing. Although sectors are still clearly apparent in Calgary's structure, the city's land-use pattern is changing and becoming more complex. The complexity arises because the patterns of land-values and economic rents are altering due mainly to changes in transport and in the techniques of handling merchandise. These trends towards multi-nuclei structure are likely to continue and it is significant that, following pressure from the business community, the city's Zoning By-law has recently been amended to permit the construction of large office blocks outside the CBD.

Smith's study of Calgary emphasizes the importance of transport as a catalyst of urban change and of outward expansion. At the edge of a city growth seems to take place in the form

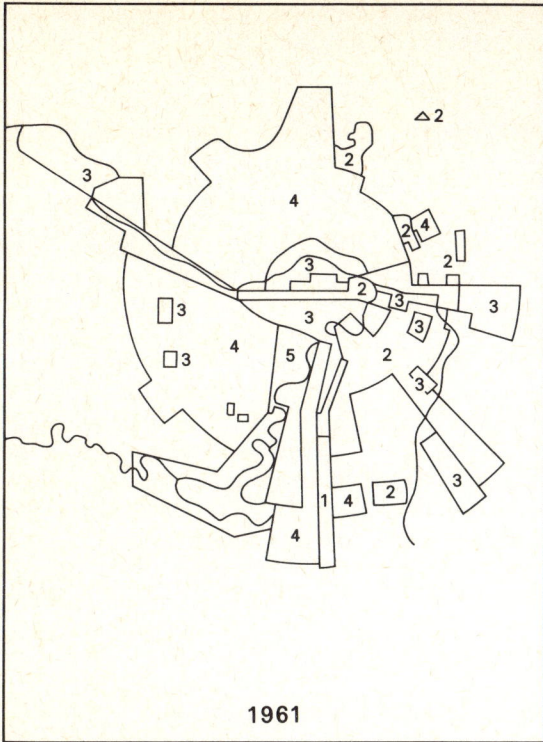

Figure 43 (c)
Hoyt's sector theory applied to Calgary, 1961, when the metropolitan population was approximately 270,000. (*Source:* Field Survey *after* P. J. Smith)

of waves. Garner* suggests a model in which growth first pushes out along arterial routes and then gradually infills the intervening land. Figure 44 presents evidence in support of this hypothesis. It shows trends in surburban house construction on radial routes and in intervening areas at various distances from central Chicago between 1946 and 1956. In Zone I, at the edge of the central city, the number of new houses is much greater in the intervening suburbs (I_1) than at places on radial routes (R_1). In Zone II the rate of house construction in the intervening areas lagged behind that on radial routes (R_2) except in 1956. In Zone III, i.e. that farthest out from

*B. J. Garner, *Differential Residential Growth of Incorporated Municipalities in the Chicago Suburban Region.* (Mimeographed).

the city, **growth** is predominantly along the radial routes (R_3), with comparatively little house building in intervening areas (I_3). From this one may deduce the following: (i) growth is initiated in sectors which have good accessibility to the central city; (ii) growth in these radial sectors is liable to wax and wane and (iii) growth in the intervening areas is also sporadic but lags behind that in the radial sectors. This suggests that the way in which a city grows outwards is more in accord with the sector theory than with the concentric theory of urban development. This view is supported by Chapman and Weiss who made a detailed study of growth in a cluster of towns in North Carolina. They also concluded that

Figure 44
Differential residential growth of incorporated municipalities in the Chicago suburban region. (*After* B. J. Garner)

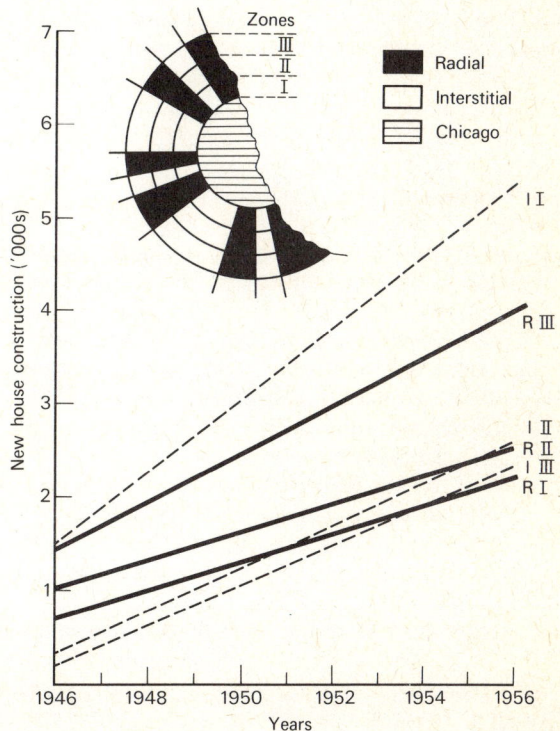

in America the intensity of urban development is greatest in areas adjacent to large centres of employment and in suburban settlements served by a wide range of community facilities. Conversely development is discouraged by poor drainage and by proximity to 'twilight' zones and black ghettoes.

11 The size and spacing of settlements

Central Place Theory
The previous section has dealt with the internal structure of cities and with various theories which seek to explain the distribution of functions within an urban area. Here the distribution of the cities themselves is analysed and an attempt is made to see whether there is any correlation between their location, spacing and size.

The basis of much modern research in this respect is Central Place Theory, which originated in Germany with the work of Walter Christaller.* Christaller studied the settlements of South Germany from the point of view of the provision they made of goods and services for the community. A convenient method of illustrating Christaller's ideas is to consider the hypothetical settlement pattern which would evolve following the occupation of a virgin landscape by a farming society. Like all theories that of Central Place makes certain basic assumptions. For the purpose of this illustration let us therefore assume that:
(1) the farming community is at first entirely self-sufficient;
(2) it is divided into equal-sized groups, with each group establishing a village in the centre of its own farmland;
(3) the landscape being settled is *isotropic*, i.e. it is absolutely uniform with no variation in relief, climate, drainage, fertility and so on;

*Walter Christaller, *Die Zentralen Ortz in Suddeutschland.* 1933.

(4) the community has a common culture and a common level of technological achievement.

It will be clear from these assumptions that each separate village community will require the same area of farmland to achieve a common level of economic well-being. At first the individual settlements may be quite separate one from the other, but as more immigrants arrive the landscape begins to fill up. It can be shown by mathematical *packing theory* that if the land is to be occupied to optimum advantage the distribution of villages must ultimately be as shown in figure 45, i.e. at the corners of a regular pattern of equilateral triangles. This assumes that each village requires the same area of land from which to obtain its supplies of food, water, timber, building stone, fuel and so on.

What will be the most satisfactory boundary between the land of each village? Clearly a circle is unsatisfactory, for this will lead either to some land remaining uncleared as in figure 46, or to some land being claimed by more than one village. Yet a circular boundary would maximize accessibility between each village and its farming hinterland. The shape most nearly circular which avoids the boundary frictions indicated in figure 46 is a hexagon, as shown in figure 47. Thus it is assumed

Figure 45
Ideal distribution of hamlets on an isotrophic surface. The hamlets are spaced three kilometres apart on an equilateral grid.

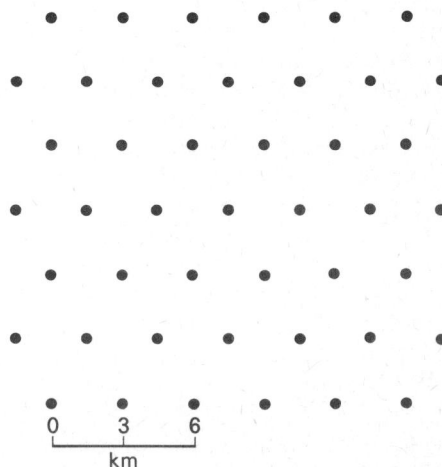

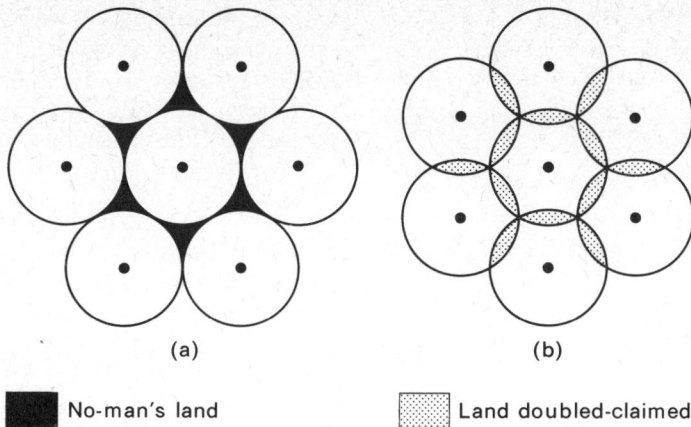

No-man's land   Land doubled-claimed

Figure 46
Boundary problems arising when each hamlet has a circular hinterland.

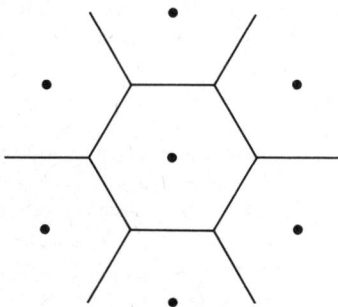

Figure 47
Hexagonal boundaries demarcate each hamlet's land and allow a maximum density of self-sufficing settlements.

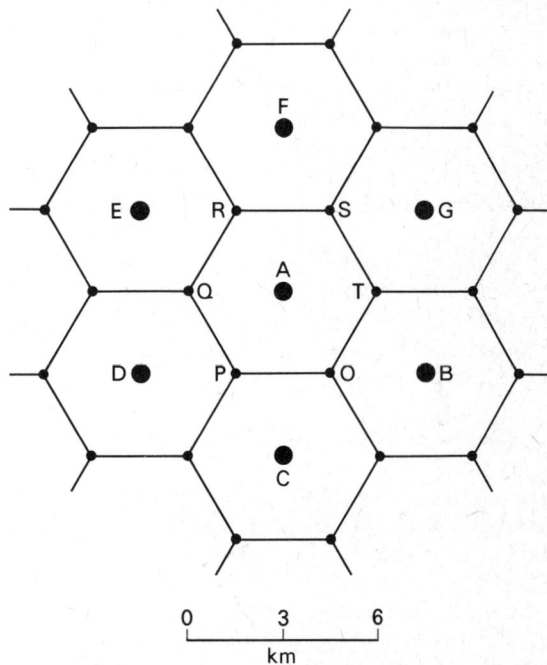

0   3   6
km

Figure 48
The sharing of customers as village functions evolve in a *k* = 3 network of hamlets and villages. (*For explanation see text*)

that the boundaries of the villages would ultimately interlock in a regular pattern of hexagons.

Various entrepreneurs, for example bakers and butchers, might set up shop in each settlement, but initially such businesses would serve only their own village population. Imagine now that in village A *(figure 48)* there is a particularly enterprising blacksmith who invents a revolutionary type of plough, an implement more efficient than that traditionally used and one with obvious advantages in terms of increased crop yields. Let us also assume that the new plough can only be produced at a profit if the blacksmith can rely upon the custom of the equivalent of three whole village populations: in other words this is the *threshold population* which ensures that the manufacture of new ploughs will be

economically viable. Other blacksmiths will of course copy the new invention but not all of them can rely on tapping a threshold population. In fact the maximum possible density of such enterprises is shown in figure 49. This

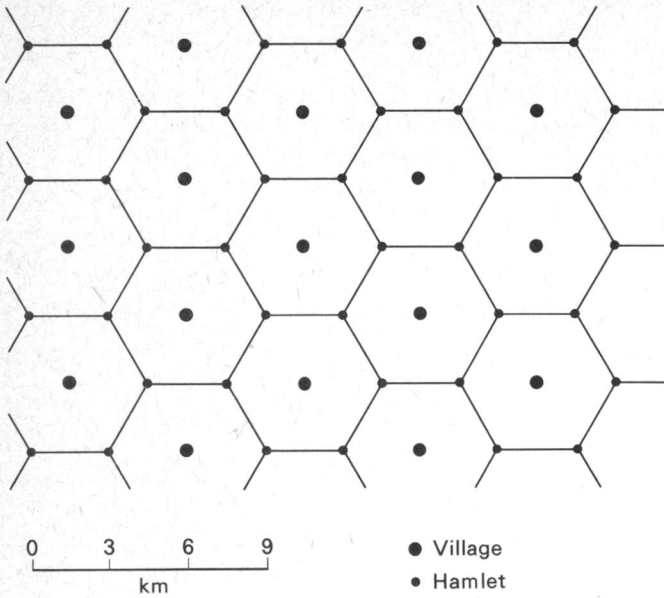

Figure 49
Pattern of villages' service areas governed by a $k = 3$ hierarchy.

Figure 50
Pattern of service areas of villages in a $k = 4$ hierarchy.
(*For explanation see text*)

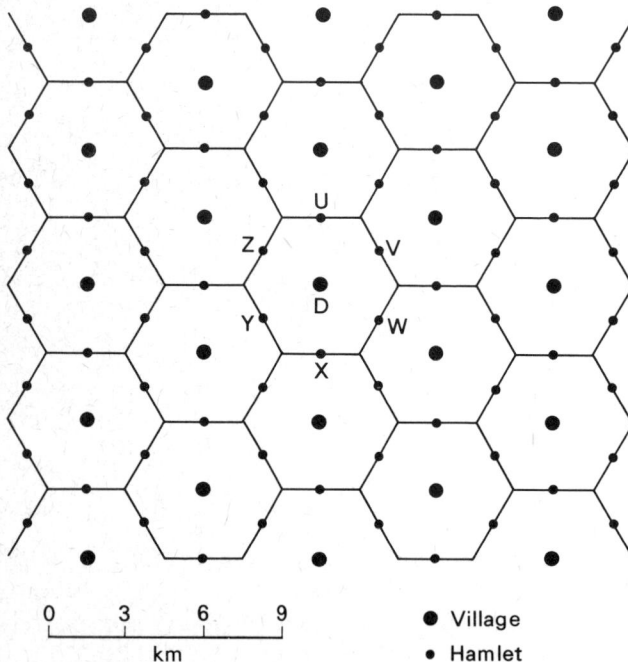

0   3   6   9
km

● Village
• Hamlet

assumes that buyers of the new plough will wish to minimize the distance they must travel to make their purchase. The blacksmith in village A can rely on all the custom of his own village. The villagers at O, P, Q, R, S and T, however, are equidistant from village A and two other plough-producing villages. For example the villagers at O are equidistant from A, B and C and it is assumed that they will share their custom equally between these three villages. The villagers at P, Q, R, S and T share their allegiances in a similar fashion. Thus the blacksmith at A obtains the custom of one whole village (his own) plus six-thirds (i.e. one third from each of villages O, P, Q, R, S and T. Similarly the blacksmiths at B, C, D, etc. have access to the equivalent of three whole village populations.

'Higher-order' central places in which the manufacture of new ploughs is added to their normal functions thus develop in a more widely-spaced pattern superimposed on the basic village grid. It will be apparent that central places of the next higher order will cater for a market hinterland of nine whole villages, the next for twenty-seven and so on in multiples of three. This multiple Christaller called the *k value* and the pattern shown in figure 49 is said to be a *k*3 settlement hierarchy. Christaller also recognized that, by rotating the hexagonal grid, it was possible to vary the *k* value. In figure 50, for example, the marginal settlements U, V, W, X, Y and Z each share their allegiance between only two main villages and each central village therefore gains access to a threshold population equal to that of four whole villages. For example, the main village D has the custom of one whole village (its own) plus six halves. This is therefore a *k*4 hierarchy in which the threshold populations of higher order settlements increase to 4, 16, 64 and so on. Yet another variation is shown in figure 51 where the *k* value is 7.

Christaller maintained that settlement hierarchies evolve with their *k* values fixed, the particular value in any one case being determined by the nature of the society involved. A *k*3 hierarchy, for example, maximizes the number of central places in a hypothetical landscape and thus brings the supply of higher order goods and services as near as possible to all dependent settlements.

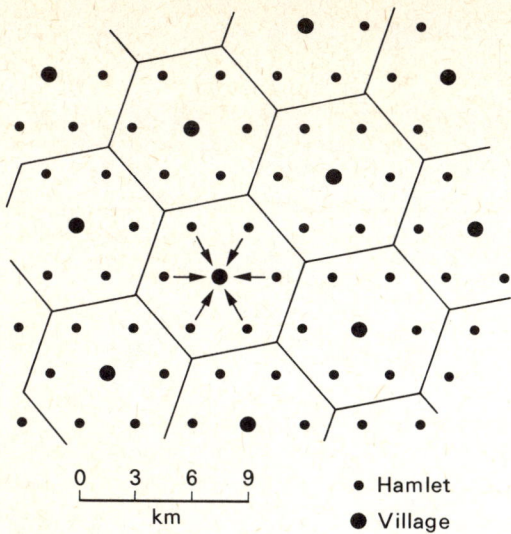

Figure 51
Pattern of service areas of villages in a $k = 7$ hierarchy.

This is Christaller's *'market principle'*. A trading society in which maximum accessibility to central market places is vital would thus tend to evolve a $k3$ hierarchy. A $k4$ hierarchy, by contrast, is likely to develop where the cost of building transport networks is an important consideration. On figure 53 it can be seen that as many important places as possible are located on any one traffic route. As regards the $k7$ hierarchy, Christaller considered that this suited the needs of a feudal society in which strong centralized administration was of paramount importance. In figure 54 notice that all six tributary villages give their allegiance to the one higher order central place. The hinterlands of all other higher order places in the $k7$ pattern are not quite exclusive, however, for a few marginal settlements must share their allegiances. This problem would be overcome if the marginal settlements realign their allegiances in the manner explained in figures 55(a) and (b), an

Figure 52
Location of urban areas and major routes according to Christaller's marketing principle. ($k = 3$).

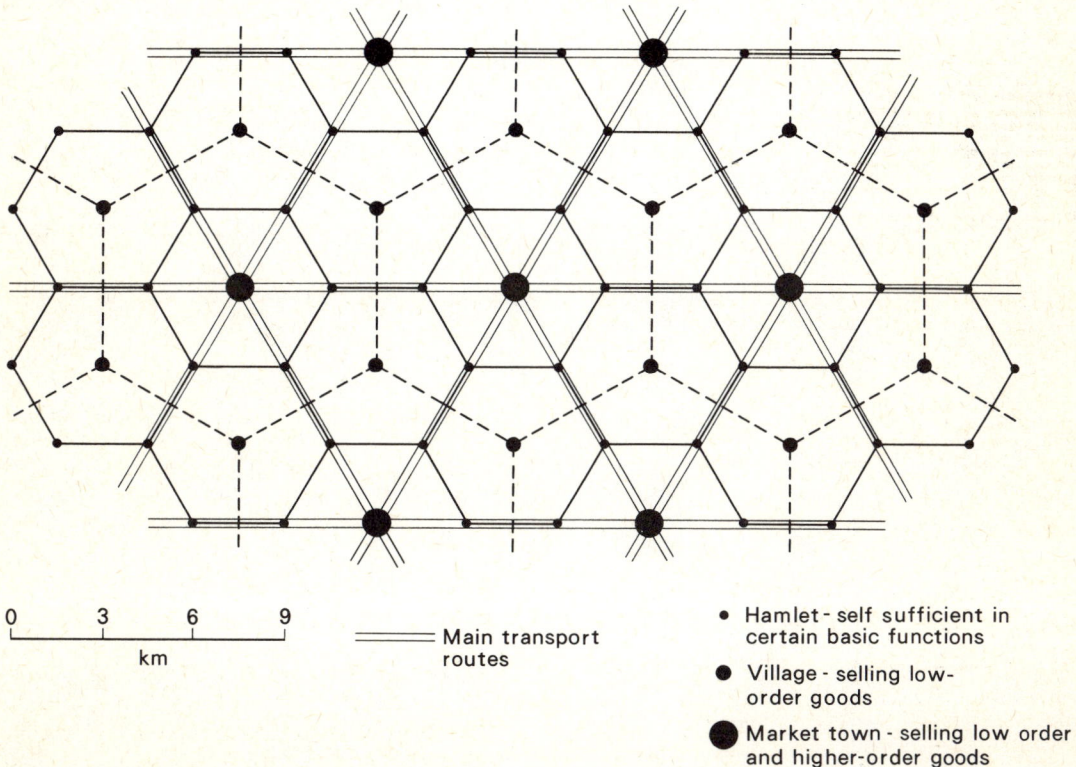

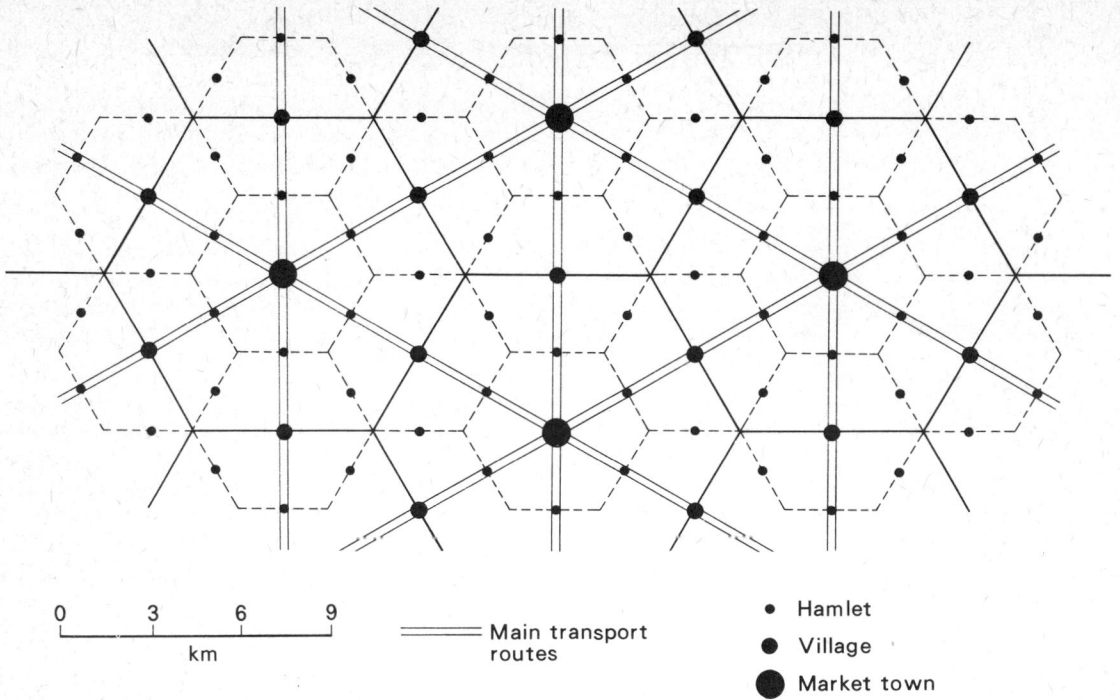

Figure 53
Distribution of hamlets, villages and towns in a fixed hierarchy where $k = 4$.
(Christaller's transport principle)

Figure 54
Location of urban areas and major routes according to Christaller's administrative
principle. ($k = 7$).

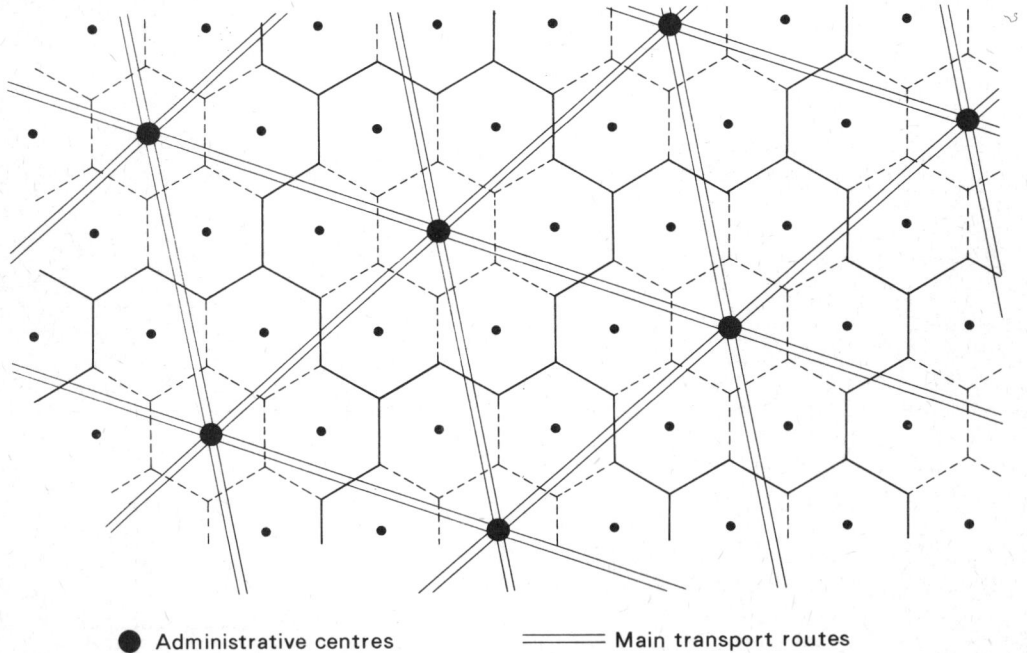

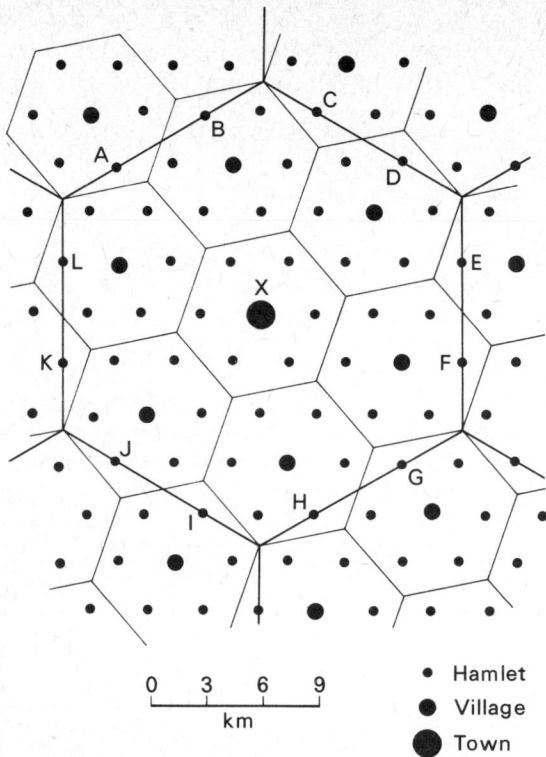

Figure 55 (a)
Pattern of service areas of villages and market towns in a
$k = 7$ hierarchy.

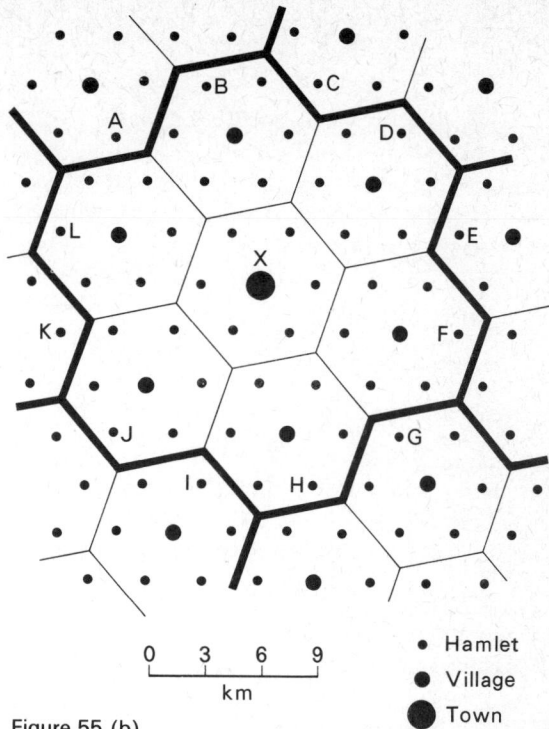

Figure 55 (b)
Nesting in a $k = 7$ hierarchy.

Figure 56
Nesting in a $k = 3$ hierarchy—an alternative way of
sharing customers. Compare with figure 48, p. 83.

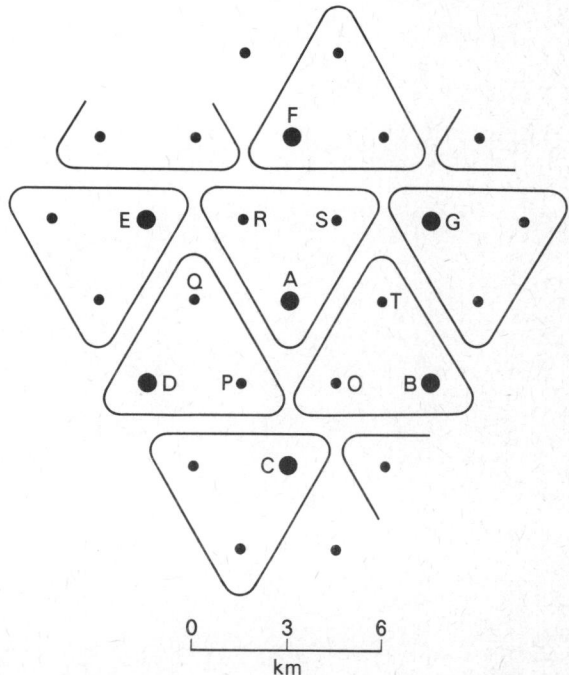

arrangement referred to by Christaller as
'nesting'. Figures 56 and 57 show that 'nesting' is also possible within $k3$ and $k4$ hierarchies.

Any hypothetical settlement pattern developed on a fixed k principle gives rise to a
hierarchy of central places with marked
'steps' between each order of settlement.
These 'steps' consist of increases in the total
number of goods and services—i.e. central
place functions—as one ascends the settlement
hierarchy. It should be noted that the theory
outlined so far does not postulate any variation
in the *populations* of the various orders of
settlement, for the more important central
places obtain access to high threshold populations by tapping the custom of tributary settlements. Providing a society has a net population increase, however, it is reasonable to
assume that the higher order settlements
would attract migrants to man their new
industries and service trades. Certain towns

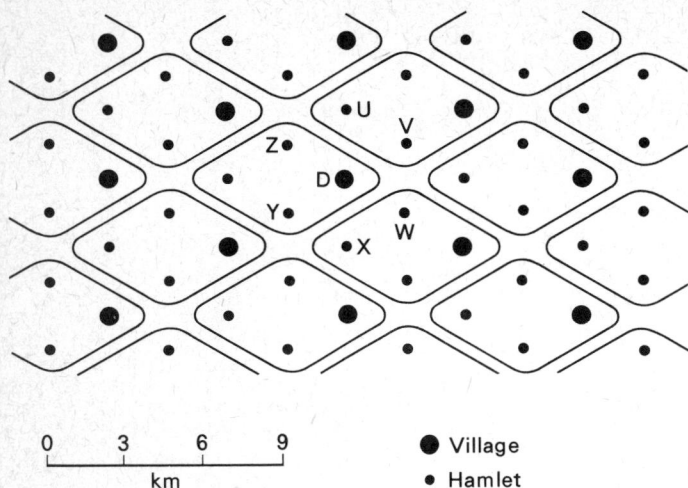

Figure 57
Nesting in a *k* = 4 hierarchy. Compare with figure 50, p. 84.

● Village
• Hamlet

0 3 6 9
km

would then gain in numbers and high threshold populations would eventually be accessible locally. The links suggested by Christaller between settlement functions, population and spacing in his hypothetical landscape are shown in Table Q *(p. 105)*.

Field studies tend *not* to support fully Christaller's hypothesis concerning fixed *k* hierarchies. Table M, for example, shows the populations in rank order of 354 settlements in the region to the south-west of Norwich. There are few, if any clearcut natural breaks in this order, except possibly between settlements 49 and 48, 10 and 9, and 2 and 1. If Christaller's ideas were completely valid one might expect to find a more definite grouping of settlements into categories by size. This problem appears to have been resolved in the theories of the German geographer Lösch (1954), who developed the ideas of Christaller

Table M

Population and rank of settlements in part of East Anglia to the south-west of Norwich

Rank	Population	Rank	Population	Rank	Population	Rank	Population
1	120 096 (Norwich)	36	1252	71	782	106	515
2	27 536	37	1237	72	769	107	511
3	21 179	38	1219	73	763	108	504
4	11 227	39	1215	74	763	109	502
5	9744	40	1209	75	762	110	500
6	7795	41	1177	76	753	111	498
7	7199	42	1136	77	739	112	494
8	7132	43	1134	78	735	113	493
9	7051	44	1124	79	734	114	492
10	5904	45	1071	80	723	115	492
11	5399	46	1070	81	712	116	492
12	4512	47	1069	82	709	117	491
13	3681	48	1054	83	683	118	487
14	3344	49	1002	84	680	119	478
15	3202	50	979	85	677	120	476
16	3192	51	978	86	676	121	475
17	3027	52	964	87	666	122	469
18	3021	53	963	88	666	123	466
19	2835	54	942	89	665	124	465
20	2592	55	940	90	637	125	464
21	2462	56	940	91	636	126	464
22	1809	57	933	92	624	127	464
23	1775	58	927	93	624	128	462
24	1709	59	921	94	620	129	461
25	1674	60	904	95	596	130	461
26	1624	61	902	96	592	131	460
27	1613	62	883	97	592	132	460
28	1583	63	872	98	591	133	449
29	1560	64	866	99	590	134	448
30	1546	65	862	100	569	135	447
31	1392	66	856	101	545	136	444
32	1388	67	854	102	542	137	431
33	1361	68	843	103	534	138	426
34	1346	69	812	104	528	139	424
35	1343	70	791	105	520	140	424

Table M (contd.)

Rank	Population	Rank	Population	Rank	Population	Rank	Population
141	423	194	330	247	237	301	148
142	423	195	329	248	235	302	146
143	416	196	328	249	235	303	146
144	414	197	327	250	233	304	145
145	411	198	326	251	232	305	144
146	402	199	314	252	231	306	144
147	400	200	312	253	230	307	143
148	400	201	311	254	229	308	141
149	396	202	310	255	227	309	140
150	394	203	309	256	218	310	140
151	381	204	309	257	218	311	138
152	381	205	306	258	216	312	136
153	381	206	303	259	216	313	136
154	378	207	298	260	216	314	133
155	376	208	297	261	214	315	129
156	375	209	292	262	213	316	126
157	375	210	291	263	213	317	126
158	374	211	289	264	213	318	117
159	374	212	289	265	211	319	114
160	373	213	288	266	210	320	111
161	371	214	288	267	210	321	108
162	371	215	286	268	207	322	107
163	370	216	285	269	206	323	106
164	370	217	282	270	205	324	103
165	369	218	282	271	205	325	100
166	366	219	277	272	204	326	99
167	364	220	276	273	200	327	97
168	364	221	273	274	198	328	97
169	364	222	273	275	195	329	92
170	359	223	271	276	195	330	89
171	359	224	270	277	189	331	86
172	357	225	269	278	188	332	84
173	357	226	268	279	185	333	84
174	353	227	266	280	184	334	77
175	351	228	265	281	184	335	76
176	350	229	262	282	182	336	74
177	350	230	261	283	182	337	73
178	350	231	261	284	182	338	70
179	347	232	255	285	182	339	69
180	347	233	255	286	179	340	66
181	345	234	255	287	179	341	66
182	341	235	254	288	176	342	65
183	340	236	254	289	175	343	61
184	339	237	253	290	172	344	58
185	337	238	251	291	172	345	58
186	337	239	351	292	169	346	53
187	337	240	248	293	165	347	45
188	335	241	246	294	159	348	42
189	334	242	245	295	158	349	40
190	334	243	245	296	157	350	39
191	332	244	243	297	156	351	38
192	331	245	240	298	153	352	37
193	331	246	238	299	151	353	36
				300	149	354	30

Source: *Census Returns 1961*
The relationship between population and rank of these settlements is analysed in detail in Chapter 5 of *Settlement Patterns* by J. A. Everson and B. P. Fitzgerald, Longman.

Photo 58
Burford (1255), an Oxfordshire village with lower-order retail and service functions which have changed relatively little since medieval times.

Photo 59
Guildford (67 000) is a city with many higher-order functions, including a university, theatre, cathedral, many large retail stores and a regional cattle market. See also photographs on page 72.

Type of service **Associated zone of influence** **Type of service** **Associated zone of influence**

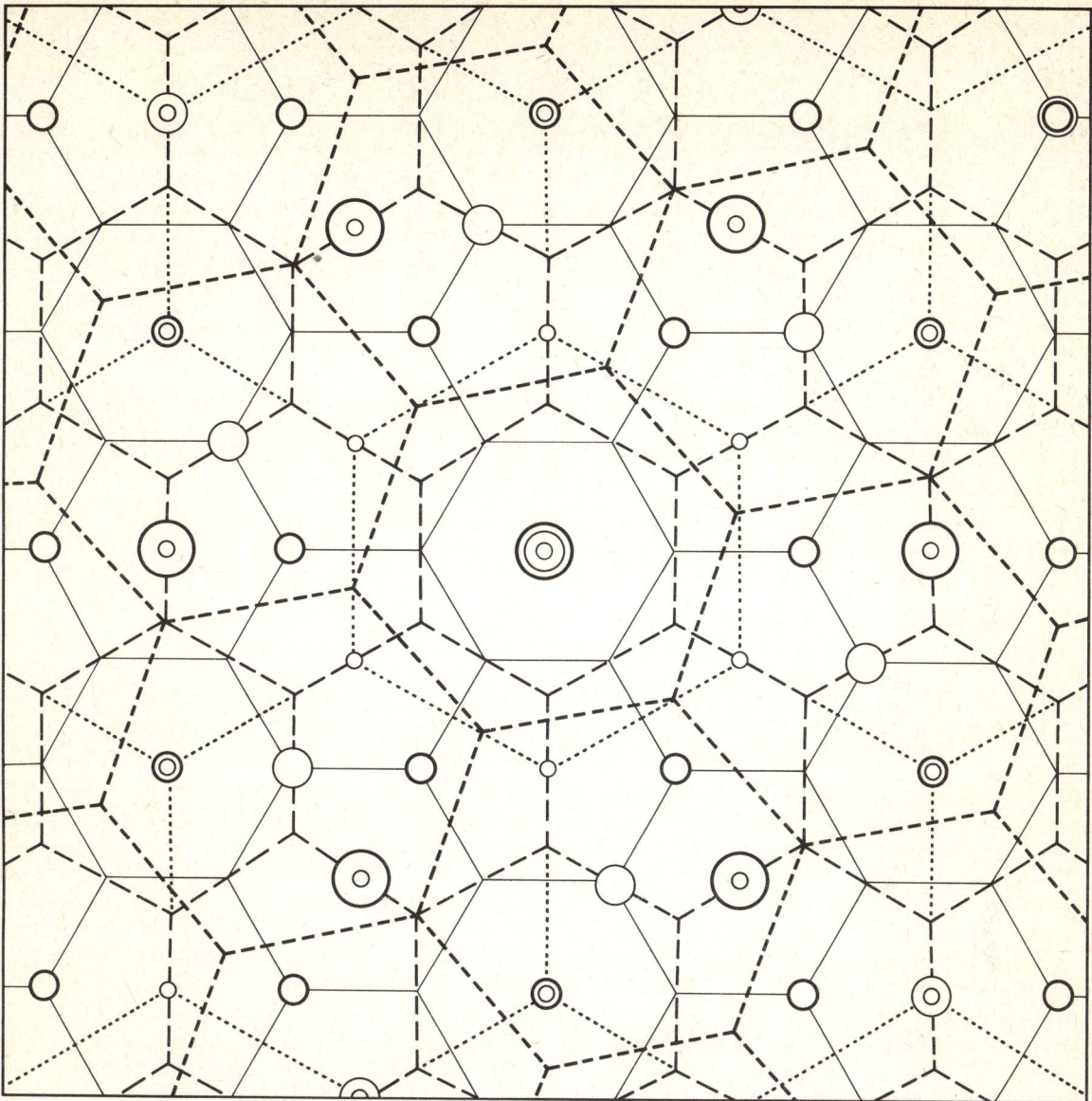

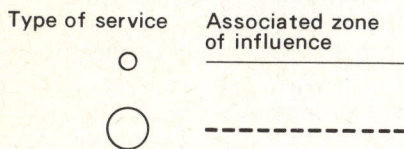

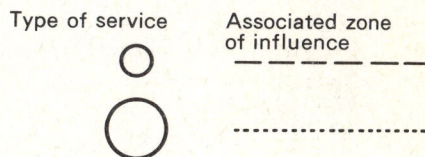

Figure 58
Simplified version of Lösch's theory of the arrangement of trade centres.

but abandoned the concept of fixed k hierarchies. Lösch built up a theoretical settlement pattern by superimposing a whole series of hierarchies, each with a different k value, on the same triangular grid. This is illustrated in figure 58, in which $k3$, $k4$ and $k7$ hierarchies

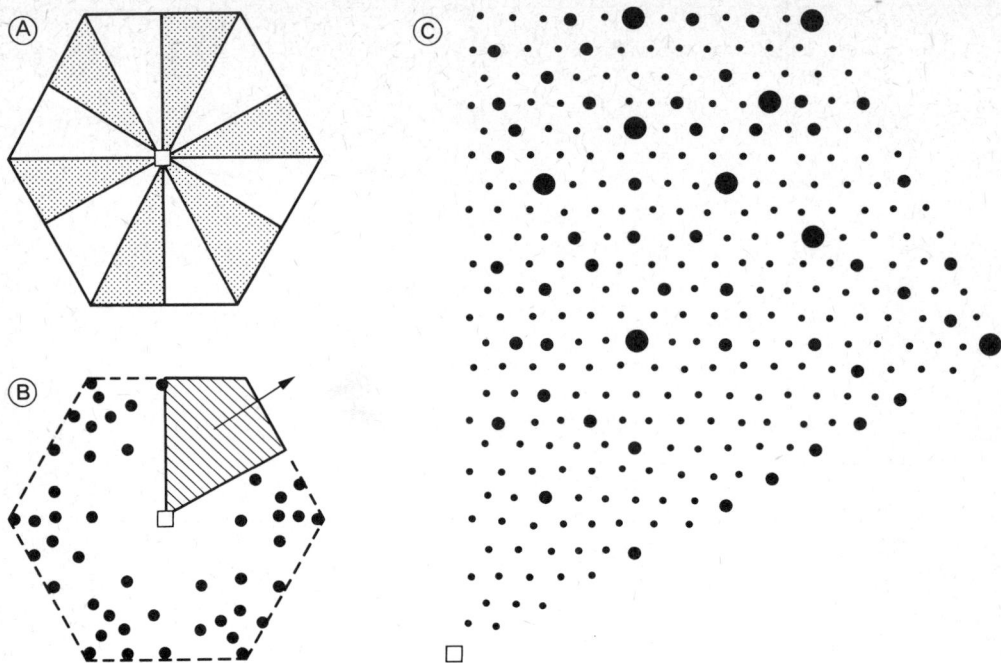

Figure 59
City-rich and city-poor sectors around a metropolis. Sectors of denser population and larger places (stippled areas in A, dots in B, detail in C) tend to develop. In C, note the concentration of the largest places along the lines connected by vertices of the sector. (*After* Lösch)

are meshed together. Clearly the gradation between settlements in this model is much more gentle than that of a fixed k hierarchy, for there is a multiplicity of overlapping population thresholds. Figure 59 shows part of a more complex Löschian landscape in which another peculiarity becomes apparent, namely the existence of 'city rich' and 'city poor' segments. One can see that the 'city rich' zones resemble incipient conurbations and that the Löschian landscapes appear to be much more akin to reality than are the simpler patterns devised by Christaller.

It is true, of course, that even Löschian landscapes are bound to deviate from real-life settlement patterns whenever the latter are developed on non-isotropic surfaces. Few, if any, landscapes are entirely uniform, though portions of the American prairies, Chinese river flood plains and English clay vales may approximate to this condition. Real-life settlement patterns may therefore be expected to deviate from Löschian predictions because of 'imperfections', i.e. variations in the physical and cultural make up of the landscapes upon

which they evolve. Such variations include soil fertility, aspect, relief, water supply, mineral resources, climate and so on, as well as social differences (for example in the attitude of people to work) amongst the population. Field research suggests that Central Place Theory is more obviously capable of interpreting the settlement patterns of unsophisticated rural societies (*see, for example, figure 62*) than those of industrial and technologically advanced communities. The latter depart so frequently from uniformity that generalized hypotheses have to be endlessly modified to accommodate 'imperfections'. Some geographers argue in consequence that Central Place Theory is an ingenious irrelevance. A more general view is that it is a valuable aid to the understanding of the growth, size, spacing and functions of settlements, providing it is supplemented by detailed field studies of local landscape idiosyncracies. Some examples of Central Place analysis and of the uses and limitations of the theory are given below.

One of the basic assumptions of Central Place Theory is that each central place is surrounded by an hexagonal market area or hinterland. Striking evidence to support this assumption has been put forward by G. W. Skinner in his 'Marketing and Social Structure in Rural China'. Figure 60 shows part of Skinner's study area in Szechwan, near

market areas are distorted polygons rather than regular hexagons. Arthur Getis, for example, studied the distribution of retail grocery markets in the American city of South Tacoma.* One of his objectives was to determine whether it was possible to predict

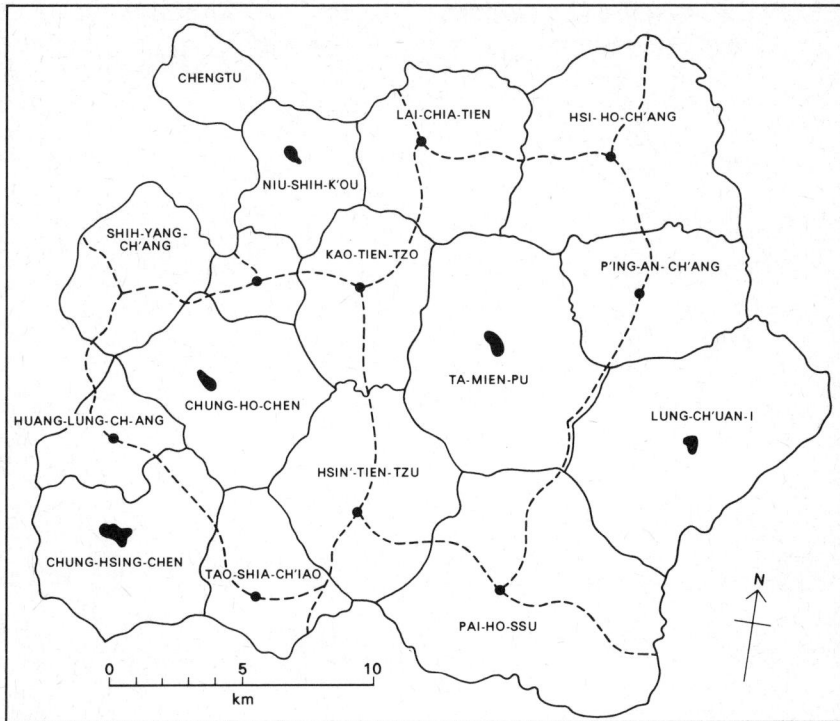

Figure 60
Part of Szechwan, near Chengtu, China. (*After* G. W. Skinner)

Chengtu. Skinner identifies two categories of market centres in this area, *viz.* smaller 'standard' markets such as Tao-Shia-Ch'iao and larger 'intermediate' centres such as Ta-Mien-Pu. Figure 61 is obtained by straightening and simplifying the boundaries of the market areas. Further reduction and representation in diagrammatic form gives a perfect example of a $k = 3$ network. Figures 63–65 show another area of Szechwan where Skinner identifies a perfect $k = 4$ network.

It is true, of course, that it is precisely in rural communities such as those of interior China that Christaller-type marketing networks might be expected to operate. Recent research suggests, however, that the concept of market hinterlands is valid also in industrial cities, although in these circumstances the

the location of grocery markets, using data about the distribution of population, their total incomes and the proportion of incomes likely to be spent on groceries. Getis also assumed that groceries were supplied only by supermarkets.

The study area in South Tacoma (*see figure 66*) covered a total area of 3100 hectares (*c.* 12 square miles). The area is criss-crossed by streets, the most important of which are shown by lines on the map. Accessibility within the area is more or less uniform. The study area was divided into 48 equal-area cells (*see figure 67*) and the consumption expenditures available for groceries (including produce

*The determination of the location of retail activities with the use of a map transformation. Arthur Getis, *Economic Geography*, Vol. 39, pp. 14–22.

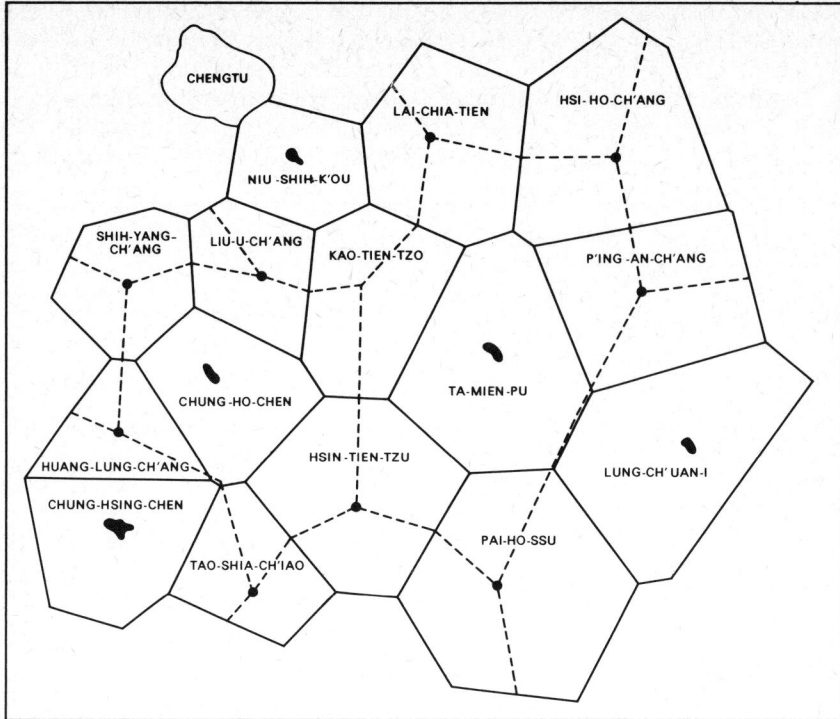

Figure 61
First abstraction of part of Szechwan. (*After* G. W. Skinner)

Figure 62
Second abstraction of part of Szechwan: the *k* = 3 network. (*After* G. W. Skinner)

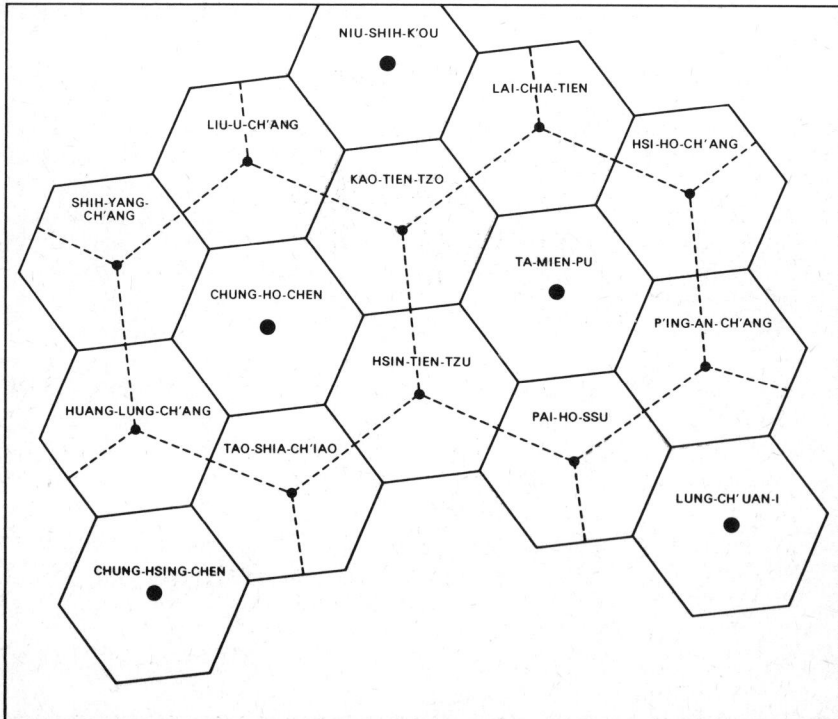

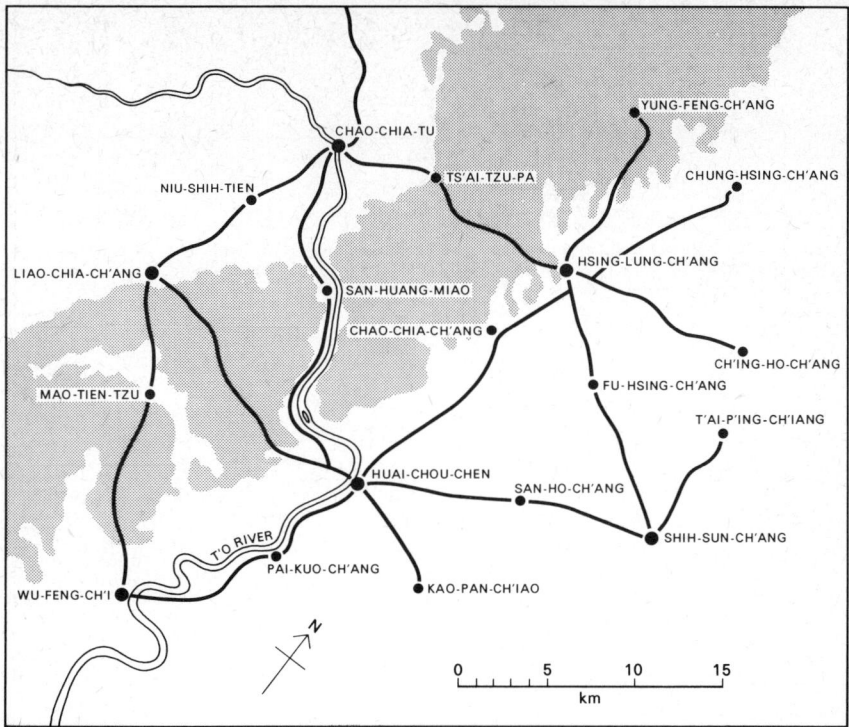

Figure 63
Part of Szechwan, north-east of Chengtu, China. (*After* G. W. Skinner)

Figure 64
First abstraction of part of Szechwan, north-east of Chengtu: the *k* = 4 network
(*After* G. W. Skinner)

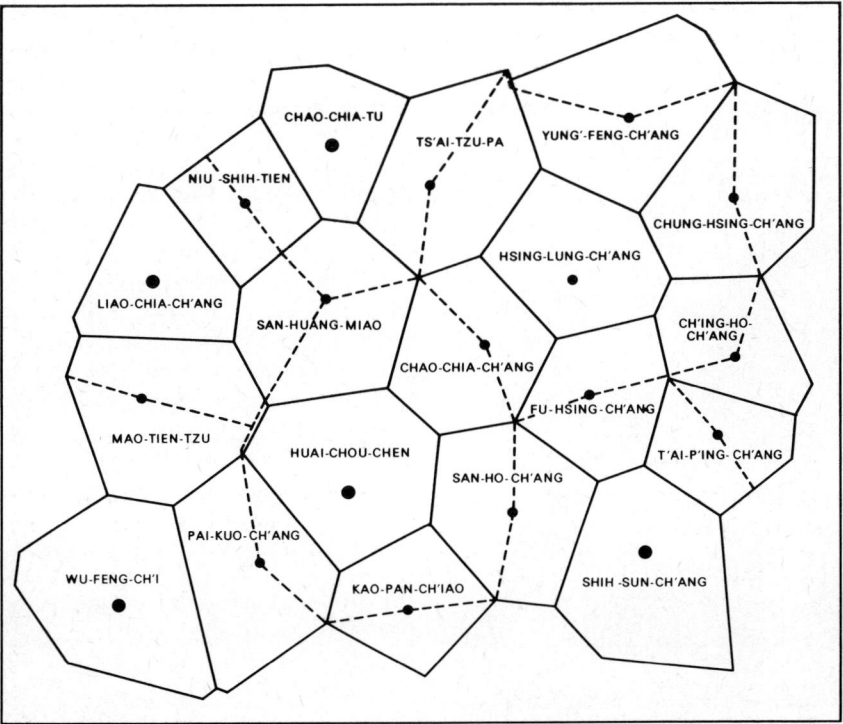

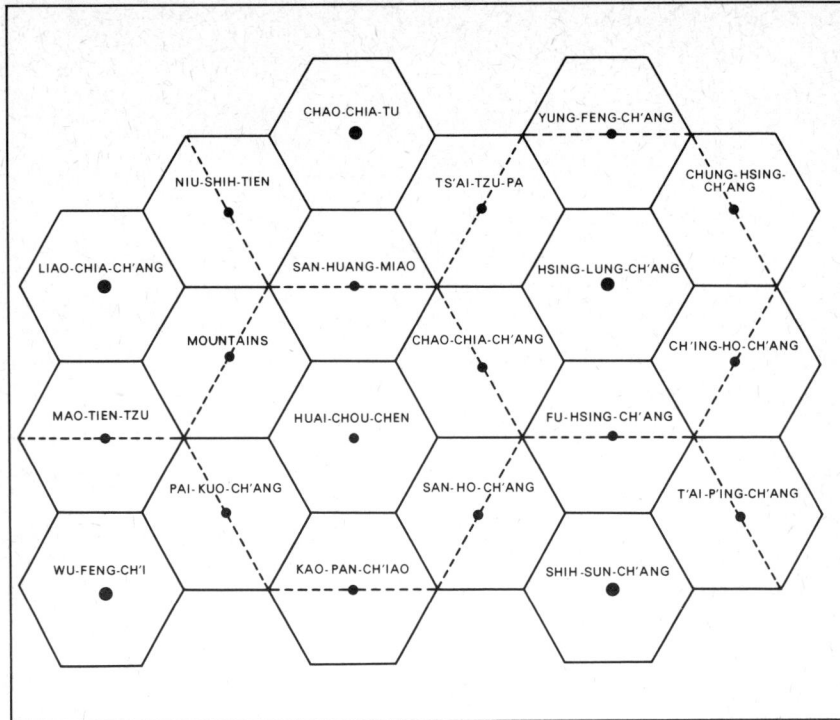

Figure 65
Second abstraction of part of Szechwan, north-east of Chengtu. (*After* G. W. Skinner)

Photo 60
A corner shop which stood in the Lee Bank district of Birmingham prior to redevelopment. Such shops catered for customers within walking distance and so had a retail trade hinterland restricted to houses in their immediate vicinity. Modern supermarkets, by contrast, cater for customers from a much wider area, many of them coming to shop by car or bus.

and meat) were computed for each cell. The cells were then distorted in such a way that their areas were proportional to the computed expenditures available for groceries in each of the original cells. The total money available for expenditure on groceries was 18 million dollars. It was known that the average value of a supermarket's grocery sales in this region amounted to 1·5 million dollars. Thus it was decided to allocate 12 supermarkets to the study area. An hexagonal grid of theoretical trade areas was then superimposed over the distorted grocery expenditure map. This was done in such a way that, starting at the geographical centre of the study area (which is also the centre of consumption expenditure available for groceries), as close to 12 hexagon centres could be included on the map as possible. Note was taken of where in the distorted cells the centres of the hexagons fell.* These centres were then relocated, *in*

*The cells were distorted to ensure that those parts of the study area with the largest quantities of money available for grocery purchases would 'attract' theoretical supermarkets.

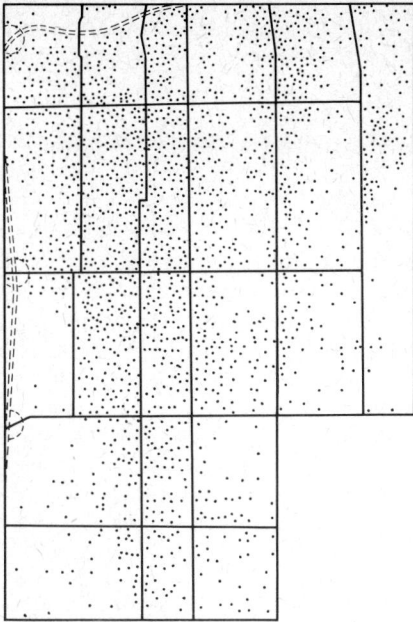

Figure 66
Study area in South Tacoma. Black lines represent main streets. (*After* Getis)

Figure 67
Central South Tacoma: total cash available (thousands of dollars) for expenditure on groceries. (*After* Getis)

	10	11	12	13	14	15
10	235	321	611	449	462	496
11	543	663	764	472	612	400
12	457	827	940	535	264	1023
13	345	827	823	420	288	162
14	194	515	680	265	298	46
15	24	397	508	336	153	99
16	35	312	300	31		
17	43	251	263	169		
18	87	147	175	88		

Figure 68
Map distortion of consumption expenditures for groceries in central South Tacoma. (*After* Getis)

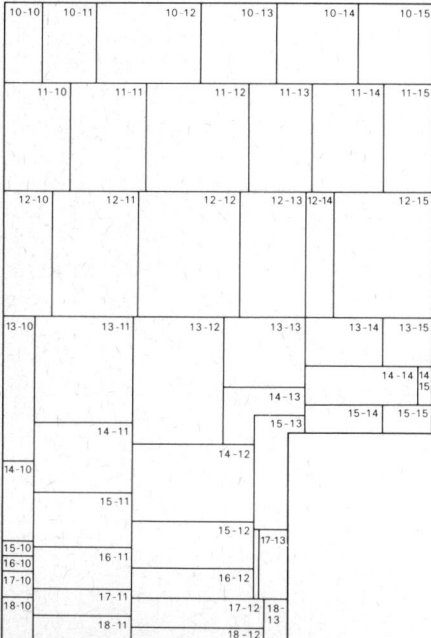

Figure 69
Theoretical trade areas in central South Tacoma. (*After* Getis)

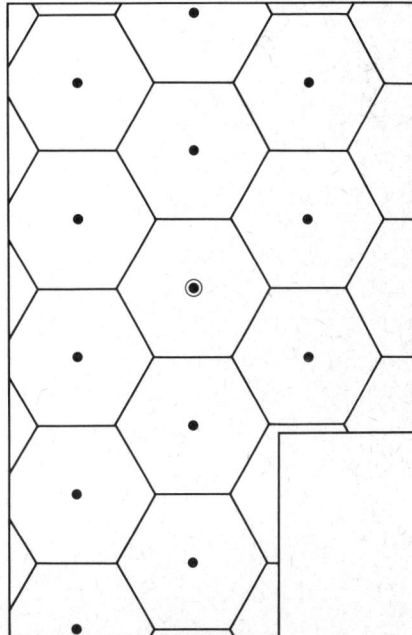

97

equivalent positions, within the corresponding original cells in figure 67. Finally these centres were transferred to the map of the study area. Distorted hexagons (six-sided polygons) were not drawn to represent the theoretical market areas. This was not necessary for, if 12 supermarkets are shown to exist in the study area at the theoretically derived locations, then the existence of their market areas, represented by distorted hexagons, would be implied.

Figures 70–73 show the results of this method of theoretically determining grocery store locations. Figure 70 compares the theoretical store locations with the location of the 12 largest actual supermarkets. Figure 72 compares theoretical store locations with the location of the 12 largest existing grocery stores. For the latter purpose non-supermarket grocery sales were included and all stores selling groceries within a single city block were considered as a single store. On both of figures 70 and 72 the theoretical pattern and the actual pattern are rather similar. The similarities are considerably improved when,

as in maps 71 and 73, each theoretical location is adjusted to fall on the nearest land upon which commercial building is permitted by the city planning authority.

This method appears to be remarkably accurate in predicting market areas and store locations but Getis draws attention to certain limitations. When buying groceries shoppers mostly go to the nearest available store and so the market areas for groceries are rather definite. This does not necessarily apply with other types of retail goods, nor with the provision of services (such as insurance or banking) in both of which cases a customer may prefer to go farther afield and to 'shop around' before making a purchase. The map transformation technique also suffers because there is an infinite number of ways of transforming the map and of placing the theoretical hexagonal trading areas over the map area. The range for possible variations in both cases is quite small, but nevertheless it is impossible to obtain absolute precision.

Figure 70
Theoretical and actual locations of supermarkets in central South Tacoma. (*After* Getis)

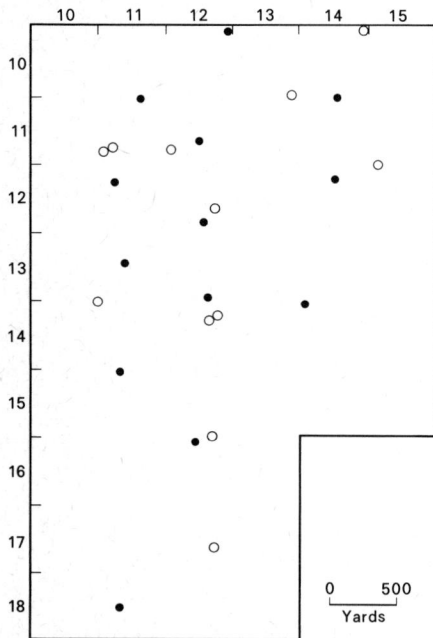

○ Actual   • Theoretical

Figure 71
Theoretical locations of supermarkets in central South Tacoma adjusted to nearest commercially-zoned land, and actual locations of supermarkets in study area. (*After* Getis)

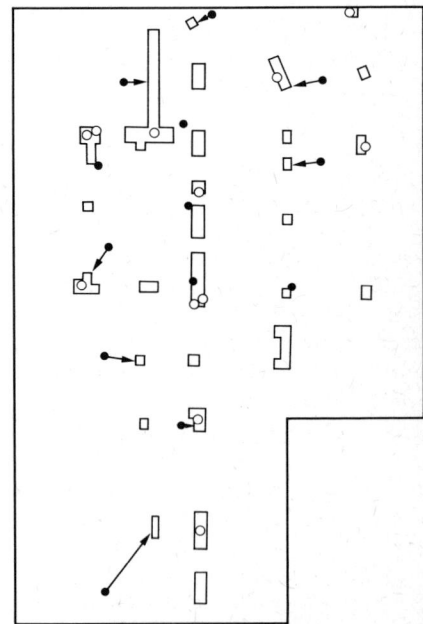

◄——— Line connecting theoretical location with nearest commercially zoned land

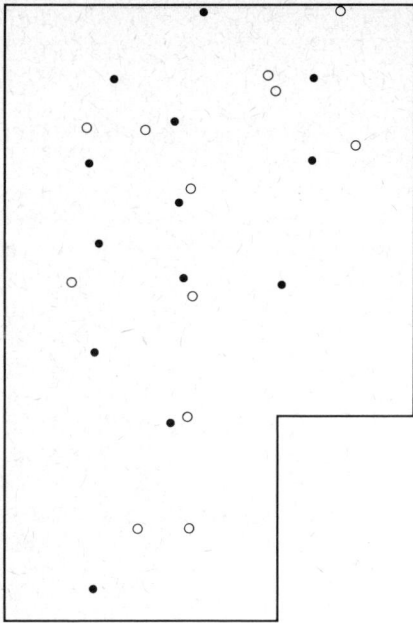

○ Actual   ● Theoretical

Figure 72
Theoretical and actual locations of largest centres of grocery stores sales in central South Tacoma. (*After* Getis)

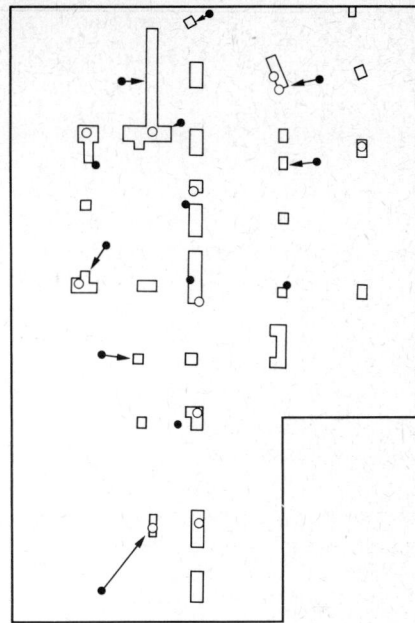

○ Actual   ● Theoretical
⟵ Line connecting theoretical location with nearest commercially zoned land

Figure 73
Theoretical locations of largest centres of grocery store sales adjusted to nearest commercially-zoned land, and actual locations of largest centres of grocery store sales in central South Tacoma. (*After* Getis).

Another implication of Central Place Theory is the existence of a hierarchy of settlements, one in which basic needs are provided for locally by all settlements, but sophisticated functions are located at more widely spaced intervals in *higher order* settlements. Within a given network each central place belongs to a particular class according to the category of the highest function which it provides. For example, in a $k = 3$ network containing 243 central places the numbers of settlements in each class would be as shown in Table N. As explained on page 87, the higher order settlements might also reasonably be expected to acquire larger populations by inward migration. Thus higher order settlements should ultimately contain a variety of functions and many inhabitants. To what extent do empirical studies support this hypothesis?

Table O shows the number and nature of central place functions in 33 of the smaller settlements in Snohomish County, Washington USA. The largest centre in the county,

Table N
Hypothetical $k = 3$ network containing 243 central places

Number of Settlements	Functions provided (classified by number of whole settlement populations needed for economic viability)
243	1
81	3+1
27	9+3+1
9	27+9+3+1
3	81+27+9+3+1
1	243+81+27+9+3+1

N.B. Each higher order settlement also provides the full range of functions of settlements below it in rank.

Everett, was excluded from the study.* The Table shows that settlements of less than 390 inhabitants contain relatively very few func-

*B. J. L. Berry and W. L. Garrison, 'The functional bases of the central place hierarchy', *Economic Geography*, Vol. 34, pp. 145–54.

Table O

Place	Pop.	A. Accountants	Animal feed stores	Apparel stores	Appliance stores	Automobile dealers	Automobile parts dealers	Automobile repair shops	Bakeries	Banks	Barbers	Beauticians	Billiards & bowling alleys	Bulk oil distributors	B. Churches	Cinemas	C. Dentists	Department stores	Drug stores	Dry cleaners	D. Electrical repair shops	Electricity distribution	Elementary schools	E. Farm implement dealers	Feed mills	Filling stations	Florists	F. Food stores	Freight stores	Frozen foods	Fuel dealers
Snohomish	3491	2	2	3	10	3	3	6	1	1	4	1	3	5	17	1	5	2	3	1	1	1	6	1	1	3	2	6	3	—	2
Edmonds	2996	—	—	2	4	2	2	1	1	2	2	4	—	—	8	—	4	1	3	3	1	1	1	—	—	7	—	6	—	—	5
Lake Stephens	2586	—	—	—	—	—	—	—	—	1	2	—	—	—	2	—	—	1	1	—	—	—	1	—	—	3	—	2	—	—	—
Marysville	2460	1	4	3	2	2	3	4	1	1	4	5	1	6	5	1	1	1	3	2	1	1	6	—	1	9	1	5	4	1	4
Arlington	1915	—	2	1	4	10	4	1	1	2	4	1	2	5	9	1	4	2	2	2	2	1	4	—	1	6	2	4	2	2	4
Monroe	1684	1	4	2	1	4	1	—	1	1	3	3	—	2	8	1	3	1	2	1	3	1	2	1	1	8	3	6	3	1	1
Lowell	1600	—	—	—	—	—	—	1	—	—	1	—	—	—	1	—	—	—	—	—	—	—	1	—	—	1	—	1	—	1	—
Darington	974	—	—	1	1	—	—	1	—	1	1	—	—	1	2	1	—	1	1	—	—	—	1	—	—	3	—	2	2	—	2
Mukilteo	900	—	—	1	—	—	—	—	1	—	1	1	1	—	2	—	—	—	1	—	—	1	2	—	—	3	—	1	—	—	—
Sultan	850	—	—	1	1	—	—	—	—	1	1	1	—	2	4	—	—	—	1	—	1	1	1	—	1	6	—	3	—	—	—
Beverly Park	725	—	—	—	—	—	—	1	—	—	1	1	—	—	1	—	—	1	1	—	—	1	—	—	1	1	—	1	—	—	—
Stanwood	720	—	—	1	1	1	2	2	—	2	2	—	—	3	3	1	1	1	1	—	1	1	3	2	—	4	—	2	1	—	1
Maltby	700	—	—	—	—	—	—	—	—	—	—	—	—	—	1	—	—	—	—	—	—	—	1	—	—	2	—	—	—	—	—
Granite Falls	600	—	—	1	—	—	—	—	—	1	1	—	—	1	2	—	—	1	1	—	—	1	1	—	—	4	—	3	—	—	—
Alderwood Manor	600	—	1	—	1	—	—	—	1	—	1	2	—	—	2	—	—	1	1	—	—	—	1	—	1	4	—	3	—	1	1
Lynnwood	560	—	—	—	1	2	2	1	1	1	1	—	—	—	3	—	5	—	1	1	1	1	1	2	—	9	—	3	—	—	3
East Stanwood	390	—	—	2	2	4	2	1	1	1	1	1	—	1	3	—	1	—	1	—	1	—	1	—	—	3	—	2	1	—	—
Gold Bar	325	—	—	—	—	—	1	—	—	—	1	—	—	—	—	—	—	—	—	—	—	—	1	—	—	1	—	2	—	—	—
Warm Beach	314	—	—	—	—	—	—	—	—	1	—	—	—	—	1	—	—	—	—	—	—	—	1	—	—	1	—	—	—	—	—
Silvana	300	—	—	—	—	—	—	—	—	—	—	—	—	—	1	—	—	—	—	—	—	—	1	—	1	1	—	2	—	—	—
Startup	300	—	—	—	—	—	—	—	—	—	—	—	—	—	2	—	—	—	—	—	—	—	1	—	—	2	—	—	—	—	—
Florence	300	—	—	—	—	—	—	—	—	—	—	—	—	—	—	—	—	—	—	—	—	—	—	—	—	—	—	—	—	—	—
Index	220	—	—	—	—	—	—	—	—	—	—	—	—	—	—	—	—	—	—	—	—	—	1	—	—	—	—	—	—	—	—
Machias	200	—	—	—	—	—	—	—	—	—	—	—	—	—	1	—	—	—	—	—	—	—	1	—	—	2	—	—	—	—	—
Oso	200	—	—	—	—	—	—	—	—	—	—	—	—	—	—	—	—	—	—	—	—	—	1	—	—	2	—	—	—	—	—
Cathcart	175	—	—	—	—	—	1	—	—	1	—	—	—	—	—	—	—	—	—	—	—	—	1	—	—	—	—	—	—	—	—
Bryant	150	—	—	—	—	—	—	—	—	—	—	—	—	—	—	—	—	—	—	—	—	—	1	—	—	1	—	1	—	—	—
Cedarhome	100	—	—	—	—	—	—	—	—	—	—	—	—	—	1	—	—	—	—	—	—	—	1	—	—	1	—	—	—	—	—
Robe	50	—	—	—	—	—	—	—	—	—	—	—	—	—	—	—	—	—	—	—	—	—	1	—	—	—	—	—	—	—	—
Getchell	25	—	—	—	—	—	1	—	—	—	—	—	—	—	—	—	—	—	—	—	—	—	1	—	—	—	—	—	—	—	—
Trafton	25	—	—	—	—	—	—	—	—	—	—	—	—	—	—	—	—	—	—	—	—	—	1	—	—	—	—	—	—	—	—
Verlot	20	—	—	—	—	—	—	—	—	—	—	—	—	—	—	—	—	—	—	—	—	—	—	—	—	—	—	—	—	—	—
Silverton	15	—	—	—	—	—	—	—	—	—	—	—	—	—	—	—	—	—	—	—	—	—	—	—	1	—	—	—	—	—	—

Furniture stores	General stores	Hardware stores	Health practitioner	High schools	Hospitals	Hotels	Insurance agencies	Jewellery stores	Laundries	Lawyers	Lumberyards	Meeting halls	Motels	Opticians	Photographers	Physicians	Post offices	Printing presses	Public libraries	Real estate offices	Restaurants	Sewage systems	Sheet metal works	Shoe repairs	Sporting goods stores	Taverns	Used furniture stores	Veterinary surgeons	Water supply systems	Weekly newspapers
—	6	2	2	1	1	—	10	2	—	3	3	3	—	1	2	5	1	1	1	7	7	1	1	—	2	5	1	1	1	1
—	3	1	1	—	—	—	1	1	2	1	—	4	—	5	—	11	1	1	1	—	5	1	—	3	—	5	—	—	1	—
1	1	—	1	—	—	—	—	—	—	—	1	—	—	—	—	—	1	—	1	—	—	—	—	2	—	—	1	—	—	—
—	2	1	2	1	1	—	1	2	1	1	1	1	6	1	1	3	1	1	1	6	14	1	2	—	2	2	—	1	1	1
—	3	—	1	2	2	1	2	—	2	1	1	—	1	1	1	10	1	1	1	3	5	1	1	1	3	—	3	1	1	—
—	3	—	2	—	—	4	2	—	4	1	4	2	2	—	3	1	—	1	2	6	1	1	1	1	5	—	1	—	1	—
—	—	—	—	—	—	—	1	—	—	1	—	—	—	—	1	—	1	—	1	—	—	—	—	1	—	1	—	1	1	—
—	1	—	1	—	—	—	—	1	1	3	—	—	1	—	1	—	1	—	3	—	3	1	1	—	—	—	—	—	1	—
1	—	1	1	2	—	—	1	1	—	1	1	1	1	1	1	—	1	1	1	—	1	1	—	1	1	—	—	—	1	—
—	1	—	2	—	—	—	1	1	1	1	2	—	—	1	—	1	3	—	—	1	1	3	—	—	1	1	—	—	1	1
—	—	—	1	—	—	—	1	—	1	—	—	1	—	—	1	—	2	1	—	1	1	—	—	—	—	—	—	—	1	—
—	—	1	—	1	—	2	—	2	—	—	1	—	2	—	1	2	2	1	—	1	1	2	—	1	1	1	—	1	1	1
1	—	—	—	—	—	—	1	—	—	—	1	—	—	—	1	—	—	2	—	1	1	—	2	—	—	—	1	—	1	1
—	2	—	—	—	—	—	—	—	—	1	—	—	1	—	—	1	—	2	1	—	—	1	—	1	—	—	—	—	—	—
—	1	—	1	1	3	1	3	1	—	1	—	—	1	—	6	6	1	—	1	—	3	—	—	1	—	—	—	1	—	—
—	2	—	1	—	3	1	—	2	1	1	—	—	1	1	2	3	—	—	1	5	—	2	—	—	—	—	—	—	—	—
—	—	—	—	2	—	—	1	—	—	1	1	—	4	—	—	—	—	—	—	1	—	—	—	—	—	—	—	—	—	—
1	—	—	—	—	—	—	—	—	—	1	—	—	—	—	—	1	—	—	—	—	—	—	—	—	—	—	—	—	—	—
1	—	—	—	—	—	—	1	—	—	1	—	—	—	—	—	1	—	1	—	—	—	—	—	2	—	—	—	—	—	—
1	—	—	—	—	—	—	—	—	—	—	—	—	—	—	—	—	—	—	—	—	—	—	—	—	—	—	—	—	—	—
1	—	—	—	—	—	—	—	—	—	1	—	—	—	—	—	1	—	—	—	—	—	—	—	1	—	—	—	—	—	—
1	—	—	—	—	—	—	—	—	—	—	—	—	—	—	—	—	—	—	—	—	—	—	—	1	—	—	—	—	—	—
1	—	—	—	—	—	—	—	—	—	—	—	—	—	—	—	—	—	—	—	—	—	—	—	—	—	—	—	—	—	—
1	—	—	—	—	—	—	—	—	—	—	—	—	—	—	—	—	—	—	—	—	—	—	—	—	—	—	—	—	—	—
1	—	—	—	—	—	—	—	—	—	—	—	—	—	—	—	—	—	—	—	—	—	—	—	—	—	—	—	1	—	—
—	—	—	—	—	—	—	—	—	—	—	—	—	—	—	—	—	—	—	—	1	—	—	—	—	1	—	—	—	—	—
1	—	—	—	—	—	—	—	—	—	—	—	—	—	—	—	—	—	—	—	—	—	—	—	—	—	—	—	—	—	—
1	—	—	—	—	—	—	—	—	—	—	—	—	—	—	—	—	—	—	—	—	—	—	—	—	—	—	—	—	—	—
1	—	—	—	—	—	—	—	—	—	—	—	—	—	—	—	—	—	—	—	—	—	—	—	—	—	—	—	—	—	—
1	—	—	—	—	—	—	—	—	—	—	—	—	—	—	—	—	—	—	—	—	—	—	—	—	—	—	—	—	—	—

tions. Above 390, however, there is a marked increase both in the number and the variety of functions. A similar notable increase occurs in settlements of more than 1684 residents. On the basis of population and number of central place functions the Table therefore suggests the existence of a three-tier hierarchy of settlements—say hamlets, villages and towns. In particular the populations of 390 and 1684 appear to represent approximate threshold values for the appearance of many functions which are not present in lower-order settlements which contain fewer inhabitants.

Table O also suggests a method for classifying central places according to *indicator functions*. In Snohomish County, for example, the lowest order settlements (hamlets) generally have an elementary school, filling station and a general store; the next higher order settlements (villages) have an appliance store, barber, bank, drug store, hardware store and restaurant, as well as electricity, water and sewage systems; at the town level there appear department stores, florists and animal feed stores. Table O supports the general assumption of Central Place Theory that each higher order settlement offers all of the functions of lower order places plus certain additional functions. The significance of indicator functions may be represented in tabular form as in Table P, below.

Some imperfections in the classification of

these 33 central places is revealed in figure 74 (b). Beverly Park, Lowell, Lake Stephens and Edmonds have fewer functions than their relatively large populations would suggest. This is probably explained by the fact that these settlements have recently gained many new residents who commute daily to nearby Seattle. Their paucity of functions is due partly to a time-lag between the growth of a residential population and the appearance of new functions to cater for it and also because commuters tend to shop in their place of work rather than in the *dormitory towns* where they reside. Figure 74 (b) also suggests that Stanwood and East Stanwood have more than their 'fair share' of functions, considering their relatively small population. This may be because these settlements are at focal points on the County's road network and thus they attract the custom of persons passing through as well as that of residents. Such central places are referred to as *resort towns*, for they show the high ratio of functions to inhabitants which is characteristic of true resorts catering for a seasonal influx of non-residents.

Where, as frequently happens, a particular function appears at a certain population level but is missing in a larger settlement, the following method of calculating an *average threshold value* is convenient: (i) total the populations of all settlements containing the relevant function from that settlement where

Table P
Indicator functions in Snohomish County

	Elementary school	Filling station	General store*	Appliance store	Barber	Bank	Drug store	Hardware store	Dept. store	Florist	Animal feed store
Hamlet	⨯	⨯	⨯								
Village	⨯	⨯	⨯	⨯	⨯	⨯	⨯	⨯			
Town	⨯	⨯	⨯	⨯	⨯	⨯	⨯	⨯	⨯	⨯	⨯

*For higher order settlements the function of a general store is usually incorporated into that of food stores.

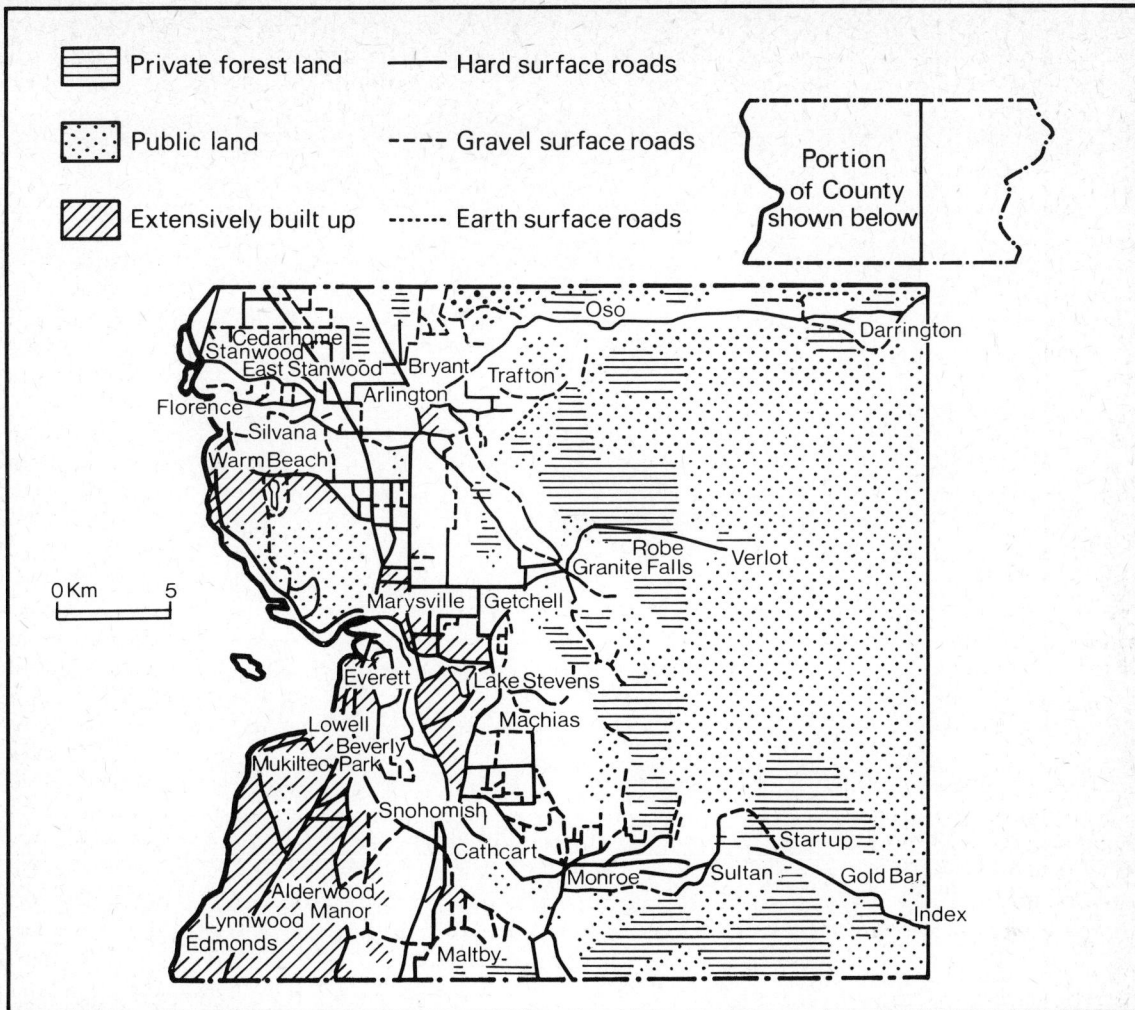

Private forest land   —— **Hard surface roads**

Public land   - - - - **Gravel surface roads**

Extensively built up   ········ **Earth surface roads**

Portion of County shown below

0 Km   5

Cedarhome
Stanwood
East Stanwood   Bryant
Florence   Arlington   Trafton
Silvana
Warm Beach
Oso   Darrington
Robe
Granite Falls   Verlot
Marysville   Getchell
Everett   Lake Stevens
Lowell   Machias
Beverly
Mukilteo   Park
Snohomish
Cathcart
Startup
Monroe   Sultan   Gold Bar
Alderwood
Manor   Index
Lynnwood
Edmonds   Maltby

Figure 74 (a)
The relationship between size and numbers of functions of settlements in
Snohomish County. (*After* Berry & Garrison).

the function first appears up to and including
those settlements above and below the final
'gap'; (ii) divide this total by the total number
of relevant functions present in the settlements
concerned. In the case of taverns in Snohomish County, for example, the relevant
settlements are Robe, Machias, Index, Startup
Silvana, Gold Bar, East Stanwood, Lynwood,
Granite Falls and Stanwood. With a combined
population of 3665 and a total of 19 taverns
this gives an average threshold population
for taverns of 193. This would explain the
tavern in Machias (population 200) but not
the one at Robe (population 50). Possibly the

latter is a 'stray' resort-type function, i.e.
one which caters mainly for non-resident
motorists.

Assuming 193 to be the valid threshold
value for a tavern one might expect to find
3491/193 = 18 taverns in Snohomish. In fact
there are only 7, but this can probably be
explained by the fact that taverns in Snohomish are larger than the one in Index. A better
criterion might be the total floor space devoted
to a function, or perhaps total business turnover, for such an index might be expected to
increase proportionally with a larger premises.

There is considerable controversy whether

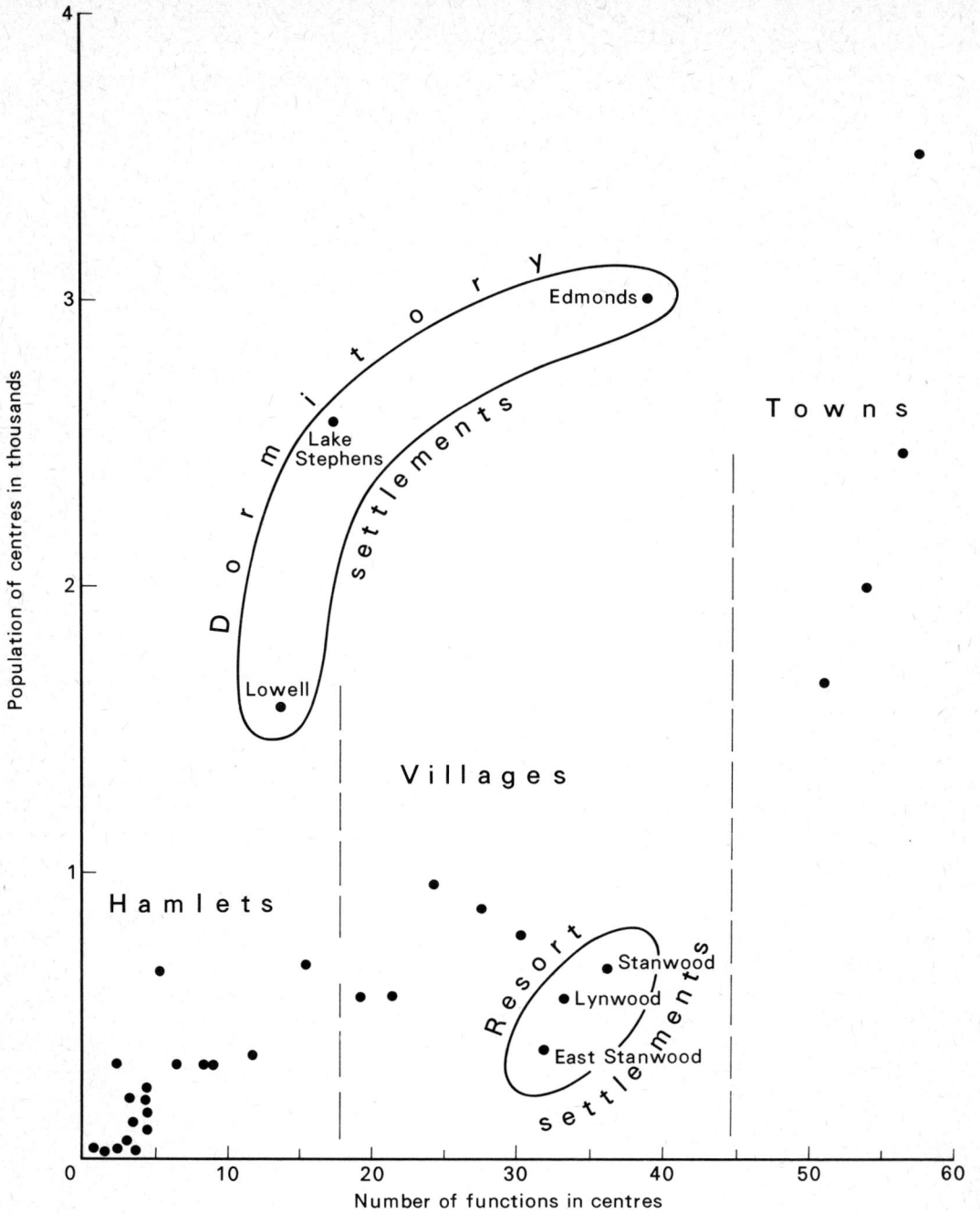

Figure 74 (b)
Rank-size relationship of 33 settlements in Snohomish County.

charts such as figure 74 (b) reveal the existence of settlement hierarchies. In the real world perfect uniformity is rarely found and the relationship between number of functions and population size varies. Berry and Mayer argue that these imperfections may so blur the issue

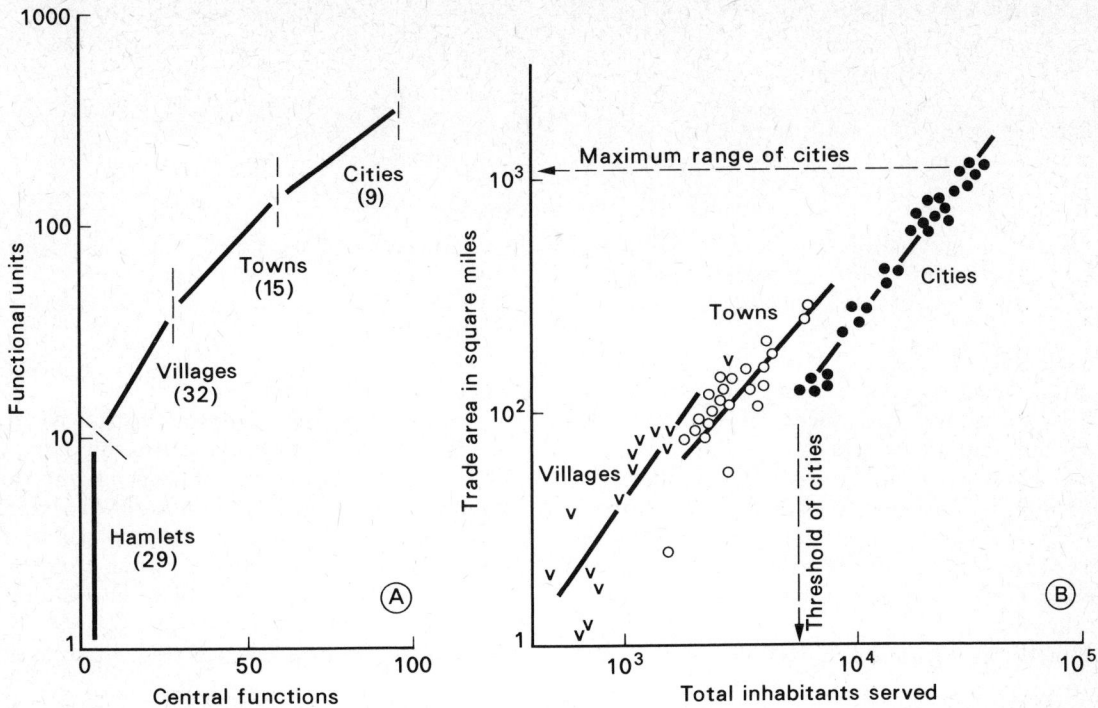

Figure 75
Four orders of central places in the settlement hierarchy, south-western Iowa.
(*After* Berry, Barnum & Tennant)

that what in fact is a hierarchy may be mistaken for a continuous linear relationship. Figure 75 (A), for example, shows four orders of central places in the settlement hierarchy of south-western Iowa, USA. In figure 75 (B) the three higher order classes are shown as a logarithmic graph in relation to the size of trade area and total population served. Despite the overlap in the graph there is general support for Christaller's hypothesis that higher order places serve larger tributary areas and populations than places at lower levels in the hierarchy.

The distance between central places is

determined, according to Christaller, by the class of settlements and by their position on an hexagonal grid. From his observations in South Germany Christaller gave 7 km as the expected distance between the smallest central places. This distance was computed on the assumption that 4–5 km, the distance one can walk in one hour, is the normal service-area limit for the smallest centres. (*See figure 48.*) On a $k = 3$ network the distance between similar centres increases by the $\sqrt{3}$ over the preceding smaller category. Christaller computed the following data for the various classes of settlements in south Germany:

Table Q		Towns		Tributary Areas	
Central place	Distance apart (km)	*Population*		Size (km²)	*Population*
Market hamlet (*Marktort*)	7	800		45	2700
Township centre (*Amtsort*)	12	1500		135	8100
County seat (*Kreisstadt*)	21	3500		400	24 000
District seat (*Bezirkstadt*)	36	9000		1200	75 000
Small state capital (*Gaustadt*)	62	27 000		3600	225 000
Provincial head city (*Provinzhauptstadt*)	108	90 000		10 800	675 000
Regional capital city (*Landeshauptstadt*)	186	300 000		32 400	2 025 000

This theoretical ideal is most nearly approached in the poor, thinly settled farm districts of south Germany, though Christaller claimed them to be typical for most of Germany and Western Europe. The validity of Christaller's hypothesis, with particular reference to the distance factor, is tested in a valuable modern study by J. E. Brush and H. E. Bracey entitled 'Rural Service Centres in South-western Wisconsin and southern England'. This study is quoted in full below.

Comparative analysis of the distribution of rural service centres in south-western Wisconsin and southern England shows that the spatial patterns are alike. Though the two areas are unlike in population density, urbanisation and transportation, and though there are profound differences in settlement history, two orders of service centres exist in both, spaced at about 21-mile and 8- or 10-mile intervals. A third, and still lower, order, spaced at 4- to 6-mile

intervals, also appears in both areas. It is impossible to equate the functional importance of rural service centres in Wisconsin and England because of economic and cultural differences. Indeed, distinctive functional types of centres should exist in every major economic or cultural realm on the earth. But the similarities in distribution pattern in Wisconsin and England suggest that there are certain common spatial relationships in the hierarchy of rural service centres.

Population distribution
The nine south-western counties of Wisconsin *(figure 76)* and the six southern counties of England *(figure 77)* that make up the two areas are situated in regions of moderate relief and fairly uniform rural population distribution. The Wisconsin area, totalling 7170 sq. miles, is a rolling plain or hill land, generally more than a thousand feet above sea level. The surface is formed by dissection

Figure 76
Rural service centres in south-western Wisconsin. (*After* J. E. Brush & H. E. Bracey)

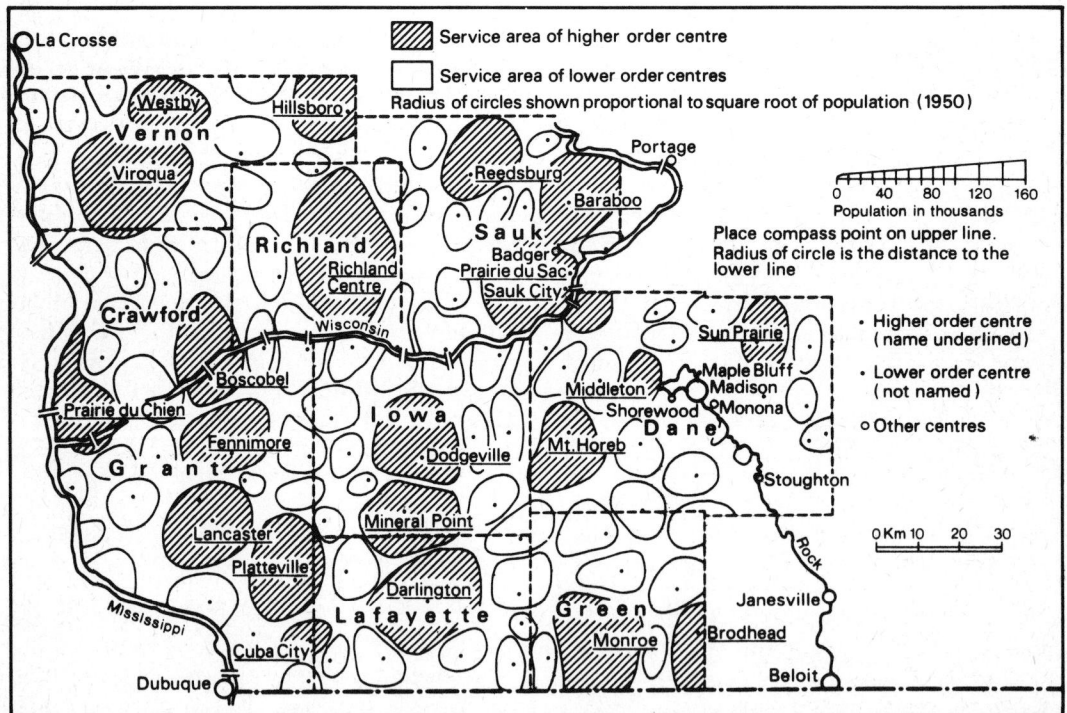

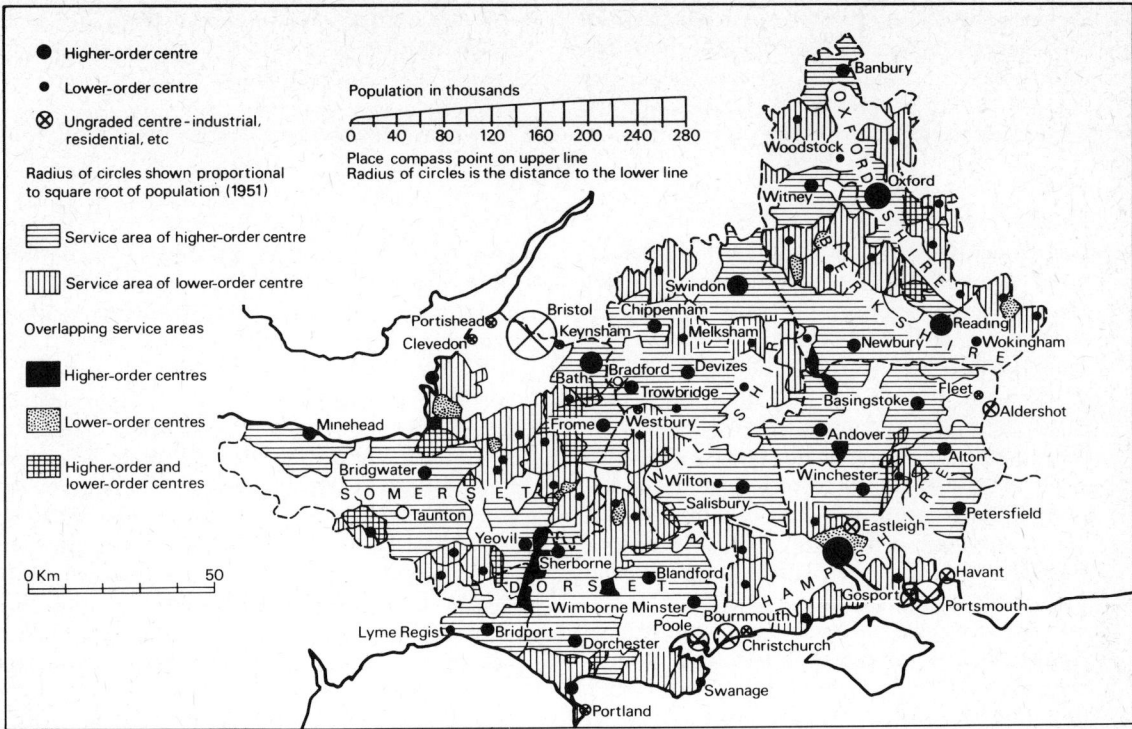

Figure 77
Rural service centres in southern England. (*After* J. E. Brush & H. E. Bracey)

of nearly horizontal strata of limestone, shale and sandstone, but has local relief of less than 200 or 300 ft, except for the rugged bluffs near the Mississippi and Wisconsin rivers. Average rural population density is 30 persons to a square mile, ranging from as low as 20 to as high as 40 or 50, especially near the city of Madison. The English area is almost the same size, 6969 sq. miles. There are stretches of highland more than 600 ft above sea level, but the predominant lowlands have local relief of less than 300 ft. The highest parts are in the chalk uplands of Wiltshire, Hampshire and Berkshire, and in the hill country of the Brendons and Exmoor in western Somerset, where abrupt slopes and altitudes of somewhat more than a thousand feet are common. The average rural population density in the six English counties is 182 to a square mile. Villages of several hundred residents and country towns of 2000–15 000 are the rule, in contrast with the single farmsteads and hamlets,

villages or small towns of fewer than 5000 in rural Wisconsin.[2] Rural densities as low as 50 to a square mile are found only over considerable areas in the hill country of western Somerset. The total rural population in the six English counties[3] is nearly five times that in the nine Wisconsin counties[4]— 998 000, as compared with 217 000.

The total urban population of the English area, 1 930 000, is more than twelve times that of the Wisconsin area, 158 000. More than two-thirds of the urban residents in the Wisconsin area are in one county, about 100 000 concentrated in Madison and its suburbs. The large cities of the English area, such as Portsmouth, Southampton and Bournemouth on the south coast and Reading and Oxford inland, have each between 100 000 and 300 000 inhabitants and account for about half the urban residents in the six counties. English country towns are generally much larger than Wisconsin towns, but in regard to rural services the dispersion of towns throughout both areas is more significant than the difference in the sizes of rural service centres or the presence of cities in the peripheral areas.

Transportation and economy

Land occupance is continuous and accessibility good throughout the two areas. Both are covered with farms and are served by close networks of improved highways and secondary roads and by numerous rail lines. The rivers of the English area are small, easily bridged and unnavigable except in their estuaries. In the Wisconsin area, only two rivers form barriers to land transportation. The Wisconsin river, no longer used for navigation, is bridged in many places. But the Mississippi, across which few bridges or ferries exist, is a navigable waterway and has had somewhat the same role in transportation as the coasts of the English area. In both areas water transportation is not now important to the development of towns and villages as local trade centres.

The functions of the land transportation system in the two areas differ markedly. In south-western Wisconsin little local use is made of the railways because of competitive services offered by trucking firms and because of the prevalence of private passenger cars and farm trucks. Although the rail lines are neglected and some have been abandoned entirely, the vehicular traffic density on the roads may well be heavier in the Wisconsin area than in the English area. Yet bus services are much better developed in southern England. English towns are served by several scheduled routes on which buses run several times a day. The residents of all except the most out-of-the-way villages can ordinarily get to one or more towns by bus. In England agricultural produce or freight is carried between farm and local market by road transport, but for longer hauls rail is more often used, though long-distance road haulage is increasing.

In both areas the economic base of the rural population is agriculture, but there are large numbers of rural non-farm people and certain urban-industrial concentrations.

South-western Wisconsin farms are predominantly of the dairy type, producing milk for cheese-making and, secondarily, livestock for slaughter. On the heavy clay lands of southern England dairying, with concentration on fresh milk supplies for London and other large cities, is also important. Large acreages, however, are devoted to the cultivation of grain and feedstuffs, stock-raising and fruit-growing.

In the Wisconsin area, Madison with its suburbs forms the only major concentration of manufacturing and other non-agricultural activities. Madison and the minor manufacturing town of Stoughton, in Dane County, mark the westernmost extension of the Rock River manufacturing region. One-half to two-thirds of the working population in the eight other counties are employed directly in agriculture and the remainder in trade, services and professions.

In southern England more persons are employed in agriculture, but they represent a smaller proportion of the total occupied population. As much as 30% of the total working population is employed in manufacturing in Somerset and Wiltshire, as compared with 12% in agriculture. Yet this has not destroyed the close relationships existing between most of the towns and the adjacent rural population. The naval shipyards of Portsmouth, the shipping services and industries of Southampton, and the resort trade of Bournemouth, Clevedon and other coastal places far outweigh their rural service functions. Bristol, with some 440 000 inhabitants, is a still larger urban-industrial concentration, but it lies just outside the limit of the study area and is exluded from consideration, though its suburbs push into Somerset and its influence as a rural service centre is felt over much of the northern part of that county. Reading, Oxford, Bath and Swindon are the only large towns in the area that function as rural service centres and also exhibit significant concentrations of manufacturing or commerce not related to rural service. All towns and villages were included in the survey, but those with slight rural service function were ignored in the subsequent detailed analysis, which embraced the seventy most important rural centres. The six counties are situated well away from the major English manufacturing districts, and the survey area is one of the largest tracts of mixed farming in England. In this respect, therefore, it is comparable with the south-western part of Wisconsin, which lies outside the main manufacturing belt of the United States.

Criteria of centrality

The role of a place as a trade centre, or its centrality, may be ascertained by either of two methods: (a) assessment of the business and services existing in the centre; or (b) measurement of the area dependent on the centre for goods and services. In other words, one may ask: Is there a given kind of retail store or service in the centre? Or, alternatively: Where do the people live who go to the centre to obtain a certain commodity or service?

The first method, followed by Dickinson and Smailes in their work in the United Kingdom, is the one applied in south-western Wisconsin.[5] All retail and whole-sale trading establishments, banking and financial agencies, trades and personal services, amusements and various other services, including professions and government administration, are considered in the determination of each centre's status. The present-day functional development of service centres in south-western Wisconsin can be assumed to be in accord with the requirements of farmers and other rural people because of the almost complete absence of other urbanizing influences. The limits of the area served by a centre are determined by the existence of traffic divides, as shown in the pattern of daily traffic movement towards the centre and towards other centres.

The second method, in which the criterion is use of the centre by rural residents, is the one applied in southern England. This is the method commonly followed by sociological investigators in the United States in the studies of rural community relationships. In the analysis of the six English counties the centres visited by village residents for medical supplies and services, clothing and household goods and banking and entertainment are determined by means of questionnaires. The importance of each service centre is measured by the number of villages partly or wholly dependent on it, and the extent of the service area is taken to include all villages using the centre for three out of the four broad groups of services. The existence of other facilities and service establishments of the kinds used is implicit in the findings, but no attempt is made to assess them directly.

The advantage of the criterion of use by rural people is not only that it results in a more accurate map of service areas but also that it separates the rural component of centrality from the urban component. This is especially important in assessing the centrality of English cities and towns, some of which have large components of centrality based on urban activities unrelated to the surrounding rural villages. However, development of a majority of the centres in the six English counties—as of those in the nine Wisconsin counties—is closely linked with satisfaction of the needs of rural people.

Working independently, the writers of this paper arranged the centres of their respective survey areas in order of importance. Each identified a group of higher-order centres, though no abrupt break in functions or facilities was recognizable. One out of every five centres in Wisconsin, and one out of three centres in the English area, appeared to belong to a higher order of centrality.

It is clear that significant differences of function exist and that a given type of retail store or specialized service may develop in one country and not in the other. Certain aspects of service function may pertain to higher-order centres in one country and to lower-order centres in the other. A differentiating feature of the higher-order centres in England is their development as shopping centres. More villages depend on the higher-order centres for shopping (retailing of clothing, household goods and various specialized types of consumers' goods) than for professions (medical services and supplies and banking). The second group appears to be fairly well represented in the towns of the lower order. Although Wisconsin towns are also well developed as retail shopping centres, medical and other professional services, except schools, and entertainment are infrequently found in villages. As a result, rural residents in south-western Wisconsin must go to town for specialized commodities except automotive equipment, lumber and hardware and farm equipment, and for all services except banking and secondary schooling.

The spatial pattern of the hierarchy

In order to demonstrate clearly the existence of higher and lower orders, it is necessary to analyse the distribution of rural centres and their areas. Figures 76 and 77 reveal for Wisconsin and England parallel patterns in spacing, service areas and arrangement of higher- and lower-order centres *(Table R)*. Similarities in the distribution patterns can be summarized as follows:

(1) Higher-order centres occur at a mean distance of 21 miles from one another in both areas.
(2) Lower-order centres occur at a mean distance of 10 miles from one another or from centres of a higher order in Wisconsin and a mean of 8 miles in England.
(3) Higher-order centres have service areas of 129 and 128 square miles in Wisconsin and England respectively; lower-order centres have service areas of 32 and 48 square miles respectively.

(4) Higher-order centres tend to form clusters or tiers with few or no centres of lower order close to them.
(5) Lower-order centres tend to form rows or belts hemmed in by the service areas of higher-order centres and crowded close to one another with their smaller service areas.

Intercentre distances would be similar in both areas if the centres were spaced hexagonally,[6] but the parallels in actual geographic patterns are more significant than this theoretical similarity. The significant features of the spatial patterns which appear in both countries are that the higher-order centres have larger service areas and that the lower-order centres exist only in the regions beyond 8–10 miles from the higher-order centres and not even there if the higher-order centres are as close to one another as 10–12 miles. The map of southern England *(figure 77)* shows overlapping of areas served by competing centres. It also shows certain territories not clearly under the influence of centres of either order but served by towns or cities whose rural service functions are too unimportant for them to be ranked with the seventy towns studied. Some of this unassigned territory is served by centres of a third and lower order, which in Wisconsin

---

Table R
Average population service areas and intercentre distances: southwestern Wisconsin* and southern England.

	Higher-order centres		Lower-order centres	
	19 towns, S.W. Wisconsin	26 higher dist. centres, S. Engl.	73 villages, S.W. Wisconsin	44 lower dist. centres, S. Engl.
Median population†	2 515	13 850	400	5 080
Mean population	3 330	25 950	480	12 425
Mean size of service areas (miles²)	129	128	32	48
Mean population of service areas	2 440	21 080	610	7 180
Mean intercentre distance (miles)	21	21	10	8

*The data for south-western Wisconsin apply only to the area west of Madison, excluding eastern Dane County and part of eastern Green County. The service area of a centre is the territory clearly demonstrated by analysis of traffic flow to be dependent for services on that town or village; the ill-defined borders of transition from one service area to another are not included. The service area of a centre in southern England is the territory that includes all villages using the centre for at least three out of four of the following groups of

services: shopping, medical supplies and services, business professions and entertainment. There is overlapping of certain adjacent service areas; there is also territory unassigned because the villages are served by very small or very large centres, not belonging in either of the two orders considered here.

†The medians of population provide a better basis for comparison than the means because of the existence of a few large centres in southern England, which unduly weight the means.

corresponds to hamlets and in England can be described as service villages. Centres of this third occur in Somerset at intervals of 4–6 miles from one another or from a centre of a higher order.[7] In Wisconsin they occur at intervals of 5–6 miles. The hamlets in Wisconsin are found chiefly in the transitional territories. left blank on the map *(figure 76)*, between the well-defined service areas dominated by higher-order centres. The people residing in these transitional territories are dependent on the nearest villages or towns for all except the rudimentary services provided by the hamlets. Service relationships are much more complex in the suburban fringe surrounding Madison and in the lake region extending southwards in Dane County towards Stoughton.

Population and centrality
These parallels in spatial hierarchy are clear, though the resident population of centres in both orders is much larger in England *(Table R)*. Towns in south-western Wisconsin have a median population only one-fifth that of the higher-order centres in southern England. The latter show a ratio of about six persons in the centre to five persons in the service area, as compared with seven to five in south-western Wisconsin. Thus it would seem that the larger town population in England correlates with the higher density of rural population. The median population of villages in south-western Wisconsin is less than one-tenth as large as that of their English counterparts. Again, this is in accord with the higher density of population in the service areas in England.

Terms denoting size and rank in the hierarchy in the two countries cannot be used interchangeably. A village of 370 in south-western Wisconsin, such as Barneveld, is a service centre for some 600 persons living on farms within a radius of 4–6 miles. This village is analogous in the hierarchy to a small country town in England, such as Castle Cary, with 2180 inhabitants, which serves the needs of ten or a dozen villages within a radius of 4–6 miles, each with several hundred inhabitants. A well-developed town of about 4600 in south-

western Wisconsin, such as Richland Center, serving some 4000 people in the rural territory as far as 10–15 miles around, is a small town by English standards. Although the English centre of Salisbury in Wiltshire, with 32 900 inhabitants, does not serve a larger rural territory, fifty-four villages, with an aggregate rural population of more than 24 000 persons, depend on it for a majority of their ordinary goods and services.

Evolution of service centres
The fact that close agricultural settlement has existed in southern England for 1500 years does not seem to have led to any significant difference in the spacing of service centres as they appear today in the two countries, though only 100–125 years have elapsed since the time of agricultural settlement in Wisconsin. Indeed, in certain respects there has been a parallel evolution of centres. During medieval times there were market towns in southern England, spaced at intervals of 4–6 miles, that served as rudimentary trade centres, accessible by cart roads from the rural villages within an hour's journey.[8] Many English villages are vestigial service centres once of a higher order. In the early nineteenth century, before the coming of railways and automotive vehicles, hamlets also developed in Wisconsin at intervals of 5–6 miles and served as rudimentary trade centres for the farmers living a journey-hour away by wagon roads.

Railway construction in the late nineteenth century had a marked effect in stimulating the growth of trade centres in Wisconsin. The effect of railways was less noticeable in England, but the improvement of roads and the spread of bus services since 1920 appear to have had much the same effect in the growth of large towns as the improvement of roads and the spread of private automobile transportation have had in Wisconsin. Development of professional services, banking and entertainment in Wisconsin has been concentrated in the centres of higher order more than in southern England. This may reflect differences in the relative case of movement in the two countries. Few English workingmen own private cars. Travel by bus increases the journey time and adds to the general inconvenience of a trip to town; this tends to reduce the length and frequency of journey. On the other hand, the persistence of services in lower-order centres may indicate a conservatism on the part of the English—a reluctance to withdraw their patronage from the business people who have served their fathers and grandfathers in satisfying their more personal needs. Some medieval market towns in England continue as service villages just as in Wisconsin the hamlets survive as relict trade centres.

Some conclusions

The fact that analogous geographic patterns have developed in these two widely separated rural territories suggests that the spatial hierarchy of central places is related to distance factors that have a dominant influence in areas of low relief and fairly uniform rural population distribution, despite differences in population density, economic functions and social or political institutions. The fact that rudimentary centres developed at about 6-mile intervals in both areas during the time of primitive transportation leads to the conclusion that the basic distance factor was the time and effort required to get to any trade centre by cart or on foot. The effect of railways was much more significant in Wisconsin than in England because rural settlement and agriculture were still undergoing rapid evolution in the last half of the nineteenth century. The similar effects of automotive vehicles and improved roads in the twentieth century are perhaps unexpected. Although the functional hierarchy is certainly much more variable from place to place and year to year than the rigid system first described by Christaller, it is probable that the spatial relationships observed in Wisconsin and England hold true throughout most of the closely settled parts of north-western Europe. There is need for further comparative analysis of the hierarchy in the countries of eastern and southern Europe and in various parts of the United States in order to determine the limits of variability. There is need also to extend the testing of the principles tentatively presented here to other regions of European settlement such as the British Dominions and Latin America and to regions of non-European settlement in Africa and Asia.

Notes
1. *Geographical Review*, Vol. 45, pp. 559–69.
2. The *rural* population in the Wisconsin counties, according to the official definition of *rural* adhered to by the United States Bureau of the Census, includes the inhabitants of small towns and villages where the number is less than 2500 persons as well as the open-country population. In England the meaning of *rural* is not strictly defined by the official census in terms of the number of residents in any closely built-up settlement. Municipal administrative areas such as cities and boroughs are considered urban, though in certain of them the number of inhabitants is only 1000. Civil parishes, some of which comprise more than one village, and some scattered dwellings are considered *rural* if administered by rural district councils, though the aggregate parish population may be as large as 3000 or 4000. One rural parish has as many as 20,000.
3. All population figures cited are taken from *Census* [of] *1951, England and Wales, Preliminary Report* (London: General Register Office, 1951).
4. All population figures cited are taken from US Census of Population, 1950, Vol. 1, *Number of Inhabitants* (Washington, DC: US Bureau of the Census, 1952) chap. 49, 'Wisconsin'.
5. R. E. Dickinson, 'The Distribution and Functions of the Smaller Settlements of East Anglia', *Geography*, Vol. 17 (1932) 19–31.
A. E. Smailes, 'The Urban Hierarchy of England and Wales' *Geography*, Vol. 29 (1944) 41–51.
6. If the seventy rural service centres in the six English counties were spaced at equal distances in a perfect hexagonal pattern, they would be 10·7 miles apart. In the part of south-western Wisconsin west of Madison, the ninety-two centres of village or town rank would be 10·0 miles apart if spaced in a perfect hexagonal pattern. The formula used in these computations is as follows:

$$D = 1·07 \sqrt{\frac{A}{n}}$$

where D is the distance between the centres, A is the total area within which the centres are dispersed and n is the number of centres. The formula calls for nothing more than the square root of the density of centres within the area multiplied by a constant factor and should not be considered as giving a true measurement of scattering or dispersion.
7. Dickinson found there are 'small towns' with 1000–2000 population in East Anglia, spaced at about 4-mile intervals.
8. A journey-hour on foot or by cart, travelling at the rate of 3 miles an hour. R. E. Dickinson, *City, Region and Regionalism* (London, 1947).

The article quoted above is concerned with the delimitation of urban spheres of influence. Other attempts to define shopping trade areas make use of *gravity models*, the most well known of which is Reilly's Law of Retail Gravitation which is usually given in this form:

$$Bb = \frac{Dab}{1 + \sqrt{Pa/Pb}}$$

where Bb is the *interaction breaking point* between city A and city B in kilometres from B, i.e. B's sphere of influence; Dab is the distance between A and B in kilometres, and Pa, Pb are the populations of A and B respectively. A worked example of the application of this model is given in figure 78.

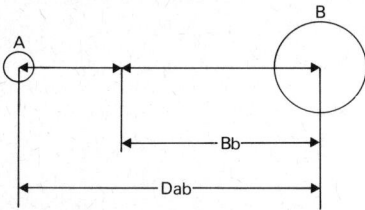

Figure 78
Let population of settlement A = 300
Let population of settlement B = 500
Let the distance between A+B = 4 km

Then $Bb = \dfrac{4}{1 + \sqrt{\frac{300}{500}}}$ km $= \dfrac{4}{1 + 0\cdot8}$

$= \dfrac{4}{1\cdot8}$ km $= 2\cdot2$ km

It is probably more realistic to consider the drawing power of an urban business district in terms of total number of shops, or the number of shops of a particular type. Thus Reilly's formula can be modified to become:

$$Bb = \frac{Dab}{1 + \sqrt{Sa/Sb}}$$

where Sa and Sb are the number of shops of a certain category in cites A and B respectively. A further modification substitutes time–distance for kilometre–distance in Reilly's formula on the assumption that shoppers are more likely to consider the time it takes them to reach competing shopping centres than the actual distances involved.

The most successful modification of the formula is that suggested by D. L. Huff as follows:

$$P(Cij) = \frac{\dfrac{Sj}{Tij^{\lambda}}}{\displaystyle\sum_{j=i}^{n} \dfrac{Sj}{Tij^{\lambda}}}$$

where $P(Cij)$ is the probability of a consumer at a given point of origin i travelling to a given shopping centre j; Sj is the area of selling space devoted to the sale of a particular class of goods by shopping centre j; Tij is the travel time involved in getting from a consumer's travel base i to shopping centre j; and λ is a parameter to be estimated empirically to reflect the effect of travel time on various kinds of shopping trips. If $P(Cij)$ is calculated for a series of points of origin (i) then isopleths, or equiprobability contours, can be drawn for each of the centres (j). A trade area can be identified by isolating points where the same equiprobability contours from different centres intersect. An example of probability contours for consumers in three retail centres is given in figure 79.

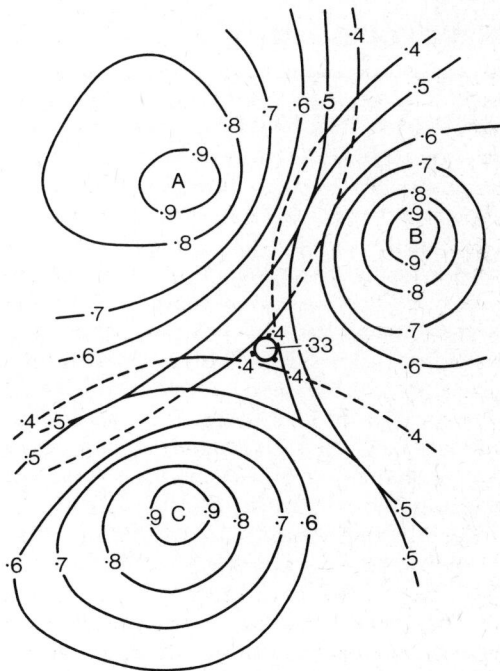

Figure 79
Probability contours for consumers shopping in three centres. (*After* B. J. L. Berry)

113

Section 6 **Some problems of urban growth**

City growth has caused problems since early times, especially the supply of food and water and the disposal of effluent. In modern industrial cities these problems are vastly magnified, and new difficulties arise such as atmospheric pollution and the contamination of rivers, lakes and the sea by toxic industrial wastes. The main problems confronting modern urban dwellers are listed on page 11. Here attention is drawn to water supply, the disposal of sewage and other effluents, air pollution, overcrowding and health hazards, all of which are to a certain extent interrelated.

12 Water supply

Water is used in a city for a wide and ever-increasing range of functions. It is needed most obviously in the home for drinking, cooking, personal cleanliness and sanitation, but also increasingly for garden- and car-hoses, washing machines and dishwashers. The present UK domestic demand for water is 164 000 litres per head per year, and this is expected to rise to 350 000 litres by the end of the century as a result of population increase and rising standards of living. Domestic water needs considerable alteration, for it must reach the consumer in a clear, odourless condition and be free from harmful bacteria. In addition it is preferable to make the water 'soft' by removing dissolved carbonates and certain other salts.

Less obviously water is used on a vast and increasing scale in industry. In England and Wales, for example, industries use 59 000 million litres daily, including 32 000 million litres per day for cooling purposes in electricity generating stations. A single coal-burning power station needs *c.* 600 tonnes of water for every tonne of coal it consumes. Some large-scale industrial consumers of water are indicated below. Others include oil-fired, hydro and nuclear power stations, non-ferrous ore refineries, textile mills, food-processing and the preparation of beverages such as beer and soft drinks. No less than 6275 million litres of beer, *c.* 98% of which is water, are marketed annually in the UK. Water is also needed in many cities for canals, swimming pools, marinas, ornamental lakes and fountains.

Another major use of water is for the disposal of wastes. Certain industries, for example meat processing, tanneries and many chemical factories, produce large quantities of effluent, much of which is both noxious and toxic. A large proportion of this waste is discharged into city sewers, augmenting the sewage disposal problems faced by municipal authorities.

The phenomenal increase in demand for water which characterizes all advanced industrial societies gives rise to two main problems, *viz.* (i) maintenance of an adequate

Iron and steel industry: 82 000 litres are required to make a 1-tonne iron ingot. A further 300 000 litres are needed to turn this ingot into a tonne of steel. Thus *c.* 100 tonnes of water are needed to make 1 tonne of steel. The total consumption of water by the UK iron and steel industry amounts to *c.* 300 million tonnes per day.

Pulp and paper manufacture: 100 tonnes of water are needed to make 1 tonne of paper. Total UK consumption by this industry is about 250 000 tonnes daily.

Oil refining: a large oil refinery requires *c.* 70 tonnes of pure water per *hour* in the refining process as well as 4000–5000 tonnes of second grade water for cooling.

Chemicals: their manufacture in the UK requires 1000 million tonnes of water per day.

Plastics: c. 30 tonnes of water are needed for every 1 tonne of finished product.

Car manufacture: each car needs *c.* 250 tonnes of water in its manufacture.

water supply and (ii) avoidance of water pollution. Annual expenditure on water supply in the UK jumped from *c*. £20 million in 1950 to more than £80 million in 1972. Much of this money is spent by hundreds of local authorities, for water supply has been a public utility in this country since the Public Health Acts of 1872–78. Local government undertakings, which include dams, reservoirs, pipelines and deep borings, have *c*. 200 days of water in hand after a moderately damp winter. This is a substantial improvement on the mere 50–100 days reserve which they held in 1950, but is insufficient for the future. Water consumption in the UK is increasing by 3% per annum, i.e. demand will have doubled by the end of this century. Total demand will then probably exceed 22 billion litres per year. The total annual precipitation in the UK is *c*. 180 billion litres, of which *c*. 60 billion litres are available for use after evaporation. At present much of this usable water returns directly to the sea, but there is obviously more than enough water potentially available to meet any foreseeable demand, especially as recycling becomes commonplace in both domestic and industrial water consumption.

Problems arise, however, because the wettest parts of Britain do not generally coincide with those urbanized regions with the greatest water demands. There is also fierce competition between water boards for control of water resources and a clash of interests of the various water users. The cheapest way to increase water supply in the UK is to build more dams across valleys in wet regions such as Wales and north-west Scotland, a policy

Photo 61
This reservoir in the Derwent Valley, Derbyshire, supplies water by pipeline to the industrial cities of Sunderland and South Shields.

which is strongly opposed by the farming community, as well as by Welsh and Scottish nationalists intent on preserving their natural landscapes and traditional rural communities. On the other hand the creation of an artificial lake may benefit a region financially by attracting tourists, especially if the lakeside can be used for camping and the water for boating, fishing and aquatic sports. This depends on how the water is to be used and on the degree of purification if it is destined for domestic supply. Future policy in Britain will be to use reservoirs mainly to 'top up' rivers, rather than to pump the water directly to consuming centres. This is partly to avoid the very high costs of pumping water over long distances and also to allow the same water to be extracted, used and returned to a river system many times during its journey towards the sea. In addition there will be an increased use and better management of water stored underground, especially in the basins of the Thames and the Great Ouse.

Another possibility is the construction of 'bunded reservoirs' in shallow estuaries to collect water discharged by local rivers. The Morecambe Bay Barrage scheme, for example, would trap 2 million cubic metres of pure fresh water daily from the Rivers Leven and Kent *(see figure 80)*. The water, distributed by

Figure 80
The proposed Morecambe Bay barrage scheme.

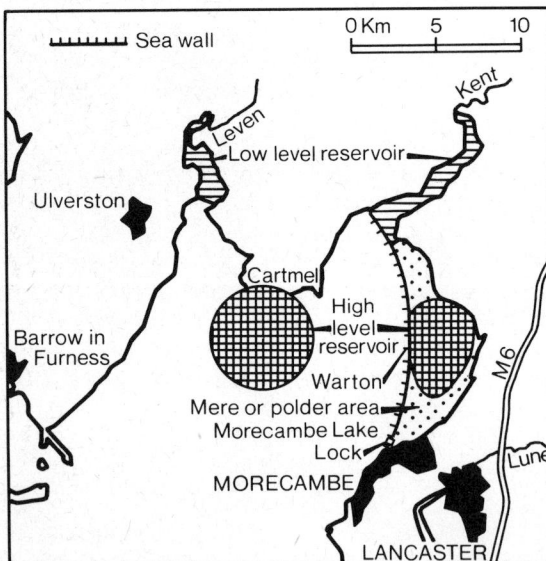

pipelines, would be sufficient to meet all foreseeable domestic and industrial demands throughout Northern England. Similar schemes have been projected for the Dee estuary and the Wash.

Desalination of sea water is a viable long-term solution to the water shortage problems of urban–industrial regions. Desalting techniques, which include multi- and flash-distillation, electrodialysis, freezing and the 'squeezing' of salt molecules through plastic pores, are all costly. In humid temperate regions none of them can at present produce fresh water for less than about double the price of conventional supplies. Even so, desalination may be an economic means of increasing the water supply of established cities where local supplies are running out and where the transport costs of bringing in water from outside are high. Under such circumstances desalination would be operated in conjunction with the conventional resources already serving the area. 'The significance of this . . . lies in the fact that many conventional surface water resources can be overdrawn during or following periods of high natural rainfall or run-off without impairing their ability to maintain their safe yield during periods of drought. Thus, for long periods of time additional supplies can be drawn at very low costs from the existing conventional resources, operation of the desalination plant—which has a high operating cost—being reserved for periods of low natural run-off. This saving in desalination plant operating costs results in the cost of meeting the additional demand from the conjunctive desalination/surface water system being as low as 60% of the comparable baseload desalination cost.'*

Desalination may also be economically advantageous because of economies of scale.

The economies of scale of desalting plant are such that it is usually preferable to choose a plant size equivalent to about five years of demand growth; thus within five years the desalting plant would be fully utilized, making for a very high average utilization over its total lifetime of 15–20 years. This, together with the relatively low capital

*P. A. Mawer, Chief Economist, Water Research Association, *The Financial Times*.

intensity of desalting processes, makes for good investment utilization. By contrast, some conventional water supply schemes have to be built with capacities which will not be fully utilized for as long as 15–20 years into the future. The necessity for such massive pre-building usually arises, again, in areas where local resources are already fully developed and water must be imported from more distant sources. The economies of scale of pipeline or tunnel transmission are such that it is only economic to consider long-distance transmission at a very large scale of operation—a scale which may be grossly over-sized in relation to local demand growth. When the greater proportion of investment in such schemes is required during initial construction and only very little can be delayed to later years, the economic penalty of initial under-utilization of investment can be severe, even though the scheme may produce water at an attractive price when fully utilized.

Under these circumstances it may be more economic to install desalination plant for some interim period of use, say ten years, as a means of delaying investment in the new conventional resource development. The large conventional scheme would only be introduced at the later date, when it could be commissioned at an immediately high utilization; the use of the desalting plant—with its high operating cost—would then be discontinued.*

Growing population centres, which are already being supplied by a complex of reservoirs, rivers and groundwater sources, are especially suitable for installing a combined desalination/conventional water supply system. Conventional supplies tend to vary seasonally and from year to year depending on the precipitation pattern. At the same time demands for water also vary seasonally and are subject to a long-term growth rate. The integration of desalination onto such an urban system requires sophisticated analysis if maximum cost benefits are to be achieved. The Water Research Association conducts such investigations; one recent study, for example, suggested that in the Barcelona region the interim use of desalination in conjunction with four existing reservoirs would allow a £100 million pipeline scheme to be delayed for up to 20 years, giving an overall saving of up to £30 million.

The world's most ambitious scheme to supplement a city's water supplies by desalination is in Hong Kong. Daily consumption of fresh water in Hong Kong runs at c. 955 million litres per day and a further 182 million litres of seawater are fed through separate mains for flushing purposes. Demand is increasing by 8% per annum, so that c. 1638 million litres a day will be required by 1980. Expanding industries such as power production and textile firms are consuming more water and domestic demand grows steadily as the colony's 4·1 million inhabitants increase annually by 2%. Hong Kong is a classic example of a city's inability to increase its local water supplies by conventional means.

At the core of the problem is the colony's limited land area of less than 400 square

Photo 62
This Israeli desalination plant produces 250 cubic metres of fresh water per day.

*P. A. Mawer, *op. cit.*

miles, which is spread over 236 islands, many uninhabited. Although it has a healthy (but erratic) rainfall, Hong Kong has no river or lake of any size. Problems of land shortage for dams and reservoirs are exacerbated by the unpredictable inflow of refugees from China, adding a strong element of guesswork to the best laid plans. 'We are at the mercy of the weather . . . All we can do here is collect and store water. But now we are running out of land and reclamation areas to do that.'*

Water storage in Hong Kong is spread over 17 reservoirs and a vast new High Island scheme will more than double storage capacity by 1979. About 25% of the water entering these reservoirs comes by pipeline from mainland China, but future supplies are to come from a £35 million seawater desalting plant. This plant, the world's biggest, will eventually give a daily output of 182 million litres of fresh water. The first of its six units came into operation in 1974.

In an urban environment one marked advantage of desalination is that it requires very little space—a plant yielding 4 million litres a day can be erected on a plot the size of a bowling green. Nor is desalination restricted to coastal regions, for there are many cities in arid and semi-arid countries whose wells have been overpumped and are now yielding water too saline to drink. Desalting by electrodialysis is the cheapest remedy for this sort of situation. Desalination will also be needed increasingly for the satisfactory treatment of effluents.

13 The disposal of wastes

Water pollution by sewage is an almost universal problem in urban societies, notably in cities of under-developed regions. In Central and South America, for example, c. 25 million people in settlements of more than 2000 have no adequate water supply: in India the analogous figure is 26 million. Drinking water is obtained from wells and streams often heavily contaminated with sewage with the result that waterborne diseases such as typhoid-fever and dysentery are endemic. In Calcutta, for example, there is no effective disposal of refuse and grossly inadequate sanitation. Rubbish is dumped in the streets and the city is interlaced with open drains carrying untreated sewage. Elsewhere human ordure seeps into the ground from open pits. Conditions are most appalling in the bustee (slum) quarters, where on average

Photo 63
Collecting water for domestic use from a street hydrant in Calcutta. Most of the city's hydrants carry polluted water intended for street-cleaning and fire-fighting.

*Barry Wain, quoting W. T. Knight. *The Financial Times*.

some 20–30 people share one water tap and one latrine. The city has two water grids: one carries an intermittent and inadequate supply of filtered tap-water intended for drinking, the other a continuous supply of unfiltered and contaminated ground water delivered through hydrants and intended for street cleaning, firefighting and flushing latrine tanks. All over Calcutta hundreds of thousands of people have no alternative but to use the hydrant water for washing, cooking and drinking, with the result that Calcutta is an endemic plague spot for cholera.

Unsatisfactory sanitation is not confined to regions which are technologically backward. Edinburgh, for example, discharges 241 million litres of untreated sewage into the Firth of Forth each *day*.

Shellfish along the city's foreshores have been found to contain salmonella, shigella and paratyphoid organisms from the city's sewage. The first two can cause acute food poisoning or dysentery. Signs on the beach warn visitors that the mussels there 'are a health hazard and should not be collected for food.' Edinburgh is not alone in its neglect. At least 50 shellfish beds around Britain's coastline are so contaminated by sewage that it is an offence to sell the shellfish at all or at least until they have been cleaned in special plants.

All over Britain local authorities, which should be showing the way, are among the worst polluters. Yet they control and finance river authorities whose job it is to stop pollution. The local authority members of the river boards help to formulate policy, and inevitably part of that policy is not to prosecute local authorities. The laws governing the discharge of domestic and industrial effluent into rivers are adequate. Standards are laid down which, if observed, would ensure the cleanliness of our waterways. But at least half the domestic and industrial effluent discharged by local authority sewage works into most major river systems in Britain is below standard.

Many local authorities drag their feet. They wait for their sewage works to become chronically overloaded by housing and industrial development and then, when

Photo 64
Untreated sewage being discharged onto the foreshore of the Firth of Forth.

Photo 65
Warning notice on the foreshore of the Firth of Forth near Edinburgh.

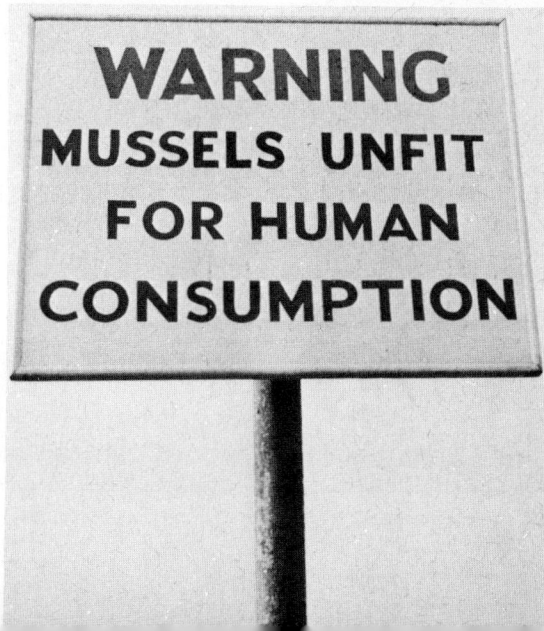

WARNING
MUSSELS UNFIT
FOR HUMAN
CONSUMPTION

pressed, complain about restrictions on capital expenditure, the high cost of borrowing, and the difficulties of getting ministerial approval for their plans.*

Furthermore councillors are well aware of the cliché 'there are no votes in sewage'. As a member of the Lothians River Board has said: 'Sewage has no glamour. People like to build monuments to themselves. Who wants to say: "Look at that lovely sewage plant?"'*

In England one of the most polluted river systems is that controlled by the Trent River Authority. The Trent and its tributaries Tame, Derwent and Soar drain large urban–industrial complexes such as Birmingham and the Black Country, Stoke-on-Trent, Leicester, Derby and Nottingham. One hundred and sixty kilometres of river, including virtually all of the Tame, are grossly polluted, the

*The Times. A News Team Enquiry. 24 March 1970.

result of foul sewage being discharged by no less than 350 of the 600 local authority sewage works. A similar state of affairs exists in the river system controlled by the Yorkshire Ouse and Hull River Authority, whose waters are so badly polluted that they are incapable of supporting fish. Yet another example may be quoted from Lancashire:

Between them local authorities and industrialists have destroyed the Douglas. Soon after it flows out of the Rivington reservoirs, near Horwich, Lancashire, all 3 240 000 gallons a day is abstracted by industry. When two companies near the river's source return the water to the river it is so grossly polluted that it is incapable of sustaining fish. . . . About two miles downstream partially treated sewage from Blackrod Urban District Council . . . slithers down a field before oozing into the Douglas.

Photo 66
River water polluted by the discharge of effluent containing detergents.

At Adlington the river receives further poor quality effluent from the Pin Croft Printing and Dyeing Co. Ironically, the water is by then so polluted that Pin Croft cannot use it and have installed a pipeline back to the source.

Further downstream the Douglas is used by the Standish Co., dyers and finishers. Although the company say they have spent 'thousands of pounds' on plans for primary treatment of their effluent, it still does not meet the standards laid down by the river authority. The company say that the danger of 'going it alone' is that they might be undercut by foreign competitors, particularly the Japanese.

At Wigan the Douglas flows sluggishly over a bed of grotesque fungus by which it is completely deoxygenated. In summer this fungus gives off gases; one is methane, which is noxious, and the other, hydrogen sulphide, smells like rotten eggs. . . . One of Wigan's main sewers is so badly misaligned by mining subsidence that the storm over-flow works continuously. As a result, untreated sewage, including blood and offal from a slaughterhouse, enters the Douglas via Poolstock Brook. Last year thousands of fish in the Leeds–Liverpool canal died when water from the Douglas was let in to maintain the level. Now at last there is some prospect of recovery thanks to a £6 million scheme drawn up by five local authorities which has received Ministry approval in principle.*

Many British coastal towns discharge untreated or partially treated sewage directly into the sea. For this to be satisfactory the Department of the Environment accept that two main conditions should be met: (i) the sewage must be broken up and sieved so that only small particles are discharged; and (ii) the sewage discharge pipe should go far enough out from the beach to prevent particles of sewage reaching bathing areas. For towns of less than 10 000 discharge should be 130 metres below low water mark; for larger cities it may be necessary to carry the sewage several kilometres out to sea. These precautions would safeguard bathers against

*The Times. op. cit.

Photo 67
Fish killed by pollution lying on the foreshore of Lake Ontario, Canada.

Photo 68
The Rhine is one of Europe's most heavily polluted waterways. This photograph shows Rhine water before and after purification in a cleansing plant near Köln.

121

gastro-enteritis, enteric fevers, typhoid and para-typhoid, the organisms of which diseases may be present in human faeces. Yet a Department of Environment report reveals that of the 333 principal discharge pipes around the coast: (i) only 30 discharged sewage anywhere near as far out as the 130 metres desirable for towns of less than 10 000 population—although the average summer population for each discharge pipe was about 14 000; (ii) six out of every ten discharged sewage at or above low water mark; (iii) four out of every ten coastal sewerage authorities admitted to some evidence of sewage on the beach or in the water close to the shore; (iv) one authority—Bridlington RDC—with a summer population of 12 500, discharges untreated sewage above high water mark.*

Figure 81 shows the 65 coastal sewage authorities who have at least one discharge pipe emitting sewage which is both untreated mechanically *and* is discharged at or above low water mark. The potential health risk of bathing in sewage-polluted sea-water is small† but dangers arise through infected sea-foods and by the transmission of fly-borne diseases where untreated sewage collects on the fore-shore.

It is clear that many British coastal waters and rivers need extra attention. A recent government survey‡ of 32 000 kilometres of main river in England and Wales found that *c*. 6% were grossly polluted, *c*. 6% were of poor quality and *c*. 15% were doubtful. The remainder were either recovering from pollution or were substantially unpolluted. The problem of pollution control is bound to worsen because the volume of pollutants discharged is expected to double by A.D. 2000. Purification costs, meanwhile, will increase *c*. $2\frac{1}{2}$ times because modern pollutants such as

detergents are very difficult to extract. The present conventional methods of treating sewage include sand filtration, micro-straining, irrigation over grassland and passage through lagoons. Additional treatment to remove ammonia is highly desirable but this increases costs by another 20%. Yet more costs are involved if river water is treated to remove industrial effluent poisons such as phenol and cyanide, minute traces of which will kill all fish.

At present it is recommended that British sewage entering inland waterways should be purified to the extent of 92% removal of Biochemical Oxygen Demand (BOD). A more stringent purification of 96% BOD removal is desirable on health grounds but this would add 15% to the costs of treatment. Overall costs to the community can be lowered, however, by returning cleansed sewage to the domestic water supply. This is done, for example, at Windhoek (S.W. Africa) where the town's potable water is derived 70% from conventional reservoirs and 30% from reclaimed sewage. Much greater use could also be made of reclaimed sewage to re-charge underground aquifers, as is done extensively in Israel.

Similar problems of water pollution exist in other advanced countries. In Belgium, for example, the river water around Ghent and Antwerp is so foul that it is not suitable even for use by industry, let alone for human consumption. This is a major difficulty because the underground aquifers from which Belgium has hitherto obtained 75% of her water cannot meet the very large increase in current demand. To counter this predicament the Government has set up three new authorities for the rivers Scheldt, Meuse and Yser, with the object of cleaning up surface waters. These authorities operate purification plants, check waste discharge and punish industrial polluters by recommending to the Ministry of Public Health that an offending plant be closed. The volume of industrial effluent has increased recently in Belgium partly as a result of a big expansion in factory farming— pig farms, for example, often pump untreated excrement directly into adjacent waterways. Belgium also suffers from such a shortage of sewage disposal plants that no less than 80% of all sewage is discharged untreated into the

*See *Which?* Bathing, sewage and illness. July 1973.

†'. . . bathing in sewage-polluted sea-water carries only a negligible risk to health, even on beaches that are aesthetically very unsatisfactory.' Public Health Laboratory Service report. This optimistic view does not meet with general approval. For example bathing was banned by the medical authorities on all beaches of the Naples region following the cholera outbreak there in the summer of 1973.

‡Report on the Condition of Inland Waterways in England and Wales. Ministry of Housing and Local Government. 1958.

Figure 81
Outfalls discharging untreated sewage at or above low water. Names in bold indicate sewage reported on the beach or in the water close inshore by either the sewage authorities or the public. (*Source: Which?* magazine)

country's rivers. The large industrial cities of Brussels, Antwerp and Ghent—with a collective population of 2 million—have no sewage works whatever.

In Japan, water pollution has become so bad that 'most of the seafood caught in Japan's fishing waters is likely to maim, paralyse or deform hearty eaters.'* The Government has warned the population of the dangers of exceeding certain weekly limits of various species of seafood. In particular one should not eat more than six prawns, 1 lb 2 oz of tuna or 1·8 flounders per week. This is because the country's coastal waters are heavily polluted with cadmium, mercury, polychlorobiphenyls and other industrial wastes. The heavily industrialized Tokyo Bay area is especially affected: the hair of some of the city's fish dealers was found to contain 64·7 parts per million (ppm) of mercury, i.e. 44·7 ppm above the safety standard.

Poisonous chemicals can also enter river water as a result of indiscriminate dumping. In the West German state of Hesse dozens of public rubbish dumps were closed by special army units in September 1973 following the illegal unloading of at least 14 200 tonnes of toxic chemicals. Over a period of more than

*The Times, 3 July 1973.

two years lethal substances such as cyanide, arsenic, sulphuric acid, nitro-benzine, hydrochloric acid, bromine, nitric acid and mustard gas had been tipped on to municipal dumps or simply drained into public sewage systems.

The toxic waste, stored in metal barrels, would be sufficient to kill the entire population of West Germany. . . . Just how much of the lethal material has leaked through rusted containers and seeped into the ground is not clear. What is clear, however, is that many officials still tend to view wilful pollution as a negligible offence. . . . Antipollution campaigners, who have long predicted that West Germany and other industrial countries will eventually suffocate in the waste products of industrial progress, argue that the lack of effective control of waste disposal and official lethargy are as much to blame for the present threat as anyone polluting the environment for profit.†

†The Observer, 30 September 1973.

Photo 69
A Japanese victim of minarata disease, an affliction affecting unborn children whose mothers ingest foodstuffs contaminated with mercury.

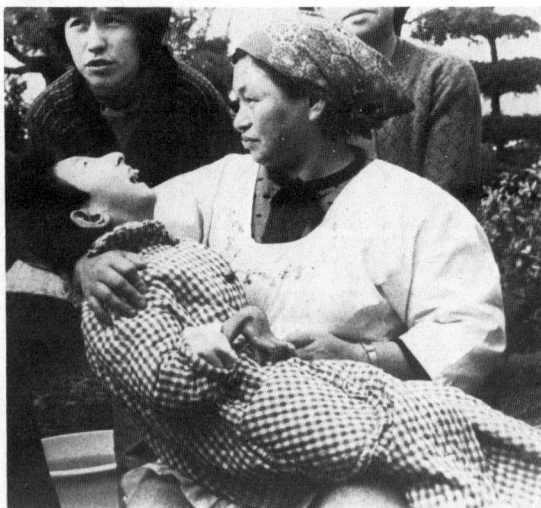

14 Health hazards and crime

Atmospheric pollution is another problem of urban–industrial growth. The discharge of gases, vapours, smoke and dust from industrial and domestic chimneys can make a city's air so foul that its inhabitants may be forced to move. This happened, for example, at Hürth, near Köln in West Germany. Knapsack, a suburban district of Hürth, is constantly enveloped by emissions from local lignite-fired power stations and chemical plants. Phosphine, fluorine, hydrogen-chloride and steam are constantly blown across Knapsack by prevailing westerly winds. The resulting health risks, combined with dangers of poisoning in the event of an industrial accident, plus constant noxious smells and noise made evacuation the only remedy. All residents from 105 hectares of Knapsack have therefore been moved to other parts of Hürth and the blighted area will never again be used for human settlement.

Health risks of this type, though not necessarily of this degree, are faced by many city dwellers. About 80% of the solid particles emitted into the air of a city are sufficiently small to remain suspended for several days. A city is therefore covered, in calm weather, by a pall of smoke, vapours and dust. The gases in this pall are derived mainly from the incomplete combustion of fuels, especially motor fuels, and so they include a high proportion of sulphur-dioxide. Atmospheric pollution is greatly accentuated during conditions of temperature inversion, when chimney smoke

Photo 70
The white mice register the hazard from traffic exhaust fumes in a busy Tokyo street. When the mice show signs of distress the police give warning of the danger to pedestrians and drivers.

Photo 71
Tokyo school children wearing gauze masks against air pollution.

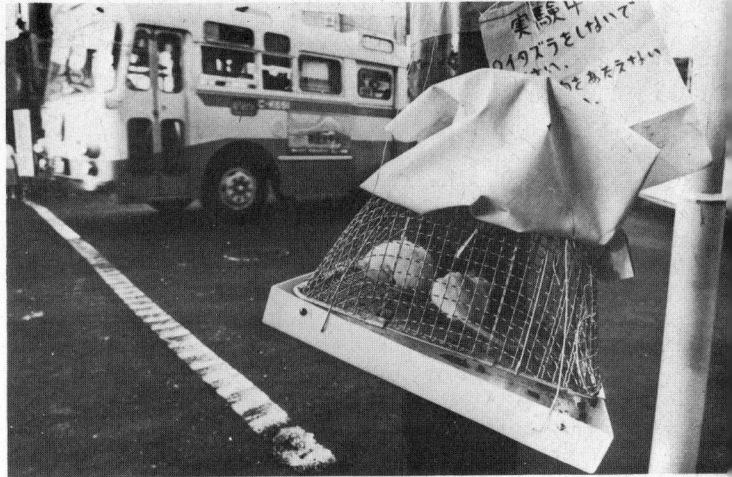

125

and exhaust fumes are chilled so rapidly that they become trapped at ground level beneath a 'capping' of less dense warmer air. Gases such as sulphur-dioxide, carbon-dioxide and phosphorus-pentoxide dissolve in water vapour in the air to form acids which cause stinging eyes, sore throats and damaged lungs. Car exhaust fumes are also dangerous because they are known to contain carcinogenetic substances. One of the most contaminated city atmospheres is that of Tokyo, where small white protective face masks *(photo 71)* are a frequent sight in the crowded streets. Vending machines in central Tokyo dispense whiffs of oxygen to pedestrians for the equivalent of 5p and policemen on point duty have their lungs cleaned regularly when they come off duty. One reason why Tokyo has such foul air is that one-half of the city's daily garbage output of 9000 tonnes is incinerated and the rest is used for land reclamation. Fumes from the burning and rotting garbage, together with those from millions of vehicles and smoke from power stations and industrial plants engulf the city in a white misty haze which the inhabitants call *kokagaku*, or *smoggu*. *Kokagaku* is a photo-chemical smog, containing poisonous aldehydes and nitrogen compounds produced by the action of sunlight on hydrocarbons and nitrogenous gases emitted by car exhausts. *Kokagaku* also contains sulphuric acid, formed by the oxidation of sulphurous fumes given off by Tokyo's oil-burning industrial heaters. The health hazards of *smoggu* were indicated dramatically in July 1970 when a party of 50 schoolgirls playing handball in central Tokyo collapsed, vomiting, with sulphur-dioxide poisoning. The Japanese Government has taken steps to combat the formation of *smoggu* and to warn citizens when it reaches dangerous concentrations. Industrial plants must limit their discharge of sulphur dioxide and car exhausts must not contain more than 5·5% of carbon monoxide. The lead content of petrol used in cars in Japan was also cut by law to zero by 1974. Public warnings are given in Tokyo when the concentration of atmospheric pollutants exceeds 0·15 ppm on calm days and 0·3 on windy ones. Warnings have also been given that, unless the situation improves dramatically, all citizens of Tokyo will have to carry respirators by 1980. In an effort to reduce pollution all traffic is forbidden at weekends in the busy shopping districts of the Ginza, Shinjuku, Shibuya and Ikebukuro. During these traffic-free periods the CO_2 content of the street air falls within an hour from 10·5 ppm to an acceptable 2·3.

In Great Britain there are strong associations between the distribution of chronic bronchitis and the level of atmospheric pollution. *(See map.)* According to the Medical Research Council's air pollution unit at St Bartholomew's Hospital the 'clean-air' legislation of recent years has resulted in fewer bronchial illnesses in London. The smoke content of London's air in fact dropped from 180 to 44 micrograms per cubic metre between 1959 and 1970. The sulphur dioxide content dropped by 5% in 1969–70 but the level of this dangerous gas remains unsatisfactorily high at 143 micrograms per cubic metre. In addition to bronchitis many other diseases have a markedly higher incidence in cities. In settlements of more than 1 million people the incidence of lung cancer, for example, is double the rural rate. Mental disorders are also more common, especially schizophrenia and other symptoms of disorientation. The increase of degenerative diseases of the heart, lung and arteries is also linked by some medical authorities with urbanization and industrialization. Although the links are not yet fully understood it is suspected that the general feelings of anxiety and stress that a city environment tends to stimulate in its inhabitants is a major contributory cause of much ill-health. Modern city life entails endless frustration—during travel to and from work in tubes, cars and buses, at work in noisy offices and factories, and after work in the 'compulsory leisure' of a shorter working week. Some observers see in city life an estrangement from the conditions and natural cycles under which human evolution took place. A city background of night shifts, central heating, air conditioning, artificial lighting and continuous stimulation by noise can disturb the functioning of the human body. Normal daily and seasonal rhythms are upset, with undesirable consequences on the composition of blood and urine, blood flow, deep body temperature and hormone secretions. One consequence of such disturbances is the advance in time of sexual

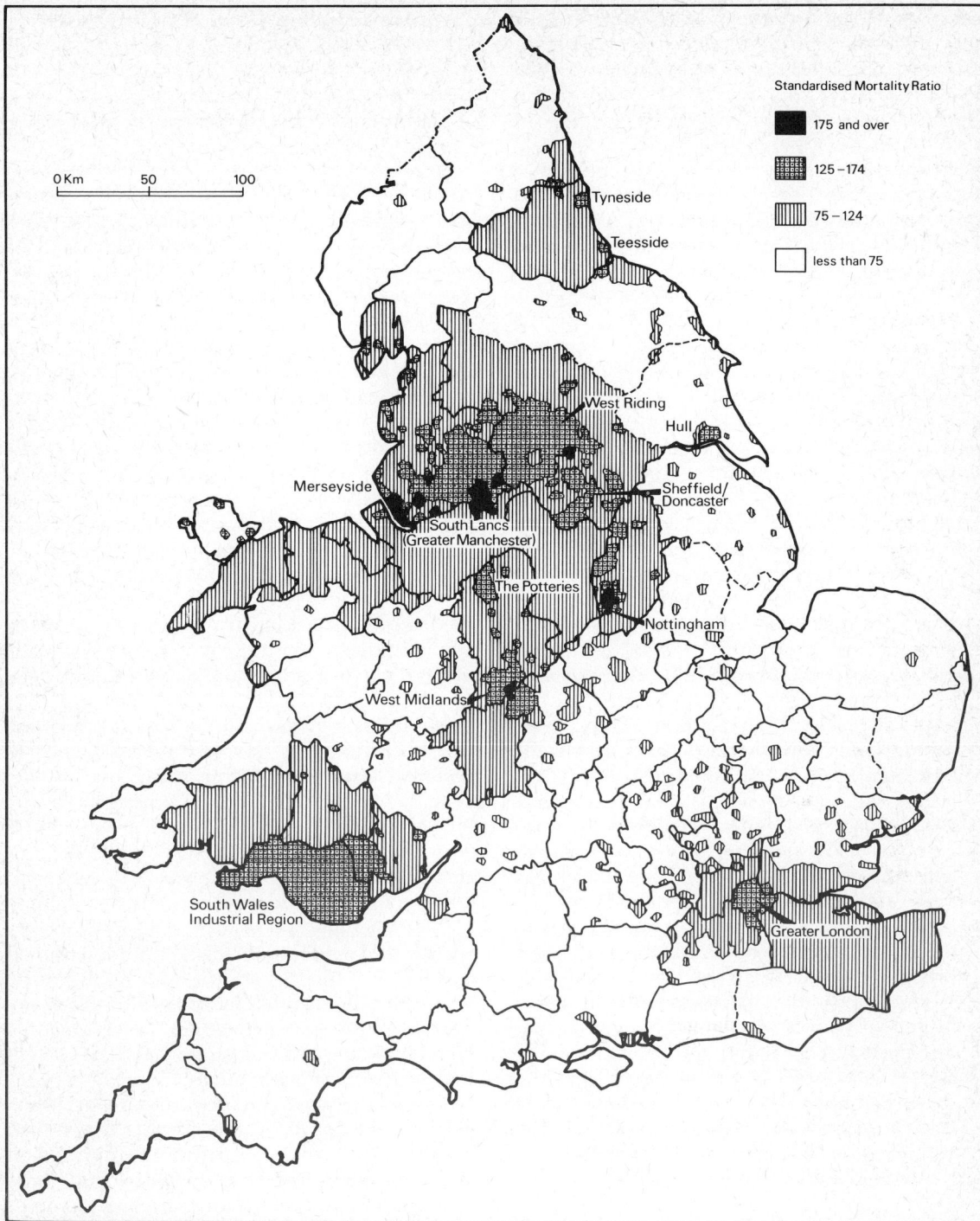

Figure 82
Incidence of bronchitis among males in the U.K. (*After* Melvyn Howe)

Standardised Mortality Ratio

- 175 and over
- 125 – 174
- 75 – 124
- less than 75

Tyneside
Teesside
West Riding
Hull
Merseyside
Sheffield/
Doncaster
South Lancs
(Greater Manchester)
The Potteries
Nottingham
West Midlands
South Wales
Industrial Region
Greater London

0 Km   50   100

maturity, which in turn may be related to the fact that life-expectancy of persons of 45 + has not increased significantly in any urban society—earlier maturity may entail earlier death.

The relatively high incidence of mental sickness and crime in cities was recognized as long ago as the 1930s. A classic study carried out in Chicago divided the city into 11 types of area comprising 120 sub-communities, and rates were established for each.

In every case the rates were high at the centre and declined steadily as one moved further away from it. There were 362 cases per thousand of schizophrenia in the centre, grading down to 55·4 on the periphery. There were 240 cases of alcoholic psychosis per thousand in the centre, grading down to 60 at the periphery. Crime, suicide, drug-taking all showed a similar pattern. The question was at once raised whether city existence caused these high rates, or whether the insane, suicidal and alcoholic were drawn to the centre of cities. The smooth grading from the centre outward made the second seem unlikely, and closer study showed that the rates were linked with the level of social organization. Thus first-generation Polish communities, with a well-knit family life, exhibited relatively low crime and mental sickness rates; second-generation Poles, torn between the two cultures, were frequently unstable. Blacks living in all-black areas had low psychosis rates, but high ones when they lived in mixed areas. Cities evolve social structure, given time. It is rapid growth which creates the problem, especially when there is movement in and out or between different areas in the city. Exactly similar signs of dis-orientation are found on new housing estates in Britain. It seems certain that the mushrooming cities of the immediate future will be plagued by crime and mental disturbances of various kinds. These are certainly evidence of severe stress.*

Another source of stress in cities is excessive noise. In man, as in other animals, sudden noises such as that made by an accelerating motor-cycle, or a sonic boom, bring about an

*Gordon Rattray Taylor. *The Observer*, 6 September 1970.

instinctive alerting reaction accompanied by adrenalin discharges into the bloodstream. A state of tenseness is thus evolved, with a fast heart-beat and heightened blood-pressure. A condition of hyper-tension, if prolonged, may bring about heart failure and/or personality disorders. It has been shown by Dr Lester Sontag at Yellow Springs, Ohio, that sounds can be perceived by a human foetus, both directly and through the physiological effects of the noises on the mother. If, during the later weeks of pregnancy, a mother is apprehensive or emotionally disturbed, the offspring will exhibit symptoms of undue apprehension and excitability at the age of two or three; maternal anxiety, in fact can be inherited. There is also a considerable risk of a city dweller becoming deafened by traffic noise. The simple blare of a car horn reaches 115 decibels of noise intensity, above which the human ear is liable to serious damage. Recent research in Italy reveals that in the larger cities noise has reached, and in some cases has surpassed, the limits that are medically tolerable. A risk of deafness arises if the human ear is exposed for eight hours a day to a sound intensity of 87 decibels. In Milan traffic noise exceeds, on average, 95. In some parts of Rome it exceeds 100. During the rush-hour in Naples it reaches 105. Detailed studies in Rome show that in the vicinity of the city's main hospitals traffic noise reaches 85 when windows are open and 80 when shut—30–35 decibels above the limit classified as 'disturbing' for the patients. Other typical urban noise intensities include 150 for a jet aircraft taking off, 115 for a train whistle and a pneumatic drill, 110 for a moped and 95 for a bus. In addition to the ill-effects on hearing the Roman investigators blame excessive noise for damage to the endocrene glands, vision, and the cardio-vascular, digestive and respiratory systems.†

Similar findings are reported from Manchester and Southampton. Dr M. Bryan‡ for example, finds that one-fifth of the population is exceptionally sensitive to noise, and these 'noise-sensitive' people may include some of the most intelligent and creative members of society, including writers, poets, composers

†*La Stampa*, 12 July 1973.

‡Reader, Audiology Group, Salford University. See *New Scientist*, 23 September 1973.

and artists. Dr P. S. Dickinson states that some types of city buildings amplify noises, harming the people who live in them. Low-frequency noise vibrations, such as those emitted by certain generators and factory machinery, can cause illnesses ranging from brain damage to sickness in sensitive people. Legislation is urgently needed in cities to control the noise of traffic and make factories, railway goods yards, scrapyards and so on quieter than they are today. For many thousands of homes near factories working on night shift or using noisy processes, new laws on noise abatement could bring at least partial peace.

High urban crime rates are symptomatic of a disturbed social environment. In some cities the social disequilibrium is being aggravated by the return of upper-middle-class families to central metropolitan areas, a return stemming from a revulsion from the frustrations of daily commuting. In London, for example, a number of inner boroughs have been 'taken over' in this way, with single families occupying houses formerly lived in by a collection of overcrowded tenants. This process inevitably sparks off social problems as homes have to be found for all dispossessed tenants. In a decayed urban environment, moreover, marked social diversity highlights the material inequalities of different socio-economic groups living cheek-by-jowl. Some sociologists see in this situation the roots of high urban crime rates, especially crimes involving theft and offences against the person, and the seeds of future conflicts.

The broad picture tells the story. London, Birmingham, Bristol, Liverpool, Manchester are all losing population, some rapidly (like Manchester), and some more slowly (like outer London). Their rateable value is increasing more slowly than in the country as a whole; jobs, particularly in manufacturing, are moving out; new investment is either not coming in or is being directed to hotels and offices that are not ready employers for the displaced dockers or mill hands who may have been left behind. If the figures are projected forward it could be that not much more than 10 years from now more than half of inner London's population will be living on grants, rebates, subsidies, supplementary benefit or whatever. They will be housed in decaying buildings or—perhaps more damaging to the spirit of some—in those new asylum-blocks, row after row, that are called 'council estates'. Huddled together in small enclaves within and alongside the new estates or the old slums will be the rich, who even this year have been shovelling money out as fast as they can to buy and 'do up' houses in the centre of the city. The great stabilizing middle classes will long since have disappeared into the outer suburbs. It would be hard to create a potentially more explosive social situation in modern Britain if we tried. Signs that this is happening are visible in many ways already, the projection of statistical trend-lines apart. The present squabble over inner London schools is partly the consequence of the exodus of middle-class children from the central area and the sending of the children of the well-to-do to private schools, leaving the State school population heavily weighted with the children of the relatively poor. A drive around the centres of Manchester or Liverpool shows the effect on housing. Anybody with an imagination ought to be scared.*

This dangerous situation may be dealt with in a variety of ways. A completely *laissez-faire* approach would allow market forces to operate unhindered until the city centre was completely devoid of residents. A completely authoritarian planner would force people to move to bring about a pre-ordained mix of social classes. In a social democracy neither of these solutions is politically practicable and so a middle, less clear-cut way must be followed. D. Eversley, Chief Planner (Strategy) at the Greater London Council, suggests† that the Government must by some means encourage the middle classes to remain near the centre of cities, and that a portion of the financial help now going to new towns and development areas should be used to rescue 'twilight' zones. The destruction of existing communities (like Covent Garden) should be outlawed and all large-scale projects of redevelopment be treated with caution. Schemes

*Joe Rogaly, 'A dangerous future for our cities'. *The Financial Times.*
†See *New Society*, 3 October 1972.

for improving existing properties or for building small housing developments in scattered locations should be favoured; proposals to construct monolithic new estates should be refused. Eversley also suggests the encouragement of subsidized housing associations on the West German style, to produce good housing and a varied mix of income-groups in the same locality. According to Eversley, British house-building is the most socially divisive institution in the country, since it ensures that rich and poor are kept permanently apart. The danger lies in the likelihood that as the years go by the distinctions between social classes will become accentuated and the climate for frustration and bitterness may be worsened.

Photo 72
Congestion of railway commuters at a busy London station.

15 Traffic in cities

Traffic problems are probably the most obvious of the ills which afflict modern cities. This is particularly the case in the United Kingdom which, with a total of 15·2 million vehicles, has the most congested highways in the world—42 vehicles for every kilometre of road. This total, which includes about 12 million private cars, is expected to double by 1980 and to treble by 1990. Congestion is especially acute in the central parts of cities, notably during the morning and evening 'rush hours' when commuter traffic is at its height.

Peak-hour congestion affects both private and public transport, but presents special difficulties for the latter. This is because 80% of the total demand for public transport is confined to a mere 20 hours of the week. During brief periods each day the rolling stock is used to capacity, but at other times it is either

under-utilized or is lying idle. Overall operating costs are therefore pushed up and fares are higher than would be the case if the same total volume of traffic were spread evenly through the week. Peak problems are likely to get worse as the working week is shortened and shift work falls further out of fashion. Capacity pressures on buses and tube-trains are now the norm at peak periods in all metropolitan centres. In Paris, for example, the metro cannot cope with the 3–4 million passengers it is called upon to handle daily, with the result that it operates at 115% capacity, with an average of 7 bodies per square metre of carriage space. In Tokyo the commuter rail system has a typical morning rush-hour overload of 308% of capacity. Similarly the London suburban commuter trains and tubes are greatly overburdened with more than 800 000 passengers who enter and leave the city centre each day, so that services are irregular and deteriorating.

Commuter rail and tube services also suffer a severe disadvantage as a means of mass transportation because of the large number of stops needed to collect a payload. This makes their journeys slow and tedious, and increases fares due to the high cost of frequent braking and acceleration. Yet trains have the distinct advantage that they carry a far greater passenger load than any equivalent form of transport. One London tube train, for example, carries about 700 passengers, i.e. about 500 commuter car loads, at an average speed of more than 32 kph. One London bus carries 41 passengers at 18·4 kph. Thus 170–220 fully loaded double deckers would be needed to carry the Fleet tube line traffic one-way during the peak load period. Similar calculations of efficiency in New York reveal that commuter trains carry 43 000 seated persons per track per hour, and tube-trains (subways) carry 60 000 standing persons per track per hour: the equivalent figures for cars on (a) a normal New York street and (b) a New York urban motorway are c. 1300 and 3200 per lane per hour respectively.

Despite the inefficiency of private cars as a means of passenger transport the congestion of central urban areas is in large measure attributable to their use. In London, for example, some 140 000 people in 97 000 cars enter the central area daily between 0700 and 1000, and

Photo 73
An attempt to exclude heavy goods traffic from residential areas.

car drivers make up c. 12% of the commuting population. Traffic speeds in Central London fell by c. 1·5% each year up to the 1960s and are now c. 16 kph. Speeds in many North American downtown areas are now 6–10 kph. In Paris, where there are 2·5 million cars, increasing annually by c. 120 000, the central city streets are so congested that only c. 115 000 vehicles can be on the move at any one time and an extra 5000 brings the entire network to a standstill. As well as congestion there are mammoth problems in finding parking spaces in central areas for hundreds of thousands of cars and commercial vehicles. An apparently facile solution would be to ban vehicles from city centres but a great deal of the business and commercial life of cities can only be served by motor traffic. Essential vehicles include buses and taxis, as well as those belonging to construction and maintenance firms, public utility services (e.g. water, gas, electricity, telephones), fire brigades, police, ambulance services, doctors, nurses, business-men, salesmen and wholesale and retail merchants. Many planners agree, however, that steps should be taken to restrict the use in cities of private cars. Possible methods include the imposition of road tolls, high parking fees, costly excise licences and really punitive purchase taxes on new cars. Perhaps the most

131

Photo 74
These cracks in the ceiling of a house in Burlington Lane, Chiswick, are typical of the damage caused by vibrations as heavy goods vehicles thunder down the street.

Photo 75
Heavy goods vehicles on Burlington Lane.

practicable scheme would be road pricing, in which a meter installed in a car would be activated automatically when the vehicle entered designated urban areas. The meter would record distances in money terms. This scheme would permit the use of private cars for social purposes and shopping, but owners would avoid using them for trivial reasons. A reduction in total vehicular movements in city centres would help to eliminate on-street parking, a practice which is dangerous because it impedes traffic, is bad for business in adjacent shops and is an eye-sore. Road pricing has been suggested as an alternative to the controversial 'Motorway Box' scheme for Central London. *(See figure 83.)* The Greater London Council has also banned the through movement of 40-foot lorries from Central London. *(See figure 84.)*

Most large cities are trying to strike the right balance between public and private transport, with deliberate efforts to encourage and expand the former whilst curbing the latter. Many cities are aiming to establish

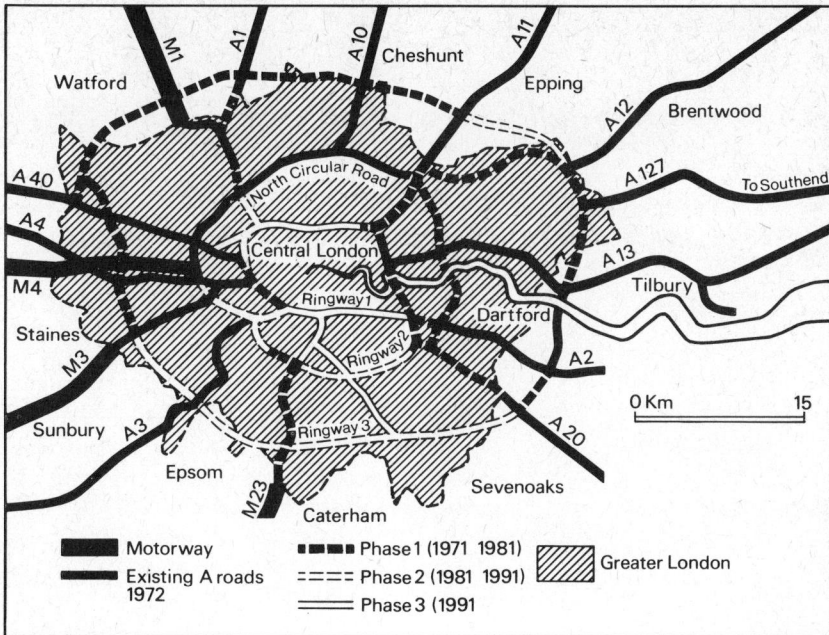

Figure 83
The proposed London Motorway Box.

vastly improved bus services as a major contribution to the transport of passengers *en masse*. In Paris, for example, 10 special bus routes have been established. Each bus lane is physically separated from other traffic lanes by small ridges in the road and by sometimes running against the prevailing traffic flow. The special lanes give buses unrestricted movement—an essential prerequisite if they are to offer the public an adequate service. Between 1952 and 1972 worsening traffic congestion in Paris reduced average bus speeds from 16 to 10 kph and the number of passengers fell from 530 million to 180 million accordingly. The London Transport Executive estimate* that it will be necessary to cut London's private car traffic by two-fifths if a reliable bus service is to be re-established there. Apart from the vexations to passengers of delays in streets jammed with traffic, the bus firms have difficulty in retaining drivers in such frustrating conditions. To ease the problem Oxford Street, one of London's busiest shopping thoroughfares, has been closed experimentally to all traffic except buses and taxis. Furthermore 500

*London Transport Executive Annual Report, 1973.

Figure 84
Area banned to heavy goods vehicles in Central London.

buses have each been fitted with a 'transponder', a device to hold traffic lights at green and to turn them from red to green quickly. Special bus lanes are also being devised from which non-bus drivers will be excluded by law.

As well as speeding up bus services, city transport authorities aim to recapture patrons by offering higher standards of comfort. Some planners suggest that services should be expanded to include fleets of mini-buses which would be available on a 'dial-a-bus' basis. West Germany is pursuing the concept of 'mini-taxis' travelling above congested city streets, The light metal and plastic 'cabinentaxi' (CAT) shown in this photo takes three people and their luggage. Powered by a linear motor the CATS are designed to travel between a city's centre and outskirts at 36 kph. The vehicles, which are driverless, are built to operate either above or below a single suspended track. Passengers enter a CAT while it is stationary on a loop. The required destination is then indicated by pressing an appropriate button. The CAT then starts automatically and is slotted into the main line. Travel to the destination is made without stopping. One advantage of this system is that the individuality and privacy of private car transport is retained, but travel speeds are at least 10 kph faster. Traffic congestion is reduced and costs to the traveller are about one-half of those of normal car driving. The short test track for CATs is at Hagen in the Ruhr, and that city is likely to adopt the

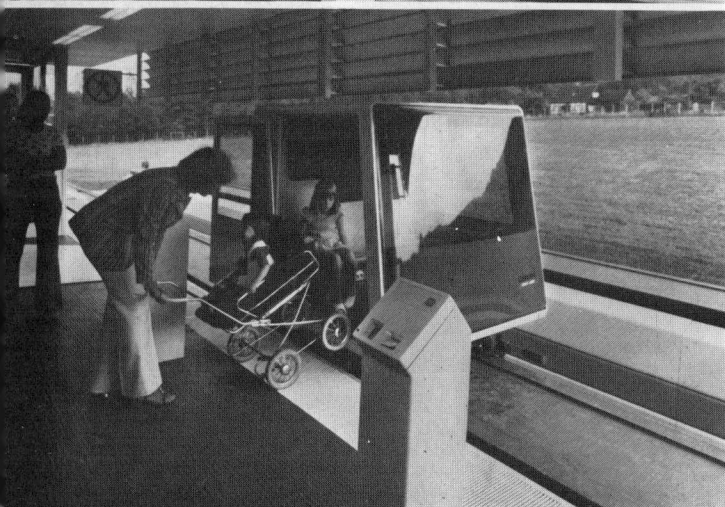

Photo 76
Cabinentaxis at Hagen, West Germany.

Photo 77
Bay Area Rapid Transport District (BARTD) Train, San Francisco. With a streamlined exterior and luxurious interior features the train is designed to draw motorists away from congested suburban and city streets. *For details see text.*

134

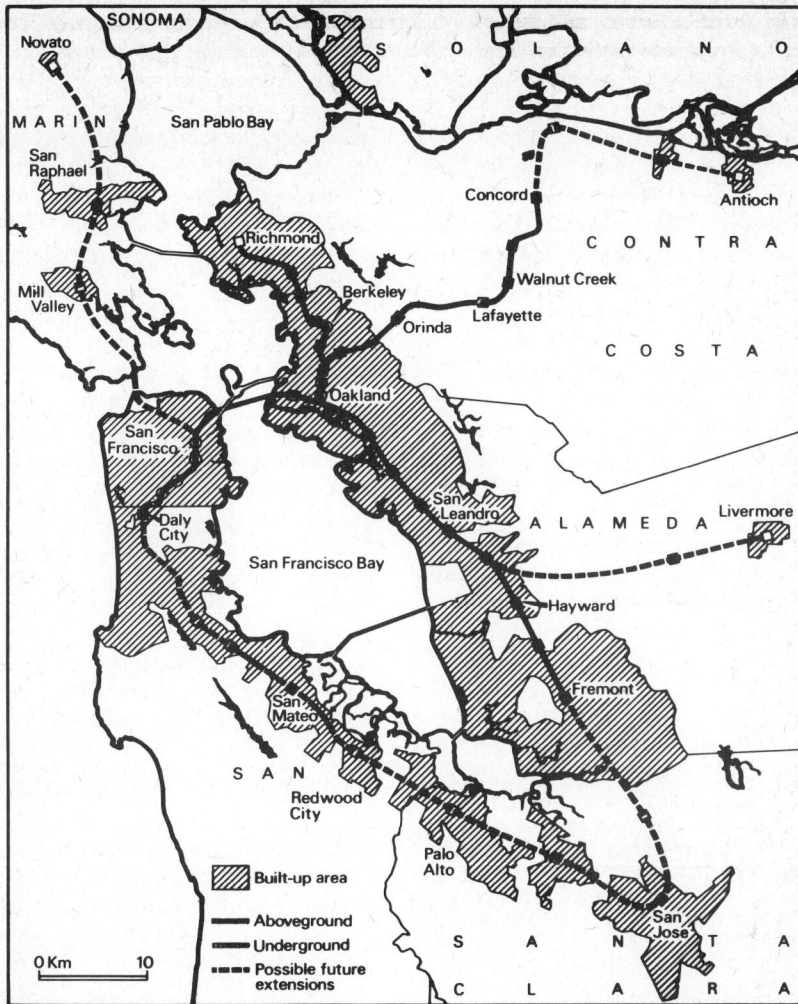

Figure 85 (a)
San Francisco Bay Area Rapid Transit District (BARTD)
currently embraces three metropolitan Bay Area counties.
San Francisco, Alameda and Contra Costa. Although
earlier studies envisaged five inner Bay counties in the
system, San Mateo County withdrew from the plan by
1962 and Marin County, joined to San Francisco by the
Golden Gate Bridge, was judged too difficult to serve
under present conditions.

system on an experimental basis. So, too, is
Freiburg and the Perlach suburb of Munich.

Other cities are placing a major emphasis on
improved rail facilities for commuters. Fore-
most in this respect is San Francisco, with its
Bay Area Rapid Transit District (BARTD).

Figure 85 (b)
BARTD: share of total daily commuter traffic. (*After
J. W. Dickman*)

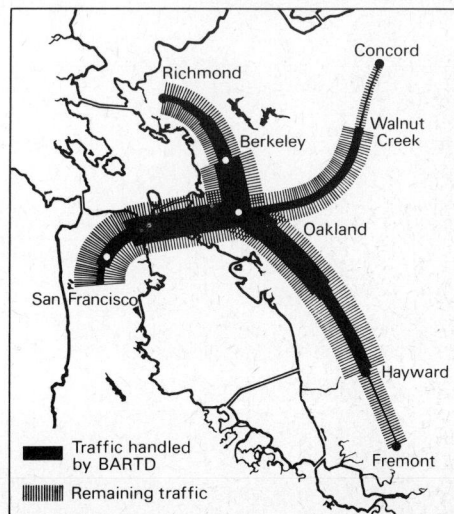

This is a newly built electric rail system specially designed to ensure the swift and comfortable conveyance of masses of commuters to and from downtown San Francisco. The aim is to provide passengers with a high-speed travel service during peak-hour periods and so to divert commuter traffic from cars to trains. The system retains some characteristics of local transit, although stations are widely spaced to avoid frequent time-consuming delays. Trains are very frequent, with intervals of only 15–20 minutes at any time of the day or night, shortening to a mere 90 seconds during the rush-hours. The whole system is geared up to be fast, comfortable and efficient—average train speeds of 72 kph are about 40 kph faster than commuter car movements in the Bay Area; station platforms are very long to avoid passenger congestion and to ensure swift boarding and alighting; there are fully automatic controls and easy ticket handling; carriages are soundless, air conditioned, carpeted and fitted with floor to ceiling windows and contoured upholstered seats. The system opened in 1972, was an instant success and aimed to carry 200 000 passengers daily by 1975. BARTD has already been hailed as the 'salvation of downtown San Francisco'. By making the central area readily accessible to a wide urban hinterland it has renewed confidence in the future of the old CBD, a fact reflected in a recent building boom, with more than 1000 million dollars being invested in new high-rise office buildings. The major criticism of BARTD is that it has not really solved the twin problems of traffic congestion and car parking, but shifted them from central San Francisco to the suburban stations. These relatively few collection points are beseiged daily by tens of thousands of cars and buses for which there is insufficient space.

Among other cities relying on improved rail services to help solve commuter traffic problems are Hong Kong and Tokyo. In Hong Kong the traditional mode of mass conveyance has hitherto been the bus, but the Colony's two major bus companies have lost many passengers in recent years due to increasing congestion of the roads by private cars. Most buses are old, creaky and 200% full, and the mountainous terrain does not favour new road construction. There is also a boom in car imports and so the very high

Photo 78
Entrance to the road tunnel which links Hong Kong island to Kowloon.

density of 185 vehicles per kilometre of road is not likely to diminish in the foreseeable future. The Government has therefore settled on mass-transit railways as the answer. A new 52 kilometre long rail track, served by 28 stations, will carry an expected 2·5 million

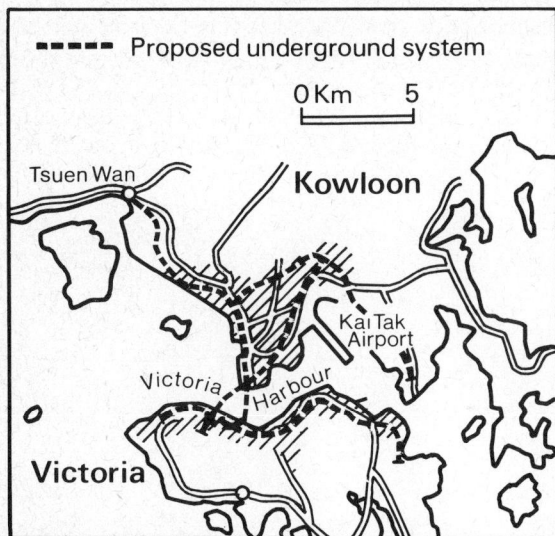

Figure 86
The proposed underground system in Hong Kong.

passengers by 1986. *(See map.)* All but 8 kilometres of the railway will be underground, including a tunnel connection between Hong Kong island and the mainland. Tunnelling provides the simplest method of penetrating the built-up parts of the Colony which comprise the most densely populated urban region in the world. The new railway will carry only 33% of the total passenger journeys, and so it is planned to blend in with a long-term road programme. Restrictions are also being placed on the use of private cars and certain downtown roads are closed to vehicles on Sundays.

In Tokyo there is an urgent need to provide mass transit facilities between the centre and the new Suburban Redevelopment Districts. *(See map.)* Seven new rapid-transit railways are to be built in the decade ending in 1983. In addition new urban motorways will provide radial arteries and three concentric ringways, plus a loop highway around the shores of Tokyo Bay. These major improvements in transportation are expected to reduce by one-half the time-distance values in the Tokyo Metropolitan Region. Similar urban ringways have been proposed for central London, but the plan is fiercely controversial, with a clash of interests between those who seek improved accessibility and those who wish to preserve the environment. The main objections to such roads are that they are visually unattractive, noisy, a source of fumes, dirt and vibration. They are also said to destroy community relationships in the districts through which they pass because they constitute a physical and social barrier. Modern planners argue, however, that the impact of urban motorways can be minimized by acquiring land astride the motorway routes so that redevelopment can be carried out in depth. Such planning involves the full integration of buildings and landscaped spaces over, under and adjoining a new motorway as well as the restoration of an adequate number of pedestrian and vehicular links.

Figure 87
The Tokyo metropolitan region. Transportation proposals. See also photo 79, overleaf. (*After* Withenick)

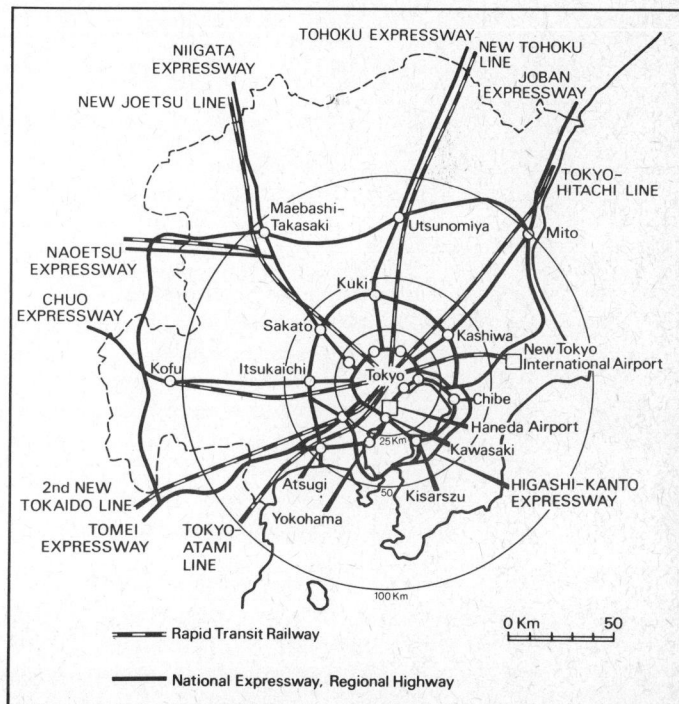

137

Photo 79
Part of the Tokyo metropolis.

The classic example of such planning is in the West German city of Dusseldorf, where new roads are partially hidden to avoid intrusion on the landscape and to minimize noise. New techniques in tunnel construction currently being developed will make it more feasible to hide urban motorways by burrowing beneath congested cities, so avoiding dislocation and the displacement of residents. One new device uses bentonite clay to form a sealing skin on a tunnel's face: this prevents its collapse and makes it possible to pierce economically through water-bearing sands and gravels. The purpose of constructing urban motorways is to provide a system of primary roads on to which all but local traffic can be diverted, thus reducing or eliminating vehicular traffic from shopping streets and residential areas.

The problem of traffic in cities is obviously complex. Policy decisions in Britain have in recent years been influenced by the 'Buchanan Report'*, the central theme of which is that it is possible to define a minimum environmental standard in terms of noise, fumes, danger and inconvenience, for any street or street network. This standard would then automatically

*_Traffic in Towns_ (The Buchanan Report), London, HMSO, 1963.

determine the volume and nature of traffic permitted to use that street. Any increase in the volume of traffic would only be allowed after costly reconstruction work designed to maintain an adequate standard. Buchanan's main objective is to maintain environmental standards and to adapt traffic flows to the amount of investment that society can divert into urban reconstruction. The Report's proposals include the separation of express and local traffic; the separation of pedestrians from traffic and the separation of certain freight movements. It also advocates the construction of urban expressways *below* street level, the storage of vehicles *at* street level and the lifting of pedestrians *above* street level to the first floor. In a similar way it wishes to see rows of arcaded shops above the main freight service traffic lanes.

The main criticism of Buchanan is that he finds no reasonable alternative to the auto-

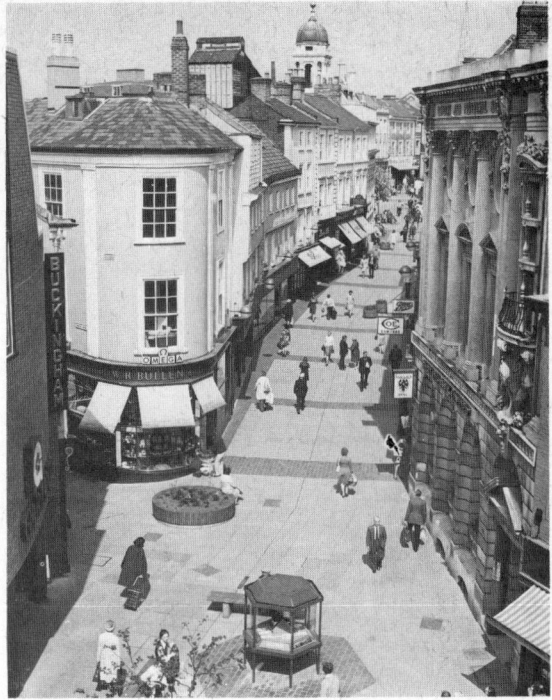

Photo 80
A pedestrian precinct in Norwich formed by closing a former street to traffic.

Photo 81
A planned pedestrian precinct in a new shopping arcade, Stockholm.

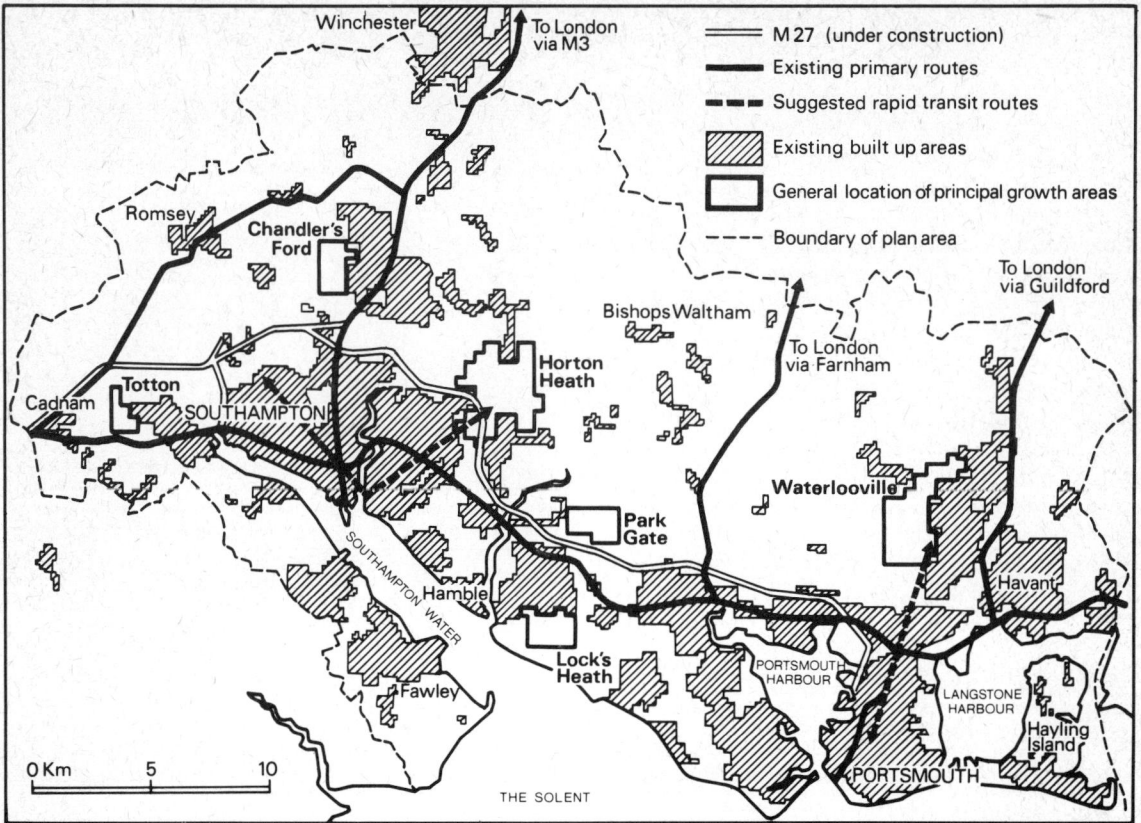

Figure 88
Southampton–Portsmouth: main urban roads and suggested rapid transit routes.

mobile, that his proposals for urban reconstruction are too car-orientated. This assumption is said by some planners to be both futile and unnecessary. The extraordinary increase in the number of private cars makes it imperative to keep them out of cities rather than try to accommodate them by building elaborate and costly parking and underpass projects. Efforts should rather be directed to providing alternative mass-transit facilities, whether by rail, bus, tube or by a combination of all three. Attempts should also be made to minimize traffic by locating alongside one another those land-use zones which require much interaction. Perhaps the most helpful

step in this direction would be to abandon the conventional concept of a Central Business District by removing CBD functions from the city centre. There is no doubt that massive central office blocks constitute a major source of traffic congestion. The deliberate location of motels, shopping parades, industries and offices in suburban settings, together with the creation of inter-city hypermarkets in the American style, would possibly do more to solve traffic problems in British cities than any amount of Buchanan-style tinkering with existing city centres. *(Photos, p. 75.)* On the other hand there is a widespread and strongly felt antipathy against 'turning cities inside out'.

140

Section 7 Urban planning

---

16 The garden idea

Urban planning seeks to solve, or at least to ameliorate, the various problems which result from city growth. Many of the basic concepts of modern planning stem from the late eighteenth and early nineteenth centuries, when certain British factory owners concerned themselves to improve the appalling living and working conditions of their employees. That the initiative in this respect should have been taken in Britain is not surprising, for it was in this country that the squalid results of *laissez-faire* urban expansion first became manifest. Some of the more notable achievements of these paternalistic industrialists are noted opposite. The form of these early factory towns reflected not only a desire to give workers more comfort but also the Utopian ideas of reforming society by encouraging a sense of human dignity and communal responsibility. Thus homes and factories were kept apart by open land, parks and gardens, buildings were of improved and varied designs and there was a general trend towards lower-density housing.

These trends were given added impetus by the garden suburb and Garden City concepts. The first garden suburb, designed by the famous Victorian architect Norman Shaw, was built in 1875 at Bedford Park, Acton. Bedford Park was created in a romantic semi-rural style, its red brick houses being decorated with casement windows, Dutch gables and tiles. Furthermore its streets were curved and many old trees were preserved to add to the illusion of living in the country. Another garden suburb, built at Hampstead in 1907, was largely inspired by the architectural and social ideas of Dame Henrietta Barnet, who aimed to attract a variety of social classes by building houses of different sizes. Hampstead Garden Suburb was destined to have a

1769. Josiah Wedgwood surrounded his Etruria pottery works in Stoke-on-Trent with 'model cottages' which were markedly better in design and convenience than most other houses of that period.

1816. Robert Owen planned a model factory village for New Lanark, designed as a co-operative community of 1200 people, with industrial buildings and houses surrounded by a belt of farmland.

1846. J. G. Richardson, a Quaker industrialist laid out a factory village around his linen mill at Bessbrook, near Newry. It is probable that Richardson's work influenced a fellow Quaker George Cadbury who in 1879 began building his famous town of Bournville. This settlement, with many amenities, was pleasantly laid out in a rural setting around Cadbury's chocolate factory which had been relocated from central Birmingham. Bournville eventually provided homes for some 2000 families.

1886. Lever Brothers, the soap manufacturers, built Port Sunlight on Merseyside. This was a low-density development notable for its gardens and children's playgrounds.

1905. Sir Joseph Rowntree built Earswick near York for the employees of his cocoa factory.

profound influence on future British town planning, largely because this suburb's housing density of eight dwellings per acre came to be the generally accepted standard. The garden suburbs were pleasantly laid out residential estates but because they contained no industry they could not form the basis of comprehensive urban expansion. The Garden Cities, by contrast, included factories and were designed to show that an industrial town need not be dreary, congested or soulless. Proposed by Ebenezer Howard in 1898, the first Garden City was begun at Letchworth in 1903. Factories and houses were kept separate, although in a pre-car era they had to be within walking distance. Another Garden City, built at Welwyn in 1919, retained the semi-rural romantic ideals of Letchworth and the garden suburbs but had a slightly higher housing density of twelve dwellings per acre. Both Welwyn and Hampstead are still thriving communities and Welwyn ultimately became the core of a New Town. The fact that they incorporated industry from the start enabled them to expand and diversify, mainly by attracting new light engineering firms.

17 New towns and 'overspill'

The 'garden' element common to these early British schemes influenced town planning elsewhere. In Essen, for example, the Krupp engineering firm built homes on a 'rural estate' for 16 000 workers and in Radburn (New Jersey) Stein and Wright designed a novel suburban community in which all residences *faced* on to gardens and *backed* on to streets, the latter in effect functioning as service roads. The Radburn scheme reflected the growing impact of automobiles on American planning in the 1930s. In Britain one can trace the 'garden' idea in Abercrombie's Greater London Plan of 1943 and again in the many New Towns established since the Second World War. In some respects, however, the New Towns represent a fundamental break with the immediate past. Unlike the garden suburbs, Garden Cities and 'Company Towns' the first New Towns were built for the specific purpose of stopping the unrestrained growth of London. Thus they were much bigger projects designed to be economically and socially viable in their own right. This was to be achieved by the creation of industrial estates capable of absorbing new industries attracted to the south-east of England. It was also hoped that the New Towns would provide sufficient industry outside the London Green Belt *(see map)* to break the pattern of commuting which had emerged in the late 1930s. There was greater emphasis, too, on the development of neighbourhood units, a concept which was essentially American in origin, though it had links,

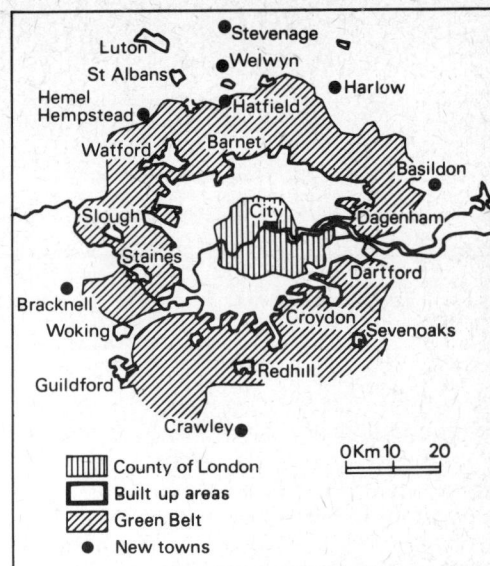

Figure 89
Greater London: New Towns and Green Belt.

too, with the aspirations of Ebenezer Howard. The aim was to create not mere aggregates of houses and factories, but living communities complete with shops, schools, churches, pubs, clubs, sports centres and so on. To this end the New Towns were subdivided into neighbourhoods containing five to twelve thousand people, on the assumption that these relatively small groups would stimulate an abundance of 'face-to-face' contacts and much social mixing. In this respect the New Towns have not been very successful, for proximity has tended to increase rather than decrease social distance, a trend which sociologists had predicted all along. Class enclaves retain their identities with extraordinary vigour, even though different socio-economic groups live cheek-by-jowl. Moreover, most New Towns have become one-class, i.e. working-class communities.

The New Towns around London have not solved the capital's commuting problems because they are too near the metropolis: people living in them need not seek local employment because they can easily commute by road and rail. Nor have the New Towns been able to solve the enormous problem of London's housing shortage. In the Greater London Council area there are at least 150 000 slums and 250 000 sub-standard dwellings

142

Photo 82
A demonstration by homeless people against the construction of high-rise office blocks in central London.

and an estimated net shortage of 250 000 homes in inner London alone. This housing shortage exists despite the fact that London's total population has fallen between 1961 and 1971 from 7 992 000 to 7 379 000 and is predicted to fall still more to 6 650 000 by 1981. This apparent anomaly arises because (a) the number of households has increased as people marry younger; (b) the density of housing is deliberately reduced in re-development and renovation schemes, thus producing a 'surplus' of people; (c) London has an enormous legacy of Victorian and Edwardian houses which are fast falling into decay; and (d) there is a desperate shortage of suitable sites in London on which to build new houses, especially near current places of work. The site problem is aggravated because old, decayed urban areas contain a multiplicity of

pipes, cables, sewers, water mains and even underground railways; this complicates and greatly increases the costs of local redevelopment.

Since 1950 the GLC, in conjunction with 33 other towns *(figure 90)*, has operated an Expanding Towns scheme in an effort to re-house would-be migrants from the capital. Potential migrants, all of whom are volunteers, are nominated by the GLC and a firm in a receiving town may have up to twenty recommended applicants for a single vacancy. The GLC also assists with the finance of industrial sites and housing in Expanding Towns and pays rents before occupation. The prospect of a new house is the big attraction for migrants; at present there are 160 000 families on London Borough Council housing lists and only about 30 000 new houses are

Photo 83
Cumbernauld New Town lies approximately half-way between Glasgow and Edinburgh. It was built to relieve housing pressures in the Clydeside conurbation.

Photo 84
La Granda Motte, a new housing project in Rousillon, Languedoc, France.

144

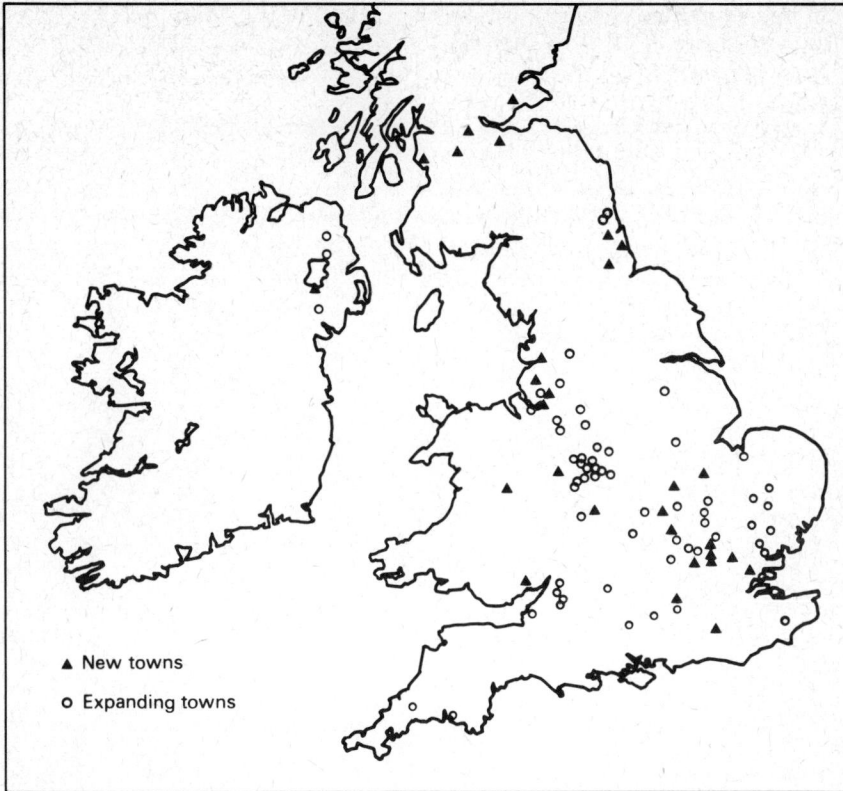

Figure 90
New and expanding towns in the United Kingdom.

built in London each year. So far about 50 000 families and more than 900 firms have moved into the Expanding Towns, with an average exodus of about 15 000 from the capital each year. The movement of this considerable body of Londoners is now beginning to have an impact on the quality of living in London and also in the 'target' areas. The scheme offers great advantages to those who move and helps ease housing problems in London. Difficulties arise, however, because the majority of migrants are young, skilled workers and the firms which leave London for the Expanding Towns are mainly in light engineering. Thus those left behind have fewer local job opportunities. Moreover, they belong mainly to lower socio-economic groups such as cleaners, road sweepers, caretakers,

bus drivers, postmen, porters and so on who find it impossible to afford decent accommodation. An added problem arises for these residual groups because the 1965 Rent Act, which was designed to keep down rents, has had the unfortunate effect of greatly reducing the total number of rented properties in London.

A more recent and grandiose plan to relieve urban congestion in south-east England involves the creation of a large new city at Milton Keynes and a massive increase in the existing populations of Northampton and Peterborough. Milton Keynes is being built on a 9000 hectare site in Buckinghamshire. With a predicted population of 250 000 by the end of the century it is the largest and most elaborately planned New Town in the history of British planning. The choice of its location midway between London and Birmingham was made in the hope that Milton Keynes would become an independent city in its own right, serving its own hinterland and immune to the proximity of those two cities. Other advantages of Milton Keynes' geographical position are listed on the right. A new urban motorway will run through the city joining the M1 to the A5. This motorway link, with five access points to the city, will be hidden by screening plants and carried in cuttings to

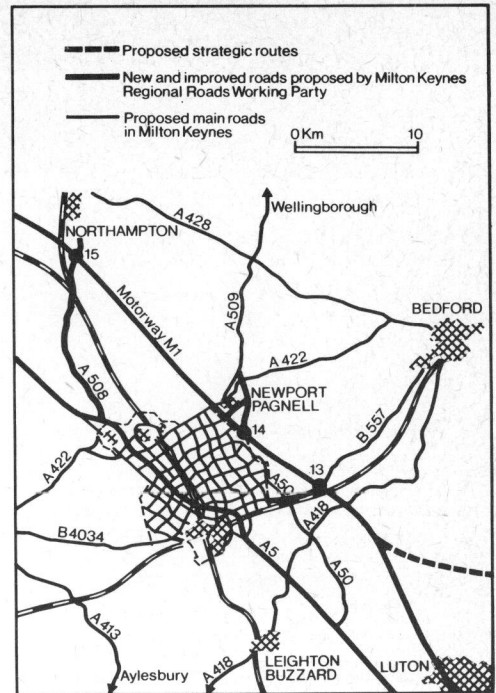

Figure 91 (a)
The location of Milton Keynes.

Figure 91 (b)
Proposed land use within Milton Keynes.

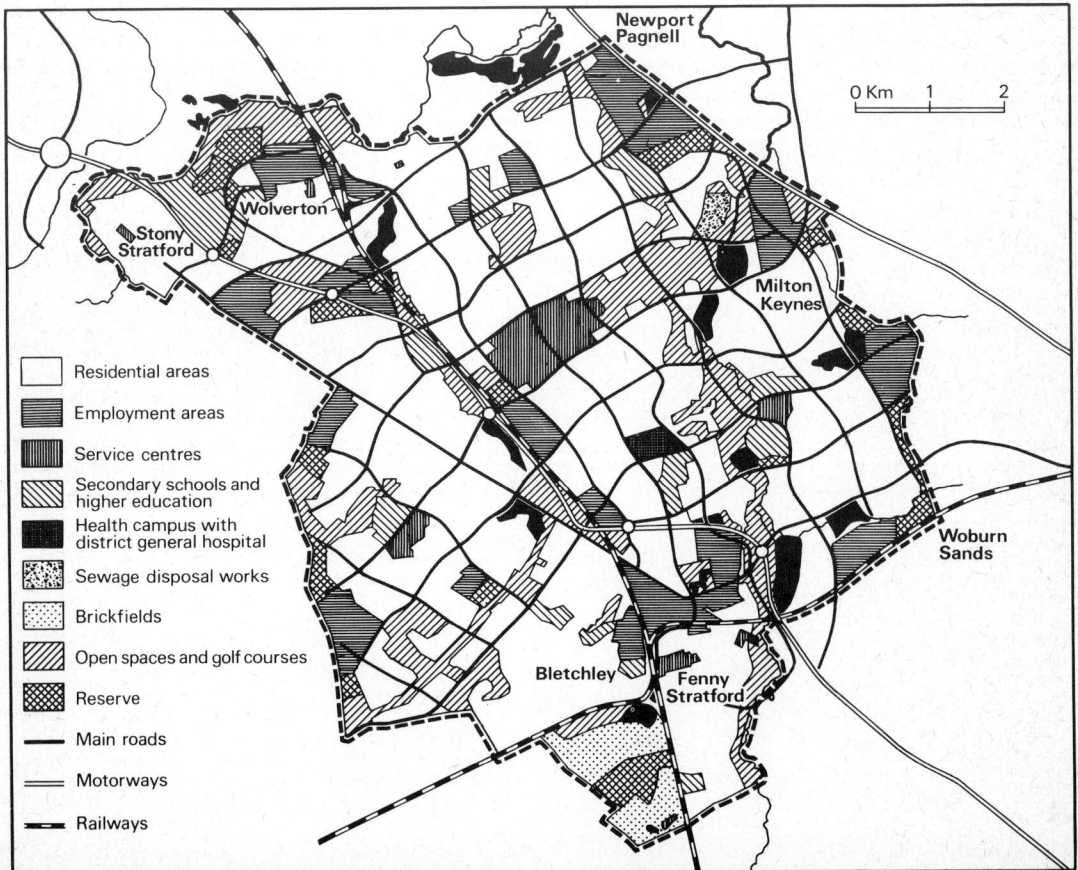

Residential areas

Employment areas

Service centres

Secondary schools and higher education

Health campus with district general hospital

Sewage disposal works

Brickfields

Open spaces and golf courses

Reserve

Main roads

Motorways

Railways

146

avoid traffic noise. This attention to planning detail epitomises the entire approach to the construction of Milton Keynes, the aim of the planners being to create a pleasant and effective living and working environment. In particular the uses and abuses of the motor car will be recognized and accepted. Milton Keynes will be divided by dual carriageways into blocks approximately 1 kilometre square, but within each block there will be complete segregation of pedestrians and traffic. Each block will contain houses, shops, offices, industrial plant as well as educational and leisure facilities.

The early growth of the city is being concentrated along a crescent-shaped area so as to include the existing settlements of Bletchley, Wolverton, Stony Stratford and New Bracknell. *(See maps.)* This is to give early immigrants easy access to existing shopping and recreational facilities. Ultimately the city will also include several small villages within its boundaries. These will be preserved as semi-rural enclaves to help retain an open feeling. A 'linear park', including 240 hectares of lakes and with direct links to the open countryside, will further augment a sense of spaciousness. There will also be a City Park within easy reach of the main shops located in the City Centre. The latter, scheduled for completion in 1991, is being planned on a scale unknown previously in Europe. It will comprise a complex of shops, offices, youth centre, museum, art galleries, cinema, swimming pool, hotels, library, pubs and bingo halls. Some 50 000 people will live within walking distance of the Centre and 25 000 parking spaces will also be available. The Centre will also house the City Club—modelled on Real Madrid—with a sports stadium to hold 40 000, a theatre, ice rinks and so on. Scattered throughout the city there will be a further 150 activity centres, each of them containing small shops, a supermarket, a communal workshop and a small meeting hall.

Milton Keynes will be mainly a light industrial centre, with electrical and mechanical engineering the greatest single source of employment, followed by chemical engineering, printing and publishing. Nearly all of the industries being attracted to the city can be fitted into commonly designed plant 'modules', but specialist firms can build factories to their

> *The new city of Milton Keynes is . . .*
> midway between London and Birmingham;
> adjacent to the M1 Motorway;
> on the Euston—Birmingham electrified railway—trains leave for London (a 37 minute journey) every 30 minutes;
> on the A5 road and linked by good roads to Bristol, Southampton and the east coast ports;
> within easy reach of the international airport at Heathrow and of Birmingham airport;
> equidistant from the universities of Oxford, Cambridge, Birmingham and London—an advantage for scientific research establishments.

own design. Well-known firms already established include British Olivetti, W. H. Smith, British Oxygen, Kodak and Hoechst who are to build the country's largest medical research centre in Milton Keynes. The city is also the home of the Open University.

The Milton Keynes project is by far the most ambitious urban planning scheme ever undertaken in the United Kingdom. Its layout clearly incorporates and amplifies many features of the 'garden-city' and 'neighbourhood' philosophies now so well established in this country. It is also notable for its deliberate retention of existing urban nodes, a policy which appears even more markedly in the master-plan for Peterborough. In fact Peterborough—planned to grow in the next 15 years from 88 000 to 188 000—will become Britain's first real polycentric city, with four separate townships of 20 000 to 30 000 clustering around the existing city. *(Map overleaf.)* Each township will have 'most of the shopping and service facilities normally found in the centre of a typical country town'.* At the same time the 'central city'—with double its present population—will contain the higher order shopping and service facilities which people within Peterborough's hinterland cannot get in their own villages or townships. Work on the first township, Bretton, began in 1970 and a wide variety of homes have been built for rent and for owner-occupation. This is in keeping with the planners' declared aim of offering 'the highest possible quality of social and family life for all, from managing director

*Master Plan for Greater Peterborough. Peterborough Development Corporation, 1970.

Photo 85
Diamond Bar, California, is typical of many urban nodes being built alongside
motorways in the Los Angeles area. Note the juxtaposition of residential and
industrial estates. Urban expansion of this type accords with the multi-nuclei
theory of city growth. (see also photograph, page 40).

to office cleaner. We are determined to make
Greater Peterborough a pre-eminently good
place in which to be born, to grow up, to make
friends, to have fun, to learn, to work, to play,
to bring up children, to lead a full adult life at
any cultural level, and to spend a contented
retirement.'* In many respects the Peterborough plan resembles that of Milton
Keynes. A local centre, for example, will be
within pram-pushing distance of every house;
the centre will contain shops, a primary
school, a pub, a women's hairdresser, a
launderette and a public meeting room. All
houses will have their garage space and a
unique district heating plant will provide
central heating for every batch of 5400
houses—the largest district heating scheme in
Britain. Each township will contain a comprehensive school and a pedestrian-only shopping

*Peterborough Development Corporation. *Op. cit.*

Figure 92
Peterborough's proposed townships: an example of
polycentric planning.

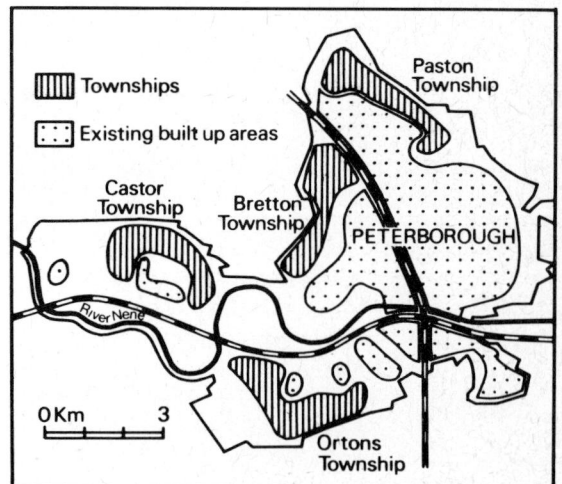

148

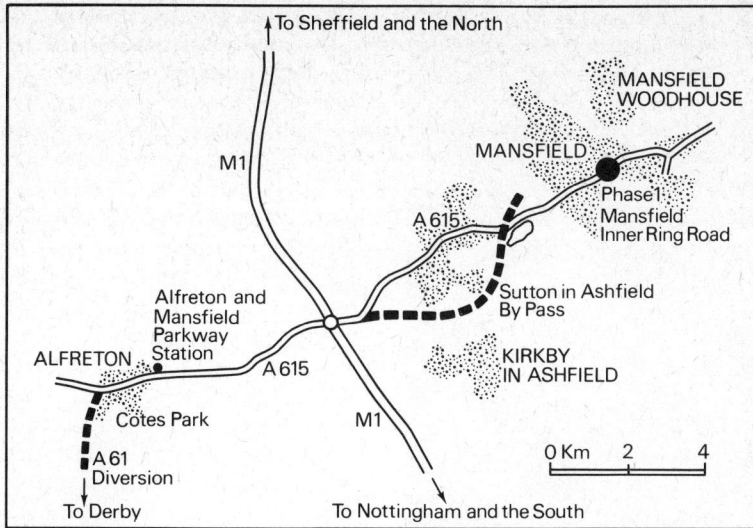

Figure 93
The Alfreton—Mansfield urban growth area.

centre with 'market town' facilities, plus a sports hall, swimming pool and library. The road system will ensure that township and local centres are easily accessible but traffic will not intrude into residential or shopping areas.

An urban planning experiment similar to that of Peterborough is taking place along the A615 between Mansfield and Alfreton. It involves the reclamation of a derelict industrial area badly affected by colliery closures. In the 10 years up to 1973 the number of collieries within a 13 kilometre radius of Alfreton fell from 30 to 11, with the loss of 9530 jobs. Urban renewal in this part of the East Midlands aims to produce a kind of open-plan city, to be called Five Towns, from the following group of towns and villages: Mansfield, Alfreton, Kirkby-in-Ashfield, Sutton-in-Ashfield and Mansfield Wood-house. *(See map.)* The existing settlements are to be linked together but open spaces will be kept to allow them to retain their separate identities. This, it is claimed, will create a polycentric urban community with most of the advantages of a city but none of the usual disadvantages such as congested roads and crowded buildings. A new railway station has been opened at Alfreton and there is an airport able to handle freight 32 kilometres to the south at Castle Donnington. A start has been

made on the Five Towns project at Kirkby-in-Ashfield, where the colliery has closed but its site and that of nearby railway sidings is being redeveloped with new light industries. Five Towns is *not* a New Town, for the local authorities wish to retain full control. Existing statutory powers are thus being used to restrict development in some places and to promote it in others. Some villages, for example, will become conservation areas. It is hoped that the reclamation scheme will halt the drift of people to Derby and Nottingham and inflate the population of Five Towns from its present 190 000 to 330 000 by the end of the century.

Most new planning projects in Britain make a deliberate point of keeping housing densities low in order to produce pleasant, open land-scaped residential areas. Most planners also assume that high density housing entails the construction of high-rise blocks of flats, with all the disadvantages attendant on living a long way above ground level. Recently, how-ever, there has been a swing of the pendulum away from the low density housing ideas of Ebenezer Howard and the New Towns. A good example of the new trend is the West-minster Council's Lillington Garden Estate in Pimlico. This redevelopment scheme shows that high density housing can be achieved without putting people a long way above the

Photo 86
11-storey blocks of flats at Wandsworth. Despite the pleasant semi-rural setting this type of residential construction is losing favour because of the psychological problems of isolation inherent in high-rise living.

Perhaps the optimal solution to the vexed problems of urban expansion and renewal is the creation of a 'ring-city' such as that emerging in the Netherlands. With an average of 378 persons per square kilometre the Netherlands is the most densely populated country in the world. Population pressures there are especially high in and around Utrecht, Amsterdam and Rotterdam (3023 per square kilometre), so that the Dutch are faced with acute problems of urban growth. The map shows that the cities of Rotterdam, The Hague, Leiden, Haarlem, Amsterdam and Utrecht have virtually coalesced to form a ring-shaped conurbation which the Dutch call *Randstad Holland*. The damp, peaty, but pleasant rural region around which the Randstad towns are grouped form a 'green heart' which planners aim to preserve at all costs. To avoid making inroads into the 'green heart' future growth will be permitted only in certain well-defined directions. The main

Photo 87 (a) and (b)
The Lillington Estate, Pimlico, attempts to provide high-density accommodation without high-rise construction. The blocks contain five or six stories, but each resident

ground. At Lillington 40% of all homes are at true ground level and each home has a private space, either a garden or a patio. The other 60% of homes emerge 3 or 4 storeys up on to a 'roof street', i.e. a pedestrian way giving easy access to ground level. There are no flats at Lillington and all homes have a front door opening on to a 'street'. *(See photo.)* This gives a high density housing of 500 bed-spaces per hectare, i.e. greater even than controversial high-rise flats such as those at Ronan Point. Yet residents at Lillington claim that there is no sense of congestion or isolation. The estate has been so planned that residents can easily use adjacent shops and services whilst non-residents find it convenient to walk through Lillington on their daily affairs. It is claimed that this arrangement makes social integration far more natural and effective than in the New Towns. A development scheme similar to that at Lillington but with even denser housing is the Marquess Estate in Islington.

150

areas scheduled for development are (a) the main transport routes leading away from the Randstad, e.g. from Ijmuiden northwards towards Alkmaar; (b) a narrow strip of land running north-east from Amsterdam through the new South Flevoland Polder and East Flevoland towards Groningen; and (c) the island of Voorne in the Delta District, where a new town Grevilingenstad is projected to absorb 250 000 'overspill' population from Rotterdam. In addition several cities remote from the Randstad are to be developed and expanded, in some cases to over 200 000. Finally, to preserve a semblance of green countryside within the Randstad, a rural buffer-zone 4 kilometres wide is to be retained between all the existing large cities.

The great advantage of a ring-city is that it permits polycentric development whilst retaining maximum accessibility across the 'green heart'. The various urban foci can also retain their existing identities and functions, and

Figure 94
Predicted Dutch conurbation for 1980.

has a front door opening onto an elevated 'street'. Note the inclined passage-way to ground level, the irregular outline of the buildings, the trees and open spaces.

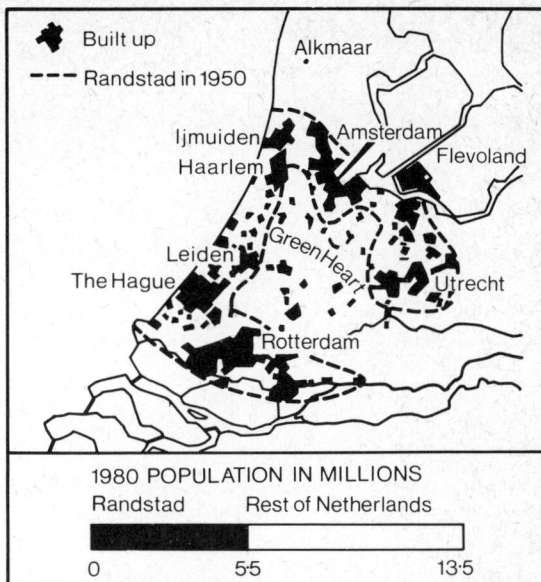

congestion is minimized. In Britain building land is in very short supply but there is an immediate need to build at least 10 million new dwellings, the equivalent of about 100 New Towns. To economize on space yet produce an acceptable urban environment it may well be that this country's best solution would be to create one or more ring-cities of high-density housing.

Figure 95
City forms: (a) core; (b) radial; (c) linear; (d) ring; (e) dispersed; (f) dispersed with nodes. (*After* Jones)

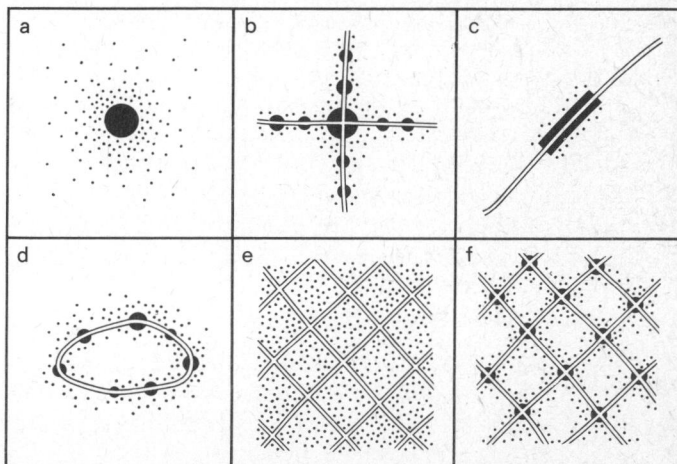

151

Bibliography

ASSOCIATION OF AMERICAN GEOGRAPHERS, *Resource Paper Series*. Commission on College Geography.
    Publication No. 1, 'Theories of urban location', 1968.
    Publication No. 2, 'Air pollution', 1968.
    Publication No. 6, 'Social processes in the city', 1969.
    Publication No. 7, 'Spatial expression of urban growth', 1969.

BERRY, B. J. L., *Geography of Market Centres and Retail Distribution*. Prentice Hall, 1967.

BERRY, B. J. L. and HORTON, F. E., *Geographic Perspectives on Urban Systems*. Prentice Hall, 1970.

BIRD, J., *The Major Seaports of the U.K.* Hutchinson, 1963.

CARTER, H., *The Study of Urban Geography*. Edward Arnold, 1971.

CHORLEY, R. J. and HAGGETT, P. (Eds), *Socio-economic Models in Geography*. Methuen, 1970. (Paperback).

DWYER, D. J. (Ed.), *The City in the Third World*. Macmillan, 1974.

EVERSON, J. A. and FITZGERALD, B. P., *Settlement Patterns*. Longman, 1969.

EVERSON, J. A., and FITZGERALD, B. P., *Inside the City*. Longman, 1972.

HAGGETT, P., *Location Analysis in Human Geography*. Edward Arnold, 1965.

HALL, P., *The World Cities*. World University Library, 1966.

JOHNSON, J. H., *Urban Geography, an Introductory Analysis*. Pergamon, 1967.

JONES, E., *Towns and Cities*. Oxford University Press, 1966.

MAYER, H. M. and KOHN, C. F., *Readings in Urban Geography*. Chicago University Press, 1959.

MUMFORD, L. *The City in History*. Secker and Warburg, 1961.

PAHL, R. E. (Ed.), *Readings in Urban Sociology*. Pergamon, 1968.

PUTNAM, R. G., *et al.*, *A Geography of Urban Places : Selected Readings*. Methuen, 1970.

ROBSON, B. T., *Urban Analysis : a Study of City Structure*. Cambridge University Press, 1969.

ROSE, A. J., *Patterns of Cities*. Nelson, 1967.

RUSSELL, J. C., *Medieval Regions and Their Cities*. David and Charles, 1971.

SCIENTIFIC AMERICAN, *Cities*. Pelican, 1966.

THE OPEN UNIVERSITY. The Open University Press :—
    The Process of Urbanization. 1973.
    The Built Environment. 1973.
    People in Cities. An Ecological Approach. 1974.
    The City as a Social System. 1973.
    The Spread of Cities. 1973.
    Spatial Aspects of Society. 1971.

WEAVER (Ed.), *The American City. An Urban Geography*. McGraw-Hill, 1966.

YEATES, M. H. and GARNER, B., *The North-American City*. Harper and Row, 1971.

Field Techniques

BRIGGS, K., *Field Work in Urban Geography*. Oliver and Boyd, 1970.

BULL, G. B. G., *A Town Study Companion*. Hulton, 1969.

BURTON, T. L. and CHERRY, G. E., *Social Research Techniques for Planners*. Allen and Unwin, 1970.

DRISCOLL, B. M. *Town Study : a Sample Urban Geography*. Philip, 1971.

HADDON, J., *Local Geography in Towns*. Philip, 1971.

Acknowledgments

Our thanks are due to the following for permission to use copyright material:

The American Geographical Society, N.Y. and Dr Howard Bracey and John E. Brush for their article 'Rural science centers in Southwestern Wisconsin and Southern England' from *Geographical Review*, Vol. 45, No. 4; The Geographical Association for an extract from Davies *et. al.* 'Directories, rate books and the commercial structure of towns' from *Geography*, Vol. 53; Cambridge University Press for an extract from B. T. Robson's *Urban Analysis*.

Our thanks are also due to the following for permission to use copyright photographs (photograph numbers in brackets):

Camera Press (cover, 5, 72, 76, 83, 84, 86); Paul Popper Ltd (1, 3, 6, 21); FAO (2); Barnaby's Picture Library (4, 34, 37, 59); J. Allan Cash (7, 33, 58); Alan Hutchison (8, 11, 12); The Oriental Institute, University of Chicago (9); Aerofilms Ltd (10, 20, 38, 39, 40, 53, 54, 56(a, b), 57(b) 79); WHO (13, 63, 68); Will Green (14, 29); Peter Fraenkel (22, 23); Keystone Press Agency (24, 32, 35, 52, 67, 70); Mansell Collection (25); Fiat (26); Bob Collins (27, 42, 46, 66); Henry Grant (28, 82); London Transport Executive (30); Stadtbildstelle, Essen (31); Robert C. Frampton (36, 85); Central Electricity Generating Board (41); Julie Stevens (42) (a, b, c, d, e, f), 73); Greater London Council (45); Shelter (47); Birmingham Development Corporation (48, 49, 60); Graveley of Birmingham (50, 51); Noeline Kelly (55); J. W. Kitchenham (57(a)); Airviews Ltd (61); Israel Desalination Engineering Ltd (62); *The Times* (64, 65, 74, 75); Associated Press (69); Orion Press (71); Bay Area Rapid Transit (77); Hong Kong Government Information Service (78); Norwich City Council (80); Swedish National Travel Association (81); Brecht-Einzig Ltd (87(a, b)).

Other photographs in the book are by the author.

Our thanks are also due to the following for permission to . base several of our figures on their original diagrams:

D. Van Nostrand Co. for a figure from Gallion & Eisner's *The Urban Pattern*, © Litton Educational Publishing Inc (Fig. 14); Prentice-Hall Inc, N. J. for a figure from Brian J. L. Berry's *Geography—Market Centers and Retail Distribution* © 1967 (Fig. 79); Routledge & Kegan Paul Ltd for a figure from Peter Mann's *An Approach to Sociology* (Fig. 35); Thomas Nelson for a figure from G. Melvyn Howe's *National Atlas of Disease Mortality in the United Kingdom* (Fig. 82); Architectural Press Ltd for a figure from *Town and Country Planning Textbook*, 1950 (Fig. 116); Hutchinson Publishing Group for the Map of the City of Birmingham from A. E. Smailes' *Geography of Towns* (Fig. 22); Oxford University Press for figures from Emrys Jones' *Towns and Cities* (Figs 21 and 95); The Geographical Association for figures from A. B. Mountjoy, *Geography* Vol. 53, 1968 (Fig. 16), J. A. Giggs and D. T. Herbert, *Geography* Vol. 53, 1968 (Fig. 19), M. B. Stedman and P. A. Wood, *Geography* Vol. 50, 1965 (Fig. 25), M. E. Witherick, *Geography* Vol. 57, 1972 (Fig. 87) and T. E. Hilton, *Geography* Vol. 55, 1970 (Fig. 7); Gerald Duckworth for a figure from J. M. Houston's *A Social Geography of Europe* (Fig. 11a); Scientific American Inc. for figures from N. K. Bose's article 'Calcutta: A premature metropolis, Vol. 213, 3 (Figs 15a and b), and J. W. Dyckman's 'Transformation in cities', Vol. 213, 3 (Figs. 85a and b); University of Chicago Press for a figure from *The City*. ed. Park, *et. al.* (Fig. 27); *Which?* for a figure from p. 197 of the July 1973 issue (Fig. 81); Longman Group for a figure from Beaujeu and Chalbot's *Urban Geography* (Fig. 3); *Economic Geography* for figures from Murphy and Vance: 'Delimiting the CBD', Vol. 38, 1954 (Figs 18a and b), from Arthur Getis, Vol. 39 (Figs 66–72), and from Smith, Vol. 38, 1962 (Fig. 42); Edward Arnold for figures from Carter's *Urban Geography* (Figs 23 and 26); *Journal of Asian Studies*, Vol. 34 for figures from Skinner's 'Marketing and social structure in rural China' (Figs 60–65) and the *Journal of the Royal Statistical Society* for a figure from Clark, A 114, 1951 (Fig. 416); the *Geographical Review* Vol. 53, 1963 for figures from Berry, Simmons and Tennant (Figs 39 and 41a); *Annals of the American Academy of Political and Social Science*, Vol. 242, 13 for figures from Harris and Ullman, 'The nature of cities' (Figs 31 and 34).

Index

Accra, 9–10
Agades, 24
Alfreton, 149
Algeria, 9
Algiers, 9

Babylon, 12
Bay Area Rapid Transport District (BARTD), 134, 135
Birmingham, 29, 47, 48, 50, 57–60, 61
Bogota, 9
Bombay, 6, 9
Börde, 15
Bournemouth, 75
Brazil, 9
Brazzaville, 5
Brussels, 32
'Buchanan Report', 136–140
Buenos Aires, 9
Burgess, E. W., 63

Cairo, 9
Calcutta, 5, 9, 26, 27, 28, 118
Calgary, 78–81
Caracas, 5, 9
Caste, 25, 26, 27
Central Business District, 37–46, 64, 65, 67, 68, 69, 70, 71, 73, 76, 79, 80, 140
Central Place Theory, 82–113
Chicago, 63, 81
Christaller, Walter, 82, 105
Christianity, 21, 22, 26
Colchester, 20
Commuting, 2, 34, 35, 36, 54, 56
Concentric Theory, 63–66, 73
Contraception, 4
Conurbations, 29, 30, 150, 151
Copenhagen, 32
Craft guilds, 26
Crime, 129

Death rates, 3
Dehli, 9
Density-decay curves, 77
'Dormitory' settlements, 2, 80, 102, 104

East Berlin, 32
Economic rent, 64, 66, 73, 74, 77, 80
Edinburgh, 24, 119
Egypt, 1, 9, 14
Essen, 36, 142
Expanding towns, 144, 145

'Filtering down', 53, 55
Friction of distance, 65, 73

Garden City, 141
Ghana, 9–10
Ghettoes, 61, 62, 82
Gradient analysis, 71–78
Gravity models, 113
Greek city-states, 15–17
Grid-iron street plan, 18, 19, 20
Guildford, 72, 90

Hamburg, 30, 32
Hanley, 44
Harris, C. D., 69
Hierarchies (of settlements), 83–112
  $k = 3$, 83, 84, 85, 93, 94, 99, 105
  $k = 4$, 84, 86, 95, 96
  $k = 7$, 85, 86, 87
High-rise flats, 150
Hong Kong, 8, 9, 117, 118, 136
House types, 53–55
Howard, Ebenezer, 141, 149

Hoyt, Homer, 66
Hydro power, 30
Hypermarkets, 75

Immigrants, 34, 61
India, 9, 11
Indicator functions, 102
Industrial Revolution, 1, 4
Industrial zones, 47–52
Indus Valley, 13, 14, 26
Iran, 9, 12
Interaction breaking points, 113

Johannesburg, 5
Joint-stock banking, 31

Kano, 25, 28
Karachi, 9
Karlsruhe, 23
Karnak, 1
Khartoum, 7
Kowloon, 9
Kumasi, 28

Lillington Garden Estate, 149, 150
London, 30, 32, 34, 35, 38, 40, 47, 52, 70, 71, 78, 131, 132, 133, 142, 143
Los Angeles, 40, 148
Lösch, August, 91, 92

Mali, 26
Manila, 5, 8
Mental illness, 128, 129
Mesopotamia, 12, 13, 14, 15, 26
Metropolitan cities, 5, 31–33, 50, 52, 137, 138
Mexico, 9
Mexico City, 7, 9
Middle Ages, 22, 23
Migration, 2, 3, 4, 5, 8, 9–10, 29, 34
Milan, 30
Million cities, 31
Milton Keynes, 145–147
Moscow, 32
Motorways, 40, 49, 50, 133, 137, 140, 146, 148
Multi-Nuclei Theory, 69–70, 73, 148
Munich, 30

Nairobi, 9
Neolithic Revolution, 12, 13, 14, 15
'Nesting', 87, 88
Net reproduction, 3
New Towns, 49, 142–149, 151
New York, 11, 30, 32, 38, 62, 131
Nile, 12, 13, 26
Noise, 128
Nomads, 13, 14

'Overspill', 60, 143–149, 151

Paestum, 17
Pakistan, 9
Paris, 32, 34, 131, 133
Pedestrian precincts, 139
Peking, 9
Persepolis, 13
Peru, 9
Peterborough, 147
Peterlee, 49
Pollution,
  atmospheric, 3, 11, 30, 50, 124–126
  water, 118–124
Pompeii, 18
Population density, 24, 77, 78
Prague, 32
Pre-historic settlements, 15
Pre-industrial cities, 26–28
Probability contours (shopping), 113

Randstad-Holland, 150, 151
Rangoon, 5

Redevelopment, 57–60
Reilly's Law of Retail Gravitation, 113
Resort settlements, 102, 104
Rio de Janeiro, 5
Roman cities, 17–22
Rome, 20, 21, 32
Rotterdam, 30, 150

Saigon, 7
San Francisco, 40, 135, 136
Santiago, 9
São Paulo, 9, 32, 39
Science Parks, 49
Sector Theory, 66–69, 73, 79–81
Segregation, 60, 61
Seoul, 9
Service occupations, 7, 33
Sheffield, 33, 64
Shopping precincts, 75, 139
Silchester, 19

Sjoberg, G., 24
Slums, 33, 57, 60, 61, 62
Southampton–Portsmouth, 107, 140
Southeast Asia, 7
South Korea, 9
South Tacoma, 93, 98, 99
Subdivision of dwellings, 34, 35
Sunderland, 67–69
Supermarkets, 75, 96, 98, 99
Sydney, 32, 39

Teheran, 9
Threshold population, 83, 102
Tidewater sites, 49, 50
Timbuctu, 28
Tokyo, 32, 125, 126, 136, 137, 138
Traffic problems, 130–140
Turin, 30
'Twilight' zones, 34, 35, 55, 56, 57,
    64, 82, 129

Ullmann, E. L., 69

Versailles, 23
Vertical construction, 37–40
Venezuela, 9

Water,
    demand for, 114–116
    desalination, 116–118
    pollution, 118–124
West Africa, 28
West Berlin, 32
Wisconsin, 106–112
Worcester (USA), 42–43

Yellow River, 13

Zambia, 9
Zanzibar, 9

For Sebastian and Oliver

OUR *President* WAS CALLED BARACK

A "Yes We Can" Book for Kids

By Laura Olin

with illustrations by Franziska Barczyk

Not too long ago, our president was called Barack.

If you think that's a funny name, well, he agreed with you.

He was kind. He fought for fairness and equality. He called on people to be their best selves. He was black.

Barack's wife, Michelle, was his partner in all things.

He thought his two girls, Malia and Sasha, should have all the same opportunities as boys.

Who was this man? Where did he come from?

Well, he started out as a pirate. (Just for Halloween.)

His dad was from Kenya and his mom was from Kansas.

He was born in Hawaii—it's a group of islands that are part of the United States—and grew up all over the world.

KANSAS

HAWAII

INDONESIA

Barack went to school and
worked hard.
When he graduated, he decided
to become a community organizer.

A community organizer is someone who brings neighbors together to change things for the better where they live.

TOGETHER

COMMUNITY ORGANIZING

Barack decided to go to law school, and after he graduated he met a woman called Michelle Robinson at a law firm in Chicago.

For their first date, they went to a movie and afterwards they sat on a curb and ate ice cream.

Barack and Michelle got married and began to build a life together in Chicago.

Over the next few years, Barack taught law and became a state senator in Illinois.

In 2004, he was asked to speak at a big gathering of Democrats called the Democratic National Convention.

Now even as we speak, there are those who are preparing to divide us, the spin masters and negative ad peddlers who embrace the politics of anything goes.

Well, I say to them tonight, there's not a liberal America and a conservative America; there's the United States of America.

There's not a black America and white America and Latino America and Asian America; there's the United States of America.

Barack ran for the U.S. Senate and won. In 2007, he thought about running for president.

The country was not doing well. A long, bad war and a lot of greed had led the economy to collapse. People felt helpless and afraid.

And we wondered: could regular people really do anything to change things?

FORECLOSED

Barack stood up and said
something simple:

Yes, we can make sure everyone has a fair shot at the American dream.

Yes, we can save the economy. We can get people health care. We can end the wars.

Yes, we can, Barack said.

And we started to believe it.

Barack would have been the first black president the country ever had. Was the country ready?

Millions of people decided to pitch in and make sure the country was ready.

We knocked on doors. We talked to friends. Yes we can.

We registered people to vote. Yes we can.

We drove people to the polls on Election Day. Yes we can.

And then something amazing happened: We won.

We couldn't believe we had done it. But by working together, bit by bit, we made it possible.

Barack Hussein Obama became president of the United States.

Yes we did.

Barack got right to work.

He did the things he said he would. He saved the economy. He rescued the American auto industry. He got more Americans health care. He ended the war. He appointed two brilliant women to the Supreme Court.

But he did a lot more than that.

He said that everybody is equal, like a president should: Black people and brown people, women and men, gay people and straight people and trans people.

He asked us to act with compassion and care for our fellow citizens. Like a president should.

He asked us to leave a better world for the people who come after us. Like a president should.

Barack was re-elected in 2012
and served eight years total.
Somewhere in there, he got two
dogs and a best friend called Joe.

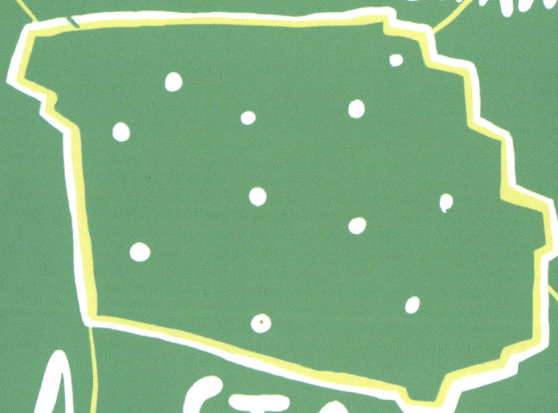

And if it can change a nation,
it can change the world.

And as he left office in 2017, he
reminded us of what he'd been saying
from the beginning:

That the power to change the
country lies within all of us. (That
means you.)

Remember:

Your voice can change the world.

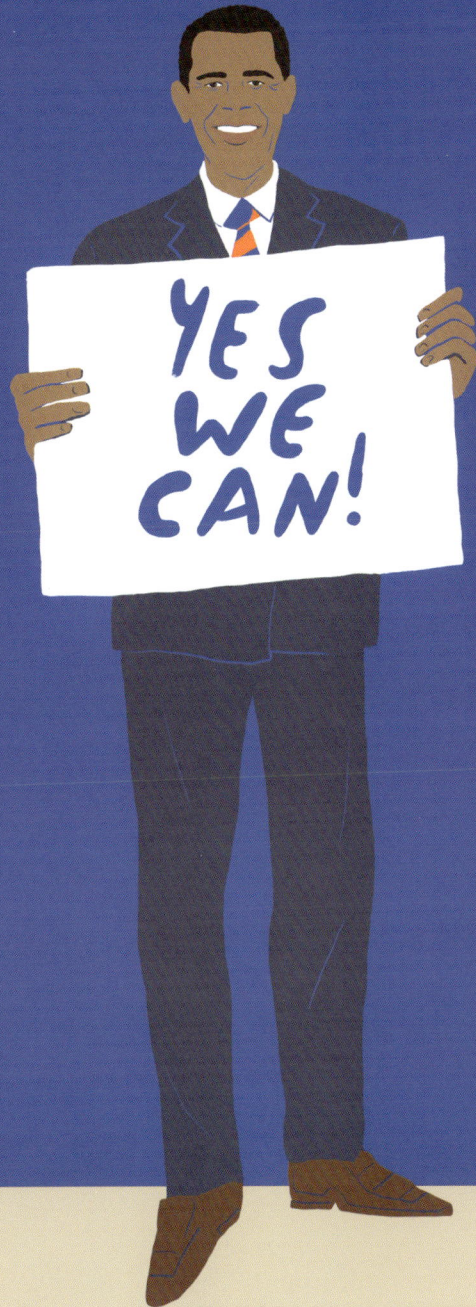

CHANGEMAKER HALL OF FAME

Aziza Ahmed Hersi

Sameer Ahmed Hersi

Abshir Mohamed Hersi

Iman Mohamed Hersi

Kylie C. Scott

Kaitlyn M. Scott

Dexter Barton

Pippa Barton

Aminatou Sow

Lily Hough McGregor

Chloe Miller-Steadman

Olivia Edna Wolvek-McKoy

Henry Wallace Houston Voss

Luther Hills-Stegner

Mae Korpics

Mary Dillon

Katie Dillon

Brennan O'Malley

Makenna O'Malley

Honorable Frances Perkins, 4th U.S. Secretary of Labor

Frances Liberty Rospars

Magnus McDonald

Dawn "Mom" Rausch

Jessica Borell

Emily Krucoff

Emmaline Nazemgoff

Lila Nazemgoff

Chance Addis

Rosemary Tilley-Taylor

Karim Al-Zayed

Geo Logan Cameron-Felty

Perrin Murphy

Noa Copeland Durocher-Pyun

Alex and Zach

Caroline Collins

Elias Konstantopoulos

Emma Athena Konstantopoulos

Olive Jones

Bryn Jones

Jonathan Yordan

Isabel Yordan

Violet Yael Sager

Erin Sager Weinstein

Bumblee Bees R Us Class 108

Jullian Xavier Maximus Detwiler

Sadie James Magdaline Detwiler

Barak Tabb Herold-Carmon

Tommy Williamson

Chris Williamson

Taylor Williamson

Finleigh Kraus Hopkinson

Milo Richard

Felix Richard

Michelle Jones, former principal
at Craig Elementary School

Ruby Madeline Ganci

Owen Beyreuther

Lily Beyreuther

Hadley Beyreuther

Elliot Beyreuther

Isalanne Gyetvai Ferguson Fox